MW00608889

Nostradamus
and the Lost Templar Legacy

Frontier Publishing

Adventures Unlimited Press

Rudy Cambier

Nostradamus
and the Lost Templar Legacy

Adventures Unlimited Press
Frontier Publishing

© Rudy Cambier 2002
ISBN 1-931882-11-8

All rights reserved. No part of this book may be reproduced in any form or by any electronic, magical, or mechanical means including information storage and retrieval without written permission from the publisher, except by a reviewer, who may quote brief passages of no longer than fifty words at a time in a review.

Every effort to trace the copyright owners of drawings and photographs in this publication was made. For further information, please contact the publishers.

Frontier Publishing
PO Box 48
1600 AA Enkhuizen
the Netherlands
Tel. +31-(0)228-324076
Fax +31-(0)228-312081
fp@fsf.nl
http://www.fsf.nl

INTRODUCTION

The poem, containing ten *Centuries* and known as the "Prophecies of Nostradamus", was not written in the 1550s by the Provençal Michel Notredame. It was written between 1323 and 1328 by a Cistercian monk, whose mother tongue was Picard, the vernacular spoken in a region of Flanders between the Dendre and the Escaut. The story of this text that flowed from the pen of Yves de Lessines, Prior of the Cistercian Abbey of Cambron, in Hainaut, in the beginning of the 14th Century, is more extraordinary than the most extraordinary prophecies that the disciples and translators of Nostradamus have ever been able to think up.

The life of the *Centuries* can be compared to a diptych, of which one panel would be very dark, the other luminously bright. The dark one represents the first 220 years – from 1330 to 1550 – during which the work remained in the Abbey library, almost unknown and certainly not understood. The second panel would symbolise the stroke of luck that started with Nostradamus in the middle of the 16th century. Misled by the imagery, the syntax and the style of the old poem, the old monk's use of the future tense for telling facts from the past and being sure of having stumbled across unheard-of prophecies, the doctor from Provence took advantage of the troubles caused by the war that raged through Flanders and Hainaut, stole the work of an unknown author, carried it away with him, and claimed to have written it himself. He had it published under his own name, and, by a rare combination of circumstances, found himself suddenly centre-stage as the greatest among prophets.

The various steps in this questionable behaviour reveal the true nature of the individual. I know it may be hard for you open-minded readers to believe me, and I am not addressing to the mage's unconditional devotees whose arguments are limited to insults, sarcasm, sneering credulity and deliberate lies. Often, at the precise moment when I conclude that Nostradamus stole the manuscript from Cambron, I can see my listener's eyes glaze over with the wispy shadow of a vague reticence, never conveyed in an idea, never discussed out loud and hence never filtered and rejected as being irrelevant. This reticence erected as a barrier against my reasoning does not proceed from reasoned thinking. It is not even a result of doubt. Rather, it is a vague sentiment hidden somewhere in the depths of the brain, triggered, not by the fact that I state that the Provençal is a thief, nor that the "prophecies" are stolen property but by the very nature of the object of the larceny.

I am not in the habit of speaking lightly on historical or literary matters; and although an interlocutor of goodwill will readily admit Nostradamus' soul was not exactly crystal clear, he cannot conceive that, having taken the risk in stealing, he stole something as strange and weird as a poem. In other words, what bothers him deeply is not the theft in itself, but the idiocy of the theft!

Impression should not be confounded with argument.

Let us therefore dig into the matter somewhat more deeply. Once we form a historical perspective, it usually remains with us, becoming a certainty in our minds. However, to change our point of view, we must return to the moment when the perspective was formed. When looking back on days long past, we must have clearly in mind that the passing of time, year after year, works as a decanter distilling the day-to-day events. Only a few drops of distillate represent our whole knowledge of a particular period and, even for a careful watcher, traps cannot always be avoided. We need to acknowledge that our errors are rooted in our mistake of looking into the past through the eyes of our own era, without building in the necessary corrections to allow for the changes in the experience of life. Because of our time-determined short-sightedness, we consider odd, strange, incongruous, exotic, foolish or inexplicable, admirable or stupid things that were quite normal in those days. Conversely, we tend to consider something that enjoyed overall admiration to be a bunch of platitudes. The logical conclusion of all this is that Nostradamus' theft is stupid only from our point of view. But was it also stupid in 1550 when Michel roved freely around northern Gaule?

As a consequence, the only question that really needs to be asked is the following: Why did Nostradamus only steal what he thought were prophecies? The answer is simple: because this kind of writings enjoyed great success in his time. They were an obsession bordering on madness.

We should bear in mind that in the 16th century the market of the printed word was devoted almost exclusively to the publication of an overwhelming quantity of almanacs, predictions and horoscopes, in which a few rare pearls were drowned in the worst and the less-than-worthless. Pious publications, in the broadest meaning of the word, came second, though far behind; alchemy came in third. For publishers and booksellers the books on "prognostications" played the role of the novel today. It was the cornerstone of the business, the only genre that would assure renown and relative wealth for its author. To envisage devoting oneself to a different genre, one had to be very wealthy or enjoy the protection of a patron. Authors living off their writing were very few. One of them was Nostradamus' contemporary Louise Labé, who was supported by a battalion of Lyonnais poets. Even Rabelais was secretary to two cardinals, doctor of medicine in the town of Metz, and was finally granted the revenues of two parishes: Saint-Martin de Meudon and Saint-Christophe du Jamblet, in the neighbourhood of Le Mans. Jean Racine and Nicolas Boileau both drew a pension granted by Louis XIV who also provided them with offices.

Hence, if Nostradamus stole prophecies, it was not at all because he believed himself to be a visionary. He would create this legend later on, when the revenues from his horoscopes largely surpassed those of his medical profession. It was because he was a thief at heart. From the foggy writings of his son, Caesar, emerges the fact that, strangely, his prophetic talent was revealed to him in the period of his thieving. I very much doubt that the "prophet" himself believed this fairy tale. More likely his deceit and tardy vocation was triggered by the inordinate desire for more and more pennies and by a taste for the illusory power that comes from renown.

However, that is not the abnormality in Nostradamus' life. Neither is it the fact that Michel professed to be very intelligent when he was in fact only a great opportunist, and unduly convinced of his ability to be the adroit helmsman of his destiny when he was nothing more than a stupid tool in the hands of a greater, more clairvoyant Destiny. Like so many others, Nostradamus forgot to become somebody by *per force* wanting to be something in the eyes of the public. To him, like to many others, "to be" equalled "appearing to be".

The abnormality – and the unexpected – show up in the destiny of the thief and his so-called personal oeuvre. The place he occupies in the history of mankind is as difficult to situate as his character. In the course of the centuries, purveyors of doom and gloom have been legion. They have all had their hour of fame. They have all been proven wrong, even Nostradamus. They have all been forgotten, except Nostradamus.

A theft, some verses and an old monk

Chapter One – The Thief

On going into Michel Nostradamus' life history, we should also be very much aware of entering a story of lies, right from the very start. From the moment the ink starts flowing to write the very words: The Prophecies of Nostradamus, and not the *Centuries*, the whole affair takes on the colour of a lie. Even the definite article "The" is incorrect.

Why? Because when speaking of "*the* prophecies" the writers are always referring exclusively to the *Centuries*, discreetly drawing a veil of silence over the rest of his writings. In fact, this poem of four thousand lines, which they affirm to be *the* prophecies of Nostradamus, represents but a small portion of the magus' publications. Besides his recipes for making jam or plasters as well as all kinds of plagiarisms, Nostradamus produced innumerable private horoscopes, almanacs or "prognostications". They are the true and *only* prophecies of Nostradamus, prophecies he sold at a hard price and exploited indefinitely. Never has a word been said about these prophecies, although they clearly bear Nostradamus' mark and style.

Discretion being the better part of valour, Nostradamus' devotees carefully hide the fact that the great visionary was not exactly a lucky one. It goes without saying that none of his so-called predictions ever came true. His not-so-stupid contemporaries and the following generations poured endless scorn on them: his "*avis et prognostications*" were not just pathetic but were almost always an object of ridicule. When the time is ripe, I shall quote these authors at considerable length.

How can I resist the pleasure of showing you a few of these prophecies that merit applause for their delirious fantasy only? All books on Nostradamus, without exception, refer with pride to the visit Queen Catherine de Medici and her son, King Charles IX, paid him on 17th October, 1564. We are led to believe that they made the trip from Paris solely to meet the idol. The truth is rather different. Catherine and Charles had been touring the country for two years and happened to be staying for two days in the neighbourhood of Salon-de-Provence. Taking advantage of the opportunity, they summoned Nostradamus to hear him prophesy. This was his day of absolute glory. At least, that is what emerges from his son Caesar's writings fifty years after the event, conveniently omitting to mention that numerous astrologers, magi and visionaries were held in much higher esteem than his father since they resided permanently at the court and received pensions and grants.

Be that as it may, Catherine de Medici quotes Nostradamus' announcements in a letter as follows: "...*Nostradamus promises lots of good things and a long life to the King, my son, who will live to be more than 90 years...* " How wrong he was! Charles IX was born in 1550, became king in 1560 and died in 1574, i.e. slightly earlier than prophesied by the good prophet.

Taking advantage of the great numbers in the royal retinue, Nostradamus had joined the entourage. In the city of Arles, home to the Aliscans, he proudly announced to Catherine that her daughter, the Queen of Spain, who was married to Philippe II, was pregnant. Without thinking twice, the Queen of France sent a messenger to congratulate her Spanish son-in-law. Upon his return the poor man was forced to report that he had been extended a rather cool welcome; indeed, not only was the happy event awaited with growing impatience, they were still waiting for something to materialise!

Being in such a good prophesying mood, Nostradamus also predicted that Charles IX, at the age of not yet 14, would be joined in holy matrimony to Elizabeth of England, also known as the Virgin Queen and who, at the time, was a buxom thirty year old and the sworn enemy of the Valois. Believing all visionaries unconditionally, Catherine had a marriage proposal presented to the court in London. After surviving the first moments of shock and utter disbelief, England's merriment lasted for months and months. Try to imagine a request from Saddam Hussein for his son to marry Golda Meïr!

As we said, none of his predictions came true. Not even the one that, according to Caesar, caught the Constable Anne de Montmorency's eye in 1559. The latter, deluded by appearances, first believed, then made the Queen of France believe – and thereafter a lot of other people right up to the year 2000 – in the predicted death of Henri II, King of France, who was killed by a lance in his eye during a tournament. This was the same Henry II whom Nostradamus promised the greatest glory and the longest life to on countless occasions and to whom he dedicated the third partial publication of the *Centuries*, as a means of obtaining royal favours. That same Henri II died at the age of 40. And not too soon either! After the eleven years of his reign

France was completely bankrupt. No small wonder when looking at his portrait painted by Clouet. Despite the highly commendable efforts to the contrary, the whole painting exudes the certain cretinism of the regal model for which his father, François I, and his syphilis were to blame.

And that is the grandiose and invincible king (dixit Nostradamus) of this most famed among the quatrains:

> I 35 *Le Lyon jeune le vieux surmontera*
> *En champ bellique par singulier duelle*
> *Dans cage d'or les yeux lui crevera*
> *Deux classe une, puis mourir mort cruelle*

Throughout our study I shall show that the lines of the *Centuries* almost always have a triple meaning. Through interaction between the intelligence of the text and the successive layers of reading, Yves de Lessines achieves the rare feat, while using the same words and in the same quatrain, of telling a story on three different levels: one from his own past, one of his own time and on top of that he gives an invaluable indication to the one he calls *the long-awaited*. The third indication is the true reason for the existence of the text, which has only been written for that one purpose. The other two meanings are tools used to attract the attention of the *long-awaited* as well as to ward off undesirable prowlers.

This feature, even taken by itself, reveals that Prior Yves was truly a man of the Middle Ages, a period in which symbol, allegory and the intimated meaning held the greatest sway even to the point of obsession. Medieval literature is allusive. It relies upon the most subtle means of composition. To perceive the full riches of what is merely suggested, it is absolutely essential to switch one's mind to a state of total receptivity, which is an indispensable prerequisite for a holistic approach to the text. Once this is clearly understood, one does not need to be a super-genius to discern the three levels of this quatrain.

At the first level, an event from the past. Let us imagine that, as a newly-wed, you had been to Venice on your honeymoon. Today, right now, for no reason in particular, you start thinking about those halcyon days. Floating freely from one memory to another, perhaps your mind will take you to St Mark's lion, sitting on top of its column on the Piazetta, next to the Palace of the Doges, three steps away from the basilica. This bronze animal was part of the loot brought back by the Venetians after the crusaders had ransacked Byzantium on 13th April, 1204. You will then remember that the lion was the symbol – as well as one of the honorary titles – of the Roman

Emperor of the East. Your musing will then take you on to the Byzantine Imperial palace where the splendour of the throne room will take your breath away. This room was called the *Chrysotriclinos*. The Greek crusos means "gold", the yellow metal. The *cage d'or* (golden cage) is therefore this throne room. This golden room was decorated with a fresco depicting the victorious Emperor, dressed as an imperator in battle, to whom generals offered the conquered towns as a token. Bishop Liutprand and Rabbi Benjamin de Tudèle, amongst others, left us a detailed description of this *champ bellique* (battlefield).

Now let us go back to the facts reported by the chroniclers. At the end of the 12th century, the Ange family masterfully tempering murder by mutilation, got rid of the Comnène dynasty. Hardly had he seated himself on the (golden!) throne when Isaac Comnène was killed on 8th April, 1195 by his brother Alexis, who literally gouged his eyes out and then took over the reins of power. He reigned under the name of Alexis III, but not for long, however. In 1203, Isaac's son, also called Alexis, slightly displeased by his uncle's lack of good manners, hit upon the idea of buying, on credit, the crusaders' army waiting out the winter on the Dalmatian coast. Uncle fled from these soldiers of the fourth crusade, wandering from hiding place to hiding place, and was finally captured and imprisoned under dreadful conditions; he died in his pit of oblivion, most likely wondering why he was not mourned.

The words "cruel death" do most likely not allude to that other Basileus Andronic Comnène (Emperor from 1182 to 1185) who died on 12th September, 1185, torn to pieces by the furious Byzantine population. In September 1183 the late Andronic, after having had the eyes of the Protosebaste Alexis (lover of the empress) gouged out in April 1182, continued his good work of dynastic improvement by arranging the strangulation of both the young Emperor Alexis II and his mother Regent Marie. In contradiction with the event reported by Yves de Lessines, Andronic is an old lion who has vanquished a young one.

A second layer of reading of the quatrain, an event from Yves de Lessines' own time, reminds us of the Battle of the Golden Spurs, fought on 11th July, 1302. On the plains of Groeninge, beneath the walls of Courtrai, the young lion of Flanders, Guillaume de Juliers, grandson of Gui de Dampierre, defeats the old Count d'Artois, who was commanding the French army. The precious spurs of the vanquished knights, picked up from the *champ bellique* (battlefield), were hung up in the choir of the church of Sainte-Marie's.

However, by means of the third layer of reading, Yves de Lessines is, in fact, very precisely addressing the *long-awaited*. We must never forget that this is the main purpose of the author, and hence the genesis and maturing process of the lines. The stories serve to conceal and, at the same time, to reveal what the *long-awaited* needs to know. Everything is subordinated to this third level, which constitutes the real heart of the work; under the pen of Yves de Lessines, that bright, uncommonly lettered man, the rest is only a game, the mask of the antique tragedies.

At the time the author was writing, the word, *bellique* also meant "red"; the word *champ* (field) mostly designated what is now called a surface. A *caGe* meant *caVe* (cellar); the two French words derive from the Latin *"cavea"* (cavus = hollow), the diminutive of which is *"caveola"* which brings us to *"geôle"* (prison cell) and *"gayole"*, the Picard word most used in the Middle Ages for designating a "cage".

Then, at the third level, what Yves de Lessines describes is a long sculptured scene (that he calls a *laze* = an embroidered piece of cloth), on which can be seen, in the midst of other animals, two lions engaged in combat, one dominating the other – executed in black bricks on a wall of red bricks and, indeed, situated in a cellar. Various other quatrains of the *Centuries* refer more explicitly to this *laze*, which is situated at the precise spot where it indicates to the *long-awaited* that he has reached the end of his voyage. The *Centuries* refer abundantly to this less than ordinary thing. It is a cast-iron proof that the poem is not a prophecy.

The only real problem of the quatrain is philological and it arises from *"Deux classe une"*. A fact of capital importance that nostraddicts *never* mention, is that the line is one syllable short. This is not a negligible anomaly. It is of crucial importance and must be examined further.

The *Centuries* are the work of a literary goldsmith and must be treated as such. To pursue this analogy, imagine your surprise when, on buying an engagement ring, the jeweller presents you with the most superb setting, but containing a flawed diamond. The missing syllable is exactly that. The flaw has not been caused by the goldsmith, who created the jewel but by the mischief of a scoundrel, who supplied the gem.

To grasp the reason for this incongruity, we must take into account various undeniable facts gained either from the text itself, or from Nostradamus' own sayings. The first is that the *Centuries* were created by a poet who was more than a genius. The basic structure of a poem is made up of lines that have a certain rhythm when they are spoken. This rhythm is determined by the number of syllables, or feet, in the line and the natural breathing point known as the caesura. The rhythm should be steady and consistent throughout the whole poem. Who could doubt that a great poet knows instantly when a line limps? A Verlaine, Baudelaire, Hugo, not to mention Walpole, Dante or Pushkin, all these great names just feel rhythm and do not even have to count. An unbalanced line sets their teeth on edge. The lines of the *Centuries* are decasyllabic (10 feet) with a 4-6 rhythm. The most famous example of this metric style is *"La Chanson de Roland"*. The line *Deux classe une, puis mourir mort cruelle*, however, has only nine feet on a 3-6 rhythm.

Secondly, Nostradamus, by his own admission, changed the original order of the quatrains and mangled a certain number by inverting or bastardising the lines. Let me explain: imagine two quatrains where the rhyme of each of the even lines is identical or very close. We will designate these lines as A1, A2, A3, A4 and B1, B2, B3, B4. Nostradamus will take these two quatrains and switch one or more of the lines. He will then present these quatrains as follows: A1,A2,A3,**B4** and B1,B2,B3,**A4**, or A1,**A4**,A3,**A2** and B1,**B4**,B3,**B2**, or else A1,**B4**,A3,A4 and B1,B2,B3,**A2**; or even worse when using A4 and B4, he switches only the *beginning* or the *end* of the line.

These tricks are simplistic and gross, but Nostradamus very often used them and time has proved that they work. The third undeniable fact is that these three words have incited the nostraddicts to utter so much stupidity. Determined to cast light on *"Deux classe une"*, they have come up with hoards of the worst interpretations and more than the worst.

To conclude the explanation: firstly, according to grammar and logic the original Picard word of the *Centuries* transcribed by Nostradamus as *"classe"* should be a *verb* and, secondly, while *"raboutant* (piecing together) *les vers"*, as he says, he simply forgot to transcribe a word. As a result, and for the time being, "Deux classe une" remains totally inexplicable; to try to give it some meaning is a pointless exercise.

Nevertheless, having taken on, in the course of time, a contrary meaning, this quatrain has undeniably become the keystone of the whole Nostradamian set-up. A careful reading, however, is sufficient to make one realise that the totality of the demonstration meant to establish its prophetic qualities, is nothing but artfully created illusion. Moreover, the interpretation is nourished by the nostraddicts' insufficient knowledge of the language (which allows any and all errors), by approximations of all kind, and by false coincidences between the actual words of the quatrains and real events. We should no longer be impressed by the apparent self-assurance of the exponents who desperately attempt to pass off their ramblings as unassailable certainty.

In reality, not one single detail of Henri II's death is consistent with those mentioned in this quatrain. If one is really very determined to find resemblances, they will spring up by the dozens, like mushrooms after an autumn rain. There may even be some troubling ones. If the false prophets misprophesy with an exemplary constancy, this is due to the fact that they imagine the future to be a continuation of the present. All announcers of the future attempt, on the one hand, to legitimise their sayings, and on the other hand, to ensure the success of their predictions. Being short-sighted, they believe that projecting the present into the future offers them the best opportunity of being correct. This could indeed be the infallible recipe *if* time progressed in a straight line, which of course it does not. Time cannot be abstracted from the events; it develops fractally. It grows like a tree and no-one is able to foresee which little twig will end up as the main branch. Even economists and futurologists get stuck in this rut. They, however, are serious people and the vocabulary they use is formulated to prove it: they are not inclined to prophecies but to prospects.

Nostraddicts are more perverse: they build their credibility on an obscure line that they decrypt in relation to past events, professing for instance that Nostradamus had announced Napoleons I and III, and claim that this clever trick equals demonstration. Hence, they triumphantly conclude that the whole text is prophetic. When working with that regime, everything becomes possible!

A splendid example of this was demonstrated by Geneviève Mouligneau. She is one of the small number of friends who helps me with my writings. She has a ferocious sense of humour and applied it to "explaining" the said quatrain, after one of my public appearances: a televised crossing of swords in which my opponent was a nostraddict nine years my senior.

Remembering that Nostradamus called himself an astrologer as well as a prophet, she engaged in an analysis of the protagonists' chart and came up with some surprising results: two Suns conjoined in Scorpio, in a difficult aspect to Pluto, the destroyer. The younger of the two adversaries, as luck would have it, has got Pluto in the sign of Leo and in the eighth house which is the house of death and of what is hidden. As the icing on the cake, his chart shows Mars (action) joined to Mercury (thought) in Scorpio and in square from Pluto to Leo. Given such a configuration, any astrologer worth the name would suspect a rivalry likely to erupt in mortal combat.

As a reminder, let me repeat the quatrain:

I 35   *Le Lyon jeune le vieux surmontera*
       En champ bellique par singulier duelle
       Dans cage d'or les yeux lui crevera
       Deux classe une, puis mourir mort cruelle

The amazed eye of the camera did indeed register a battle of lance and spear. This *singulier duelle* was witnessed by thousands of spectators on a *cage d'or*, i.e. the luminous screen of their television set. The combat (classe) took place on what is called in Belgium *"la une"*, the first French-speaking national television network. Twice, since the broadcast was repeated the next day "sur la deux", the second TV network. The *Lyon jeune* gouged out *les yeux* of the *vieux* by giving clear evidence that the other either did not admit, or for which he claimed the right to be wrong. As the youngest of the opponents was in the process of writing a book that will totally demolish the older's thesis, the latter will view the *mort cruelle* of the ideas he has been carrying around as Holy Writ for thirty years, and which his father had been preaching before him, to wit that Nostradamus is of course the author of the *Centuries* and that the *Centuries* are of course authentic prophecies, and may all who question this roast in hell. At the end of her examination, Geneviève asked the one fundamental question: if Michel Nostradamus "visualised" the TV set as a golden cage – and for him living in the Renaissance and seeing it as we do would border on mystification – would he then have prophesied his own defeat? A superb dilemma: if we answer "yes": we agree that Nostradamus is the greatest visionary in history, although facts have proven that all his other prophecies happen to be false!

Of course, Geneviève's explanation of this tricky quatrain is only a joke.

So, back to the subject. The sum total of the Nostradamian glosses enlightening the magus' "prognostications" are but a rare collection of historical and lexical ramblings. However, contrary to a foreseeable fate, in opposition to sense and logic, Nostradamus' glory emerges again and again as if governed by a derailed destiny. It is kept alive by the vanity of an army of scribblers, self-professed Sibylls, who realise of course that the title "Prophecies *of* Nostradamus" makes for good sales. This is a statement, but not an explanation. What are the causes of such an aberration?

The first one is an anomaly. From the moment of the theft, the renown of the *Centuries* has been subordinated to the glory of Nostradamus. Normally the reverse is true. For instance, if you know Victor Hugo, this is due to the fact that he wrote *Les Misérables*. However, even if a few among you have actually read the *Centuries*, you all know who Nostradamus is. During his lifetime, he owed the greater part of his renown, not to the *Centuries* but to all the talk and rumours surrounding him. Today we would call it an outrageous publicity stunt, the impact of which was multiplied several times over by the support of Queen Catherine de Medici, who was infatuated to the point of insanity by astrological revelations.

The second reason is that even today we have not been able to do away yet with these ramblings. And this influences the reading of the *Centuries*. The number of the various interpretations, which accumulate and are repeated over and over again, weighs heavily and obscures our normal perception. In the same way as the soil can be poisoned by the residue of inept agricultural practices, a text can be polluted by the parrot-like repetition of its exponents. Happy are those people who have never known the doubt that purifies the intelligence, and who go through life never realising or admitting that mistakes, even if repeated ad infinitum, never become the truth.

That is what I hold against the nostraddicts in general: they who should have been the servants of the text, have used and abused it like heartless exploiters. They have interpreted and distorted the lines to serve their own fame, in the first place, and their material aspirations, in the second. A few were truly naive, full of conviction and with a fresh approach, but the best known are cool and scheming calculators recounting stories and counting money. With this, they walk in the footsteps of their "idol", who also abused the verses for his own fame and fortune. History repeats…

Alas, poor ticklers of prophecies; the certainty proclaimed to one generation does not usually round the cape to the next without lethal damage. It may happen that time adds insult to injury when the prophet of the Prophet outlives his published inspirations. Some gently fade away, but I am sure you all know of some artist or other who is utterly lacking all sense of decency and continues publishing imperturbably the next truth, while awaiting to preach the following that will no doubt precede yet another one. Of course, the spiritual edification of his fellow men is not the main purpose. Rather it is the filling of their own pockets. And here the fault lies with the reader who forgets too easily the ancient and peremptory inanities uttered recently or in days of yore. A re-reading of the "announcements" proffered five, ten or twenty years ago is a most enlightening, intellectually hygienic occupation that will, incidentally, deflate a few egos and pull down a few icons.

Chapter Two – The Centuries

To understand a text such as the *Centuries*, so alien to our culture and our way of thinking, one must have much sound knowledge and use a serious method. But the most important thing of all is to humble your spirit and empty it of intellectual pride and vanity. As far as the first prerequisite is concerned: we, the readers, must not be overwhelmed by any dazzling mirage. No title, however great or pompous, stands for real knowledge. We ourselves must see the proof of the erudition in each line of the commentary we read. The method, then, must be transparent and reproducible.

Then, based on what the Old Monk reveals, comforted by what history teaches us about the events and the outlook on life of the beginning of the 14th century, and strengthened by the matching of the slightest details between these two pillars, we will never try to inflict upon the text a meaning that lies outside the reach of reason and stands opposed to the veracity of historical facts. Wisdom will lead our steps along the difficult way we have to tread.

Right from the start, the opus fascinates us by its very nature. There is no need to weave a net of bogus marvel around it. The *Centuries* are something unique in world literature of any period: 4000 lines that are so many historical enigmas. You may rest assured that such a performance has never been equalled by anybody. And this is just a small start, the first step in the discovery of the many-splendoured opus of Yves de Lessines.

The whole poem exudes a religious and medieval spirit. It has moreover a three-fold construction: one must always open three doors before being deemed worthy to see. Always bear in mind that, during the Middle Ages, Paradise is attained only at great cost. It never comes as a gift and the Last Judgement is sculpted on the tympanum of the churches. In the same way, as far as the lettered people were concerned, each form of knowledge requires hard work, the first goal of which is the text itself which is *always* written and read on three different levels: the letter, the senses, the significations. Three messages will then emerge from profane texts, and four from sacred texts.

There are still medieval manuscripts on *Des Quatre Sens de l'Ecriture* to which the interested reader may refer. The treatises on medieval grammar, rhetoric and logic go into lengthy and very detailed explanations on this. Alas, they are written in Latin and that may be the reason why the nostraddicts failed to notice them and hence, never understood the true nature of the *Centuries*. And yet, these books are not at all the work of obscure mystery writers or anonymous underdogs. Chrétien de Troyes, the author of the Grail legend, indulged in the genre. Dante Alighieri himself, a contemporary with Yves de Lessines, left us a manual entitled *Dantis Alagherii de Vulgari Eloquentia*.

There is no shadow of a reason why the *Centuries* should not reflect the intellectual and aesthetic movement that, at the time and place of their conception, characterised the taste of enlightened society and channelled its creativity. Like all major works, they are an expression of their time, as well as its illustration. Once this is understood and acknowledged, all becomes very clear, and any mystery evaporates like haze in the morning sun.

Each of the thousand quatrains tells one or more different stories, in the form of enigmas, that constitute a first set of keys. They all hide a second story, and most of them also a third, each revealing other characters. Moreover, in order for their message to be conveyed, the quatrains referring more specifically to the "location of the treasure" must also be read phonetically in old Picard, and as such the most obvious meaning of the written words should be disregarded. Quite a few of them are constructed in such a way that, when read aloud, from right to left, they have yet another meaning! The literary performance is tremendous, but these procedures were not odd or unknown in the Middle Ages: pure eye reading as is the general practice now, did not exist. In former times, everybody read aloud, or at least murmured the text. And it is a fact that reading aloud adds meanings that eye reading does not enable one to grasp. These phonetic games were always present in medieval Latin poetry, as well as in poetry written in the vernacular.

Unlike the hallucinating complexity of the verbal technique of the *Centuries*, the keys to these hidden significations are handed to us by rather simple means, very classical and much used in the literature of that epoch: an intentional blunder, the permutation of two syllables or two letters, the changing of a letter, inversion of tense (future tense used to describe facts from the past), word games and an ironical use of last names... In fact, nothing unusual, but in this instance so skilfully and naturally interwoven that a casual reading of the text will yield almost no hints, even if one is alert and attentive. Besides, no understanding is possible if one is not familiar with the functioning of the mind of authors and readers at that time.

When I was young, a Professor assigned me the task of analysing an almost unknown medieval author, a song writer. At the time, I was furious; I thought I had been arbitrarily discriminated against. Afterwards, however, I realised it was quite the opposite. Since there were no previous explanations that might have helped me in my analysis, the Professor had forced me to be original, to find and to express my own ideas. I got caught up in the game. In later years, instead of burying myself in well-known texts, analysed and explained at nauseam already, I devoted 25 years of my spare time to exploring the undergrowth of the "minor works" of the Middle Ages.

Thus it was this long misunderstood good fortune that allowed to me recognise almost immediately the period in which the *Centuries* were written in: the 14th century. Its literary genre: an enigma. The original language, the historical anecdotes and even the social environment of its author: the Cistercian movement. All this long before identifying Yves de Lessines. It took me much, much longer to realise and admit that the poem was in fact intended for a Templar Knight.

The Old Monk has constructed his poem in such a manner that a first level reading reveals historical facts, the sources of which were found in manuscripts (such as Vincent de Beauvais' *Speculum Historiale*) stored at Cambron at the time Yves de Lessines lived there as a monk.

Then, a second level reading denounces the enemies of the Order of the Temple, or relates events in which the Temple was involved while alluding to other events contemporary with the author.

Finally, hidden behind these two screens that somehow must have made the task even more arduous, lies a third level that tells the epic of the Temple, particularly the circumstances in which it was destroyed, and reveals the measures taken for its revival, which, as we know, never happened.

Giving an overview of the literary instrument used by Yves de Lessines seems to be the most practical thing to do first. So I shall start by summarising what will be given in detail and justified at length in the following chapters. We should never forget that almost seven centuries have elapsed since the author wrote his work of art. For the reader to be really convinced that I am speaking the truth, ideally he should be able to return to the days of Yves de Lessines, something which is physically impossible of course.

So, to assist and corroborate my thesis, I shall be obliged to recount events and to depict people in great detail, as they were perceived by the author himself, all the while remembering the outlook prevailing in those times, and also those hundreds of large and small items of proof that have long since disappeared.

In the spirit of a medieval battle, I will aim the first cannonball at the heart of the fortress: I will start with the banner-bearing quatrain of all the nostraddicts, the one in which they all saw, in hindsight as usual, Nostradamus prophesying the birth of Napoleon Bonaparte, one of those quatrains that have made and still make the fame of the prophet.

> I 60 *Un empereur naistra près d'Italie*
> *Qui a l'empire sera vendu bien cher*
> *Diront avec quels gens il se rallie*
> *Qu'on trouvera moins prince que boucher*

An Emperor born near Italy… This obviously means Napoleon. Alas, it is the same kind of evidence that proclaimed the Earth to be the centre of the universe!

Let us adjust our binoculars.

As soon as I read this thing, by which I mean the interpretation by a someone called Pichon, usually more at home in the astrological morass and the self-professed Prince of this corporation, I could not help laughing, since I knew for certain that the quatrain referred to the German Emperor Frederic II Hohenstaufen, living in the first half of the 13th century. I also knew that the phrase, *"he is less prince than butcher"* was one of the insult most commonly directed at this Frederic II during the 13th century.

Frederic II (1194-1250) was the son of Henri VI Hohenstaufen and his wife, Constance of Sicily. At the time, this Swabian dynasty was engaged in a ferocious fight against the papacy. His grandfather, Frederic I Barbarossa, even had an "antipope" elected to counter the incumbent, whom the German clergy almost unanimously and nicely nicknamed "the Antichrist from Rome".

In those times, if it would serve the holy cause, which always sanctified the means, the ecclesiastic hierarchy handled calumny with zeal and with an enthusiasm equal to nothing but their holy cupidity. They put a lot of work into blackening the reputation of these German emperors who were heroic in their stand against a Pope selected by the maffiosi families of Rome and the surrounding areas. All things considered, the two potentates – the imperial and the papal – unwittingly did us a good turn because their dogfight (the quarrel of the Guelfes and the Gibelins) is unquestionably one of the direct origins of democracy.

Let us examine the tool and the way it was put to use.

Having reached the rightful age to marry, the son of the red-bearded Emperor, although not basking in an aura of sanctity, nevertheless aspired to get married. The Pope himself had no grounds to object as long as the wedding was canonically Catholic. Barbarossa, being his recalcitrant self, rose to the occasion and played a masterly trick on the Pope, who was still deluding himself into thinking he was sovereign.

The papacy had always managed to rally the State of Sicily against the Empire. So, unable to resist the fabulous opportunity for mischief-making, Frederic I started negotiating the marriage of his son Henri to Constance of Sicily. Constance was the sister of King Guillaume, and at that time, no-one could foresee that the Norman kingdom that extended over the south of the Italian peninsula and Trinacrie would fall apart. But now, with marriage of Henri and Constance, the Papal States were surrounded and held in a vice by the imperial territories to the north of the peninsula and the Napolitan territories to the south. In such an unfortunate location, the Pope would have nowhere to fall back to, and the total disappearance of the Pontifical State was to be feared. The papacy raged and trembled; how could it cope with the allied German and Sicilian armies? It entered the battle with its own weapons and soldiers: intrigue (demurely re-baptised "diplomacy" when handled by the great) on a European level, anathema and imprecations, flowing in torrents or surreptitiously whispered into willing ears by that part of the clergy all too eager to prove their allegiance to the Pope.

So, when his wedding with the heiress of Naples and Sicily was announced, priests and monks laughed out loud, saying this was just a trial run, the Prince not being a Man in the place where it really mattered. When it became obvious that the heir had nonetheless fulfilled his marital vows with the lady, they ridiculed his unnecessary efforts and fatigue saying that, to punish the Emperor's insolence, God who is well aware of where His interest lies and hence who His pope is, had rendered the daughter-in-law sterile. Alas, diabolical disaster continued to harass the Roman Church when the Imperial court announced Urbi et Orbi that Constance was with child. The ecclesiastic corps countered that the big belly was only a cushion and that imperial duplicity would have a substitute infant ready on the day of the staged confinement.

Hoping to put an end once and for all to the malevolent rumours, the Sicilian Queen decided to give birth in public, under a tent pitched on the main square of Jesi, near Ancona, i.e. almost under the Pope's nose. Alas! What snake would feel discouraged by such a small contretemps? The first slander was dragged out again, though slightly modified: Henri was a man, but, solely in order to cause trouble to His Holiness by insulting God, the Queen had lain with a butcher. Consequently, the " thing " born at Jesi was but a bastard of the Sicilian Queen and had no rights to the Empire.

The occupation of this male at work in the bed of the enemy of Christianity had been carefully chosen to heighten the obscenity. Apart from the job of emptying latrines, there was no task more loathed in the Middle Ages than the job of butcher.

Throughout his life, Frederic II was to suffer from the nickname of butcher's son. We should, however, not pity him too much. In the last century, the anticlerics who proclaimed that impiety was the highest form of intelligence, granted him a halo of progressiveness. In reality, he was low, mean, unpleasant and unscrupulous, attempting to pose as a lettered man, never surpassing the level of inconsistent, short-lived provocation.

Thirty years later, under a different sky, the men of the meat trade reminded him badly of their existence. Having gone on a crusade, he acted so strangely – incoherent in his strategy and disorderly in his politics, ending up by attacking those he had come to help – that the people there became really angry with him, to the point they wanted to butcher him. Frederic was cruel and vicious, but no great hero. To prevent himself from being torn to bloody pieces by his numerous victims, he took refuge in the fortress of St Jean d'Acre, having a hasty retreat to his own island in mind.

Of course, nobody volunteered to cover the flight of this villainous fiend to the embarkation point. He remained hidden till, at long last, the Knights Templar took it upon themselves to escort him. The only route from the fortress to the port went through the Street of the Butchers. As he passed by, they covered the glorified Emperor in excrement and threw waste and offal at him. Foul smelling and furious, he entered the safety of a Templar boat.

The Templars had saved his life. He thanked them in his own particular manner. Back in Sicily, burned by the hatred of feeling beholden and wishing, like all cowards, to punish the innocent to cover up his own faults, Frederic started a smear campaign against them, which nearly a hundred years later Philip the Fair reproduced against them almost word for word. He then seized their belongings and arrested the Templars stationed on his territory. With this in mind it is unlikely that the Templars living at the time of Philip the Fair, the man who would put an end to their fortunes, had already forgotten this disastrous experience?

On first reading, when I looked at the language of this verse, I made another discovery. The rhyme of lines 2 and 4 proves beyond doubt that this quatrain was definitely *not* written in the 16th century! Indeed, at the time of the Renaissance – when Nostradamus lived – the word *boucher* was pronounced, in French, exactly as today: with a closed "é". As of the second half of the 14th century the final "r" was in most cases no longer pronounced. Although there was a movement at the court of Louis IV to change the pronunciation of the infinitive of verbs such as *finir* those ending in –er, such as *aimer*, and indeed *boucher* remained as they were. In anglophonics this sounds like "aymay", "booshay". *Cher*, on the other hand, sounds like "share".

In short, the two words do not rhyme in French. There is not even an assonance: we hear an open "è" and a closed "é". In 14th century Picard though, which it is essential to know in this case, the words *cher* and *boucher* were pronounced "keere" and "boosheere".

What conclusion are we to draw? The only way to resolve the impossibility of the rhyme is to conclude that the original text was written in Picard, or rather, that it was written in *Roman* by a Picard, in the 14th century at the latest. The mix of languages will surprise no-one with a little knowledge of the Middle Ages. Outside their native region, and in writing, people used a *"lingua franca"* which they almost always called *"Roman"* and rarely *"François"*. The Paris court did not impress them in the least; they were all very proud of their own particular dialects. Philippe Mousket, the author of the *Cronique Rimée* once silenced a Queen of France quite elegantly when she had dared to ridicule his Picard. The exclusive use of the Francian started to become the norm during the 15th century. It turned into a dictatorship during the 16th and became tyrannical in the 17th thanks to the two Louis, their servant Armand Jean du Plessis, their preacher Bénigne, also known as the Morbid Orator, and the Academy of the King's retired oldies.

As a Provençal Michel Nostradamus was obviously neither a Picard writing his own language, nor a Picard writing in French. If on the other hand, he was creating a rhyme intended for the eye rather than for the ear, he contravenes the most elementary rules of versification, disclosing *ipso facto* that he is a mediocre writer. However, once the Picard key to the story is turned and the door to the enigma is opened slightly ajar, one cannot fail to notice that the *Centuries* are a pure masterpiece. The conclusion is inescapable, as well as all its consequences: the *original* text is undoubtedly the work of a Picard, one of the best authors ever.

The use of Picard and Flemish idiomatic expressions is such a very powerful reality that, this fact in itself, reverses the burden of proof. It is now up to the convinced nostraddicts to demonstrate why Nostradamus has written what he claims to be his lines, using Picard expressions and Flemish words since he has no knowledge of either language. This is clear from what is left of his correspondence.

There are a number of passages in the *Centuries* on which even the most passionate and dedicated nostraddicts have had to give up and admit they could not understand a single word, or which they tried to explain by using hare-brained Greek words that only exist in their heads. These passages, however, are so clear and simple: the words that are not understood are all Picard or Flemish.

In the quatrain we are looking at now, Nostradamus gives an example of the way he has mistreated the whole poem. He modernised and frenchified the original text without understanding its meaning. Because a poem is subject to strict rules of rhyme and feet, Nostradamus' mistakes are unavoidable as soon as he decides to use the stolen work. Indeed, the potency of the images, the whole hallucinatory element of the *Centuries* is inevitably lost if one attempts to turn them into prose. If one listens carefully to a liar of this nature, one will notice that, in spite of himself, the truth will emerge. Thus the theft itself becomes useless and we all know that a pilferer is truly unhappy when his ill-gotten gains turn out to be profitless.

Let us now get back to the quatrain. Taking it as a starter, I did not go for the easy approach since it is one of the few quatrains of the *Centuries* that does not show immediate gross historical and linguistic contradictions with the prophecies some people pretend to see in them.

When and how did Napoleon suddenly appear in this quatrain?
Although I cannot claim that he was definitely the first to do so, as these kind of people are in the nasty habit of attributing authorship of ideas to themselves when they have only copied, quite unscrupulously, one another's, a 19th century Frenchman, Eugène Bareste, was convinced for a long time that Nostradamus was The Greatest of All Prophets, having read the explanations of those who preceded him on the route of the *Centuries*. These exponents were all of the opinion that numerous quatrains prophesied the exploits of the French kings. But then the Revolution intervened and this nonsensical mishmash of erroneous and contradictory ponderings lost all of its shine and glory, and became thoroughly ridiculous. Would this set Bareste's little grey cells in motion and lead him to conclude that the *Centuries* are no prophecies? Wishful thinking! He was inspired by the line: *un empereur naistra près d'Italie.* Eugène replaced the names of the kings by Bonaparte and the trick was done. All his successors have followed this example and exploited in depth the evocative power of this admirably written quatrain.
You will find it on the first pages of their books where its psychological function is very precise: *it de-activates the reader's critical sense.* After having told you the story of Frederic II Hohenstaufen, I shall now very briefly go into the story of Napoleon so that you may see for yourself it does not fit in with the *Centuries*.

Un empereur naistra près d'Italie

To the prophecy-makers, *près d'Italie* means Corsica. Why do we accept this statement without raising the slightest eyebrow? Because, on the one hand, mixing the Corsican and the Tuscan languages together, we imagine the indigenous islander speaks Italian exactly like that spoken on the Cisalpine peninsular. On the other hand, when we look at the map of France, Corsica *seems* near Italy. Is it indeed? When I was young, on a beautiful night, I dumped my rucksack on the deck of an Italian boat. It took more than twelve hours to cross over from Livorno to Bastia. Moreover, as soon as the anchor was raised, I fell to talking with a Corsican lady who taught Philology on the continent. When the long talkative night came to an end, and before setting one foot on the island's soil, I knew quite a lot about the differences between the Corsican and Tuscan languages.

But in Nostradamus' time, as well as in Yves de Lessines', depending on the direction from which the wind blew, the crossing took at least five days; sometimes the adventure would last some weeks. Nobody in his right mind would have said it was just next door. Austria is closer to Italy than Corsica is.

A few smarter nostraddicts clearly saw the incongruity. However, did they change their minds? Well, of course, they didn't! Their reasoning goes as follows: "Just see what a subtle visionary The Great Prophet is. Indeed, Corsica is nowhere near Italy in space, but you must understand the text refers to time." The reason for this? When Nostradamus lived, the Isle of Beauty belonged to the Republic of Genoa, which sold it to the France of Louis XV in 1768. Napoleon Bonaparte was born on 15th August, 1769. Nostradamus had "seen" all this…

Qui a l'empire sera vendu bien cher

Granted, the Corsican famiglia cost France a fortune. But the Popes Innocent III, although he reigned at the end of the 12th century (1198-1216), and Honorius III, who succeeded him (1216-1227), between them also spent a vast amount to buy the votes of the German nobility and have Frederic-Roger Hohenstaufen elected King of the Romans. Then, when doubts arose regarding the results of the first election, they started all over again, paid out the same amount and re-elected and crowned Emperor, the same Frederic-Roger, better known as Frederic II. And no less of an emperor than Napoleon.

Diront avec quels gens il se rallie

Those who hark back nostalgically to the blessed time of kings of Divine Right had a lot to say about the company the Corsican Emperor kept.

It seems that, as far as Dukes are concerned, *de Magenta* is not worth *de Guise*. To cut a long story short, just like the current custom of bestowing honours and knighthoods, the usurper granted a little "*de*" too easily to erstwhile commoners who were of course endowed with a solidly-based fortune and who were thus worth imperial distinction.

Seen through the eyes of his contemporaries, Frederic II did much worse. The good fellow had the audacity to have a harem. Moreover that almost godless creature offered hospitality on Sicily to a legion of Muslim and even Jewish scientists. This misdeed was more than what was needed for him to be frowned upon. Society took him severely to task for his bad manners.

At this point I must need to add that *dire*, used in the precise way that it is here, is a typical Picard word that still lives on in our language. The terms *diso'n*, *dirî* – very often emphasised as *dirî bî* or *dirî ti bî* – and *dîron* (the stronger form of which is *dîron ko*), give a nuance of contempt and disdain that no translation can render.

Qu'on trouvera moins prince que boucher

I have already briefly explained Frederic II Hohenstaufen's trials and tribulations with the meat trade. I will leave it at that, but you will have guessed what a lot of embarrassment and pain this wretched line caused the Bonapartist nostraddicts.

I would also like to point out that the verb *trouver* also meant: "to make a song, to write verses", in the Middle Ages. It was obviously in these kind of writings that Frederic II was most criticised. The meaning of the line is clearly: *songs will be written wherein he will be called less a prince than a butcher.* Yves de Lessines would certainly have known the full import of this vocabulary.

Once this historical data is clearly established, and if one recognises that Corsica does not lie near Italy, and that Frederic-Roger was born a few kilometres away from the Old Italy – beginning at the Rubicon and including neither Sicily nor the northern part of the peninsula – it becomes obvious and logical that this quatrain of the *Centuries* is a picture of the medieval German Emperor Frederic II Hohenstaufen. No longer deceived by the prophecy chanters, the reader has access to a limpid work and he will no longer doubt that it was written in the 14th and not in the 16th century.

Chapter Three – The verses

The renown of the *Centuries* and the glory of its self-professed author are certainly partly due to the fact that, up to now, nobody has asked a simple, common sense question: to what literary genre do the *Centuries* belong? The answer to that question solves the problem and everything that has remained impenetrable suddenly becomes obvious and clear. However, today, it is not enough just to wonder why for almost half a millennium, no questioning whatsoever has been carried out. Coherent answers must be found. In order to do so, there is only one route to go down: that paved by logic and informed prudence.

The *Centuries* that are, according to some, recurrently intriguing are prophecies. However, never, in the whole history of the genre, have prophecies been stated in the form of an Enigma. Not even the Apocalypse! A flashing image is not an enigma. The richness of an image flows from symbolism, the enigma is a means to construct a discourse. A prophecy, if it wants to be more than stuff and nonsense, states facts that are to come and that must be unequivocally identifiable and impossible to foresee by logical reasoning. The prophecy is a precise vision located outside our space-time.

The enigma, on the other hand, functions in the present time. Either it asks questions that need an answer today and not tomorrow; or it reveals actual facts, contemporary or past, which acquire meaning or which must be used now. These facts are concealed only by the use of verbal constructions. Sometimes these are really simple, sometimes very elaborate. Prophets may use a metaphor, but never an enigma. It may happen that we have problems grasping the meaning of a metaphor, or that we do not understand it at all, still this does not turn it into an enigma.

Visionaries never formulate their prophecies as riddles. Let us not be blinded by the Delphic Oracle. The priests of Apollo – and their disciples – were masters in the art of always giving those, who came to consult them, answers with always at least two quite opposite meanings. By doing so, their oracles lost the quality of being prophecies. But in the eyes of the average man in the *agora* who made up their clientele, the oracle was always right. This ingeniously simple trick assured the Delphi priests of undeserved renown for one and a half thousand years. However, the fact that a formulation has two meanings is not sufficient to make it an enigma. The enigma, when all is said, is nothing more than a riddle with a more elaborate construction.

A long enigma must not be confused with a metaphoric work like *Le Roman de la Rose* by Guillaume de Lorris and Jean de Meung. A metaphor is constructed upon a logical chain of known or at least obvious symbols. The enigma reveals facts by using impossible associations. If allusions to precise and recognisable historical facts are mixed up in it, then the enigma is almost certainly a hidden story.

Are the *Centuries* an enigma in the literary meaning of the word?

A literary genre is defined by its rules of composition and its tools of expression. Together with the tale, the enigma is the most ancient genre. Its speciality is that it has but one rule of composition: a truth must be revealed without ever clearly stating it, a story must be suggested without ever clearly telling it. The genre is based solely and exclusively on astuteness. Understanding is a challenge in itself. People in the Middle Ages were fanatical about this twist of the mind and simply adored enigmas.

The tool of expression – or the form – follows the rules of the time. Like Turold when he wrote *La Chanson de Rolland*, Yves de Lessines chose the epic decasyllable and his lines, as opposed to those written by Nostradamus, are of an impeccable construction. They always count ten feet, and the caesura, or natural breathing space, always falls after the fourth. Nostradamus' decasyllables are, on the contrary, rather erratic: they count from four up to… 13 syllables, without rhyme, caesura, reason or common sense. When the *Centuries* are compared stylistically with writings that are undoubtedly those of Nostradamus – *"prognostications"*, *his jam recipes and tutti quanti* – it is absolutely crystal-clear that Nostradamus never had enough writing talent to compose the *Centuries*.

To convince ourselves that the *Centuries* are indeed an enigmatic poem, the most efficient way to start is to list a few of the typical devices always used by the authors of this genre and to determine that they are also consistently used by the Old Monk:

1)   an obvious mistake:

     a)   *Ethene* instead of "Athenes" meaning that he refers to an Athens that is in fact not Athens. Later on in this book, this will be explained.

     b)   *AntHioche* instead of Antioche because the word is not to be read literally. The "h" is dropped twice (each letter unduly doubled must be eliminated). Hence the word must be pronounced *antioke*, a Greek-Latin-Picard word play relating to Wodecq, called *Oc* or *Ok* in Picard. This is an illustrious village situated in the *Tenement d'Inde*, also know as the *Terre des Débats* (Land of the Disputations), located on the frontier between Flanders and

Hainaut. It must be noted that until Yves de Lessines' time the toponym was also spelled *Antioce*, without an "h" (both spellings are used by Guillaume de Tyr in his *Chronique*). For a Picard, it makes the recognition of the word game easier still because naturally he would have both pronunciations in mind: either *AntioCHe* à la "Francienne", or *AntioKe* à la Picard. The word means "before Wodecq" (for one coming from Ellezelles and following the route of the Old Templar) or "opposite Wodecq" (when one looks from the Croix Philosophe, a place-name at Wodecq graced with a weeping willow and a heavenly resting place for bucolic lovers).

c) *AntipoLLique* instead of *AntipoLique*.

d) *THolose* to draw the attention on the fact that the Tolosa (Toulouse) that will automatically come to mind is deceptive. In fact it refers to Lotosa or Lutosa, i.e. Leuze-en-Hainaut.

e) Is it a pure coincidence if the author writes: EtHene, AntHioche, THolose? Better even ETHene, AnTHioche, THolose? Yves de Lessines uses these words and this spelling at the same time to convey essential information and *signs of recognition*, as a signal to he who will come – of this fact he is sure – when *the time is ripe*. One cannot ignore that the letter group, TH, that is meant to be intriguing and therefore to attract the reader's attention, is one of the acronyms for the Order of the Temple: *Templum Hierosolymitanum*, i.e. the Temple of Jerusalem. When you know that the Middle Ages made an even greater (mis)use of acronyms and abbreviations of all kind than we do in our epoch, the power of the sign is undeniable. In order to fine-tune the information while playing with the spelling, the author shows us that the T must always be maintained, whereas the H must be dropped. The Temple remains, even though Jerusalem fell into the hands of the Infidels.

2)   an inversion of letters:

a) I 27   *Dessous de chaine Guien du Ciel frappe*
         Non loing de la est cache le tresor
         Qui par long siecle avoit este grape
         Trouve mourra l'oeil creve du ressor

Trouve mourra l'oeil creve du ressor (who finds will die the eye gouged by the spring) must also be read *Mouve **trouva** l'oeil creve* *du ressor* (who moves will find, the eye gouged by the spring), except that the words *oeil* (eye) and *ressor* (spring) must be also given meanings other than the most obvious but nevertheless perfectly correct and commonly used. One then understands that there is no contraption designed to kill, nor is there a curse à la Tutankhamun, as some were convinced, but a much more precise and interesting piece of information: having (re)moved something, one will find the broken pipe (*oeil*) of the drain (*ressor*), which clearly describes the real trap.

b) *osdu* standing for *dous*, the 13-14th century version of the numeral two, at the same time to be read *os du* meaning at that time " the riches of… "

3)   word-plays, particularly subtle when two, or even three different languages are used:

a)   The following line constitutes a good first example:

> I 33   *Pres d'un grand pont de plaine spacieuse*
> (near a large bridge in a spacious plain)

In Flemish, a bridge (pont) is a *brug*, the town of Bruges is *Brugge*. The great Bruges becomes *"le grand pont"* thanks to an analogy between *Brugge* and *brug*. When Yves de Lessines lived, the Flemish metropolis was one of the largest cities of the Western world. But the true subtlety of the Old Monk is only really manifest when one knows there is a slight difference of pronunciation between Bruges (*Brugge*) and the bridge (*brug*). To Dutch ears this difference is obvious but it will go unnoticed to foreigners. Now, at the time the *Centuries* were written, only twenty years had elapsed since the Bruges uprising of 1302, when the French were slaughtered during the night after having been picked out by their inability to pronounce the words *"schild en vriend"*, shield and friend, correctly. At least, that is the modern and probably erroneous version of these words potent with Justice, but which show no common sense. However, one never knows…

Personally I believe that it is more logical to believe that the overexcited crowd shouted a slogan with a pronunciation very close to the other, namely *'s gilden vriend*, meaning: friend of the guilds, i.e. friend of the people.

As I also happen to mix words of one language with another, I can testify that by using this particular play on words, the Prior of Cambron is having fun in the way any bi- or multilingual speakers might do. Moreover, he mocks the French cruelly for their incapacity to pronounce Flemish correctly. This inability caused them to be done to death in May 1302, a few weeks before the French Knights were, in turn, massacred near Groeninge. When we understand this, we even know Yves de Lessines' political inclinations: he is Klauwaert, i.e. opposed to the French. He had first-hand experience of these events since at that moment he was in charge of the large agricultural estates that the Abbey of Cambron possessed in the Polders, which I shall prove later on. Furthermore, his mission was to safeguard the secret of the Templars, whose demise had been engineered by the French… Perhaps the latter was cause enough to dislike them…

Hence, all the micro-details of the text fit perfectly with what we generally know about the period, its people and the events. Now, what has Nostradamus to do with all this? He was a Provençal doctor of medicine of the Renaissance, who had no idea, let alone knowledge, of the existence of the old Flemish language called Thiois.

When the line is considered from the point of view of Yves de Lessines, with his Cistercian outlook, perfectly at home in time and space, the reading of a line such as *Pres d'un grand pont de plaine spacieuse* is not particularly arduous. It conjures up the image of the town of Bruges lying in the fields of Flanders. No need to fall into the trap of looking for some Tancarville or Verrazzano. Again, this way of thinking and writing is not exceptional; it was common to the men of letters of the Middle Ages. I shall demonstrate this at length later on.

b) The second example reveals subtleties of the same order:

> X 47 *De Bourʒe ville a la dame Ghirlande*
> *L'on mettra sus par la trahison faite*

At this stage, I shall not discuss in any philological depth the Nostradamian spelling of *Bourʒe*; for all kinds of reasons, the word should be read Bourghe.

When the old Cistercian walked the earth, there still existed in the heart of Bruges what is today just a place-name: the *Burg* or *Burge* or *Burghe*, the fortress of Baudouin Iron Arm, the first Count of Flanders. No place can be more symbolic of Flanders than the dwelling of its founder. *Burgeville* therefore refers to the town where the *Burge* is located, in other words Bruges. As for *Ghirlande* or *Ghis'nlande*, this is literally in old Flemish and in a number of today's vernaculars *het land van Gui,* the land of Gui. In this instance, the only Count of Flanders to bear this particular Christian name and to be a contemporary of Yves de Lessines was Gui de Dampierre. Ghirlande is Flanders. And who is the Lady (dame) of the land of Gui? The town of Damme, one of the five ports of Bruges.

De Bourghe ville a la dame Ghirlande*: very simply means from Bruges to Damme. The description is an itinerary.

c) X 59 *Dedans Lyon vingt et cinq d'une halaine*
Cinq citoyens Germains, Bressans, Latins
Par dessous noble conduiront longue traine
Et descouvers par abbois de mastins

Et descouvers par abbois de mastins: the barking of matins is the noisy echo of the rivalry that very often set the Cistercians against the Preachers or the disciples of St Dominique. *Dominicani* literally means "those of Dominique". In Latin, dogs are *canes*. In common with many others in those days, Yves de Lessines calls them *Domini-canes,* the dogs of the Lord, because they were not confined to monasteries and used to roam the country like stray dogs. In the *Centuries,* the preaching and imprecations of the Inquisitors have become "*abbois de mastins*", the barking of big, ferocious, ugly, slavering and flea-bitten dogs.

These verbal games are no exception during the Middle Ages. Even the literature qualified as of little consequence by the authoritative pronouncements of the academics, is full of them. This kind of literature is indeed less pretentious than the great, but it is just as elaborate and stands in contrast in its freshness and audacity to the grandiloquence of its pompous sister. Many a poem that intimately mixes Latin with Roman, Flemish or German is to be found in its garden.

Here for example is a text from the 13th century that seems at first sight completely harmless and innocent, bordering on silly. The German parts have been underlined, but, if I mention here a few Latin-Germanic "double-entendres" such as: *siquis (look at the thigh), tetigit (touch or play with the breast, or worse), tunica crepuit (she wriggled out of her shirt), an eime loube (on my ball),* etc., while passing over the verbal acrobatics of *fura nutica, faru naticu*, I am sure you will get the drift.

Stetit puella rufa tunica	There was a girl in a red dress
Siquis eam tetigit	If somebody touched her
Tunica crepuit	The dress (itself) cried
Eia!	Eia! (Oh yes!)
Stetit puella tamquam rosula	The girl was a little rose
Facie splenduit	Her face radiated
Et os eius floruit	And her mouth was a flower
Eia!	Eia! (oh yes!)
Stetit puella bî einem boume	The girl was near a tree
Scripsit amorem an eime loube	She wrote " love " on a leaf
Dar kom Venus alsô fram	Then came Venus, so powerful
Caritatem magnam	Great tenderness
Hôhe minne bôt si ir manne	Fin'Amour gave her to the man

This just to show that Yves de Lessines is a man of his time and conforms to its customs and usages.

4)   humorous hints at the expense of surnames:

a) an easy one as appetiser:

> II 55 *Dans le conflit le grand qui peu valoit*
> *A son dernier fera cas merveilleux*

Le grand qui peu valoit (the great who was not worth much) is of course the Great de Valois, i.e. Charles de Valois, brother of Philip the Fair, the destroyer of the Templars.

b) the humour of the next one, on the contrary, might have totally escaped me, if I had not been granted a great stroke of luck:

> II 3   *Pour la chaleur solaire sus la mer*
> *De Negrepont les poissons demy cuits*
> *Les habitants les viendront entamer*
> *Quand Rhod et Gennes leur faudra le biscuit*

First of all, notice that the rhyme of lines 1 and 3 is only possible in old Picard, when the two "e" sounds were closed "é".

During the Middle Ages, the island of Eubea – after the name of its capital town – was called Nègrepont. This island which lies in the Aegean Sea, off the coast of Attica, in Greece, belonged to the Duchy of Athens. Incidentally, in 1204, the Duchy of Athens had been given to the lord of my village, Rasse de Gavre, who, to thank Heaven for such a wonderful gift, donated his land at Wodecq to the Abbey of Cambron. This is another of Yves de Lessines' subtle references to the place that is to be found. The nostraddicts are of the opinion that Nègrepont is the Black Sea, but I cannot help them with that…

So far, so good! I knew where to find Nègrepont, but I had to be the beneficiary of an amazing piece of good fortune to find its fish. My luck was in one day when I craved a casserole called in French "*carbonnades flamandes*", a Flemish stew. Musing from my abode in Wodecq, I wondered what else indeed could be said about "*carbonnades flamandes*" other than praise for flavour and succulence, except of course that it is called "*flamandes*" everywhere except in Flanders where, being Flemish by nature, it is called quite simply "stewed meat", or in Dutch *stoofvlees*.

Suddenly, I remembered that in the German Empire of the 12-13th centuries, until the Great Interregnum at least, the artistic style was known as *Staufisch*, literally meaning "of the Staufen". This appellation of "*Staufisch Stile*" comes from the family name of the Swabian Emperors, in particular Frederic Barbarossa, Henri VI and Frederic II: the above mentioned Hohenstaufen. The "*platt-Deutsch*" versions *stauen* and *staufen* mean to stew, to cook; *der Fisch* is a fish; and *Staufisch* is stewed fish, or cooked or boiled fish.

Frederic II, archenemy of the Templars eighty years before Philip the Fair took over, belonged to the Staufen family, and was thus *Staufisch*, stewed fish.

There is a small problem though: the fish worth mentioning in the *Centuries* is only half-cooked (*demi cuits*). Would this imperfect cooking point to Manfred, Frederic II's bastard son by Bianca Lancia? So it would seem! The whole quatrain becomes totally clear and refers to the maritime expedition headed by Manfred in the Mediterranean around 1260, against the allies of Charles I d'Anjou, brother of Louis IX, who intended to rob him of the throne of Naples and Sicily. Bianca Lancia (the lance, the pointed weapon) is referred to on many an implicit occasion throughout the *Centuries*.

c)   the last example will be as easy as the first:

> II 70   *Le dard du Ciel fera son estendue*
> *Morts en parlant, grande execution*
> *La pierre en l'arbre la fiere gent rendue*
> *Bruit humain monstre purge expiation*

What can we find in a tree? A bird's nest? A parasite plant? Mistletoe! Let us turn the expression around: La pierre en l'arbre = *l'arbre en pierre*, more precisely: *l'arbre dans pierre*, and replace "*arbre*" by "*gui*" (mistletoe). And who appears on stage: *gui dans pierre*, the Count of Flanders, Gui de Dampierre.

The meaning of the line immediately appears in all clarity: in order to try and stifle revolt in Flanders, Philip the Fair had not hesitated to trap and imprison Gui de Dampierre and his son, Robert de Béthune. However, he was forced to release them after the disaster encountered by the French in 1302 near Courtrai, on the meadow where Guillaume de Juliers, Gui's grandson, distinguished himself. This, of course, is only the first level of reading, but it suffices to illustrate our point.

5)   the use of a legend:

> I 76   *D'un nom farouche tel profere sera*
> *Que les trois soeurs auront fato le nom*

Ferocious-sounding? If the nostraddicts are to be believed, this means Napoleon. Because he fought a lot of wars, according to some; because the Christian name Napoléon seemed dissonant to the French ear, according to others. And then why not Farouk, the last King of Egypt? It seems as if God created heaven, earth, stars, eclipses and comets for the sole purpose of glorifying the name of Bonaparte. However, rather than identifying their blood-thirsty imperator: *le nom farouche* very literally means: *the name of a ferocious beast.*

In the period that interests us, there used to be a very important French family, the Lusignan, who claimed to be direct descendants of the fairy Melusine, the snake-woman, who had two sisters: Palatine and Melias. Together that makes three sisters (trois soeurs).

This family legend was so famous that it became the subject of two great verse tales during the years 1380-1400. The family brought forth Kings of Jerusalem and Kings of Cyprus, among others.

As for the word *fato* it is pointless to repeat, which is indeed what all nostraddicts do (without admitting to their plagiary), Anatole Le Pelletier's weird interpretation. Anatole used to be the champion of the most hilarious explanations; in this case *fato* becomes *fatum*, the Latin Fate, to prove in his own special way that the line really does concern Buonaparte Napoleone as prophesied by Nostradamus Michel.

Fato is a frequent spelling in the Middle Ages of our modern "*fait tout*" (does all). The meaning of the two lines is therefore: *D'un nom farouche celui-là sera porté en avant dont les trois soeurs auront fait toute la renommée* (The one bearing a ferocious name will be brought forward (Latin: *ferre*: carry, bring; and pro: forward) whose renown the three sisters will have fully established). Why a "ferocious name"? Because he was called Lusignan; *lus* or *luz* is the common name of the pike, the fresh-water shark! Joined to *ignan* and *agnan*: which means burning and stinging in Picard.

But the "*nom farouche*" may also refer to the worst ever master of the Temple: Gérard de Ridefort, whose true name was Rudervorde (elsewhere in the *Centuries* he is qualified as "uncultured", which he is twice since "v" was written "u"!).

Catching all and sundry in the glue of his stratagems, and extravagant intriguing, the said Gérard had managed to have Gui de Lusignan crowned King of Jerusalem on the 20th July, 1186. This Gui was called the Rudolf Valentino of the 12th century. He was such a foolish, idiotic dandy that his reputation was known all over Europe although, during the Middle Ages, rank and position tended to erase and excuse the most stupid behaviour. When his father heard of his enthronement, he exclaimed in disbelief: "If Gui has been made king, then I will end up as God!" In Prior Yves' time, this story was, of course, well known… The same cannot be said of the 16th century.

Let us now completely change tack, and try to discover how the Old Monk builds up the different levels of reading and understanding. I must stress once again that, at this stage, my purpose is to present you with a general approach and to set up a framework for reflection. There is not enough room in this particular book for a full and detailed progress of my logic with all the supporting arguments. While this may slightly weaken the evidence that would result from the systematic examination of elements of proof, a simple exposé of the facts remains legitimate, when these facts are sound.

So let us talk about serious matters, like rain and stormy weather for instance.

> I 40   *La trombe fausse dissimulant folie*
> *Fera Byzance un changement de loix:*
> *Histra d'Egypte qui veut que l'on deslie*
> *Edict changeant monoye et alloys*

The two first lines allude to the fourth crusade, the one that took place in 1203-1204 but never went to Jerusalem.

In our region, Hainaut, the *trombe* ou *trompe* (in Picard the *"bè"* sound at the end of a word softens to *"pè"*) is the name given to a harvest-destroying thunderstorm, an evocative image of the true nature of this crusade, that was in fact a plundering raid set into action by the Venetians. The nuance in *fausse* is clear: turned away from the truth, the straight path. A *"folie"* is a mad, destructive rage, especially when it comes to fighting and plundering (*sic* Dictionnaire de Godefroy). You will note that a plundering rage is exactly the right expression as far as this crusade is concerned. Before departing to lay siege to Byzantium, the Venetian Doge Dandolo had concluded a contract with the "crusaders", which secured the lion's share of the loot for this Republic. It is generally considered that in one single day, the plunder from the town on the Bosphorus augmented the total wealth of Venice tenfold.

The time has come for you to take a little rest while I tell you a small fact related to this quatrain, which will help you to understand, from the inside, how difficult it is to be convincing when one has to deal with proof that no longer exists. The greatest problem with proof is that it cannot be demonstrated, it can only be stated. With regard to the above passage, Geneviève Mouligneau commented: "How do you get from a storm to a crusade?"

Each epoch uses its own words and imagery. Ours is industry-oriented; the medieval epoch based its own on agriculture. Let us, however, revert to the text.

The nostraddicts should have known that during the Middle Ages the word *loi* primarily meant religious obedience; the word had other different meanings, of which the modern "law" was by far the least in use. The following excerpt from Guillaume de Tyr's *Chronique* will serve to illustrate my assertion. The example is taken from among dozens of others.

En cele saison avint que granz contenz sourdi entre les mes-creans degipte et les mescreans de Perse; car chascune de ces genz voloit avoir la seignoirie sur lautre. La racine de la grant haine et de la grant envie sourdi de ce que il se descordoient et encor se descordent il des poins de leur loi. *Si neis que il ont divers nons; car cil qui tiennent* la loi de Perse *si ont non en leur langage Sonni; et cil* de la loi degipte *sont appele Siha; et cist ne sont pas si loing de la vraie foi crestienne come sont li autre. Il avint que cil degipte issirent de leur terres et conquistrent toutes les terres qui sont jusquen Antioche; et avec les autres citez qui furent prises la sainte cite de Jherusalem vint en leur pooir et soz leur seignorie. Assez li estut bien selonc lese que len puet avoir en chaitivoison. Jus que il avint par la soufrance Nostre Seigneur et por son pueple chastier que uns desloiaus hom et crueus fu sires et califes degipte qui ot non Hecam: cil voult passer toute la malice et la cruaute qui avoit este en ses ancesseurs: si neis que* la gent de sa loi *le tenoet ausi come a forsene dorgueil et de rage et de cruaute.*

It is undeniable that the false crusade of 1204, by allowing the Roman Curia and the Pope's minions to supplant the Orthodox Hierarchy temporarily, brought about a change in religious obedience in Byzantium, notwithstanding the vehement misgivings of that fine politician called Henri de Hainaut or Henri d'Ancre, the second Latin Emperor.

Lines 3 and 4 translate as follows: *Il sortira d'Egypte celui qui veut que l'on publie un édit changeant les pièces de monnaie et les titres des monnaies* (out of Egypt a man will come forth, who wants that an edict be issued changing the coins and their title).

This refers to the French King Louis IX, in other words Saint Louis, who had been taken prisoner in Egypt and who had got out of that country thanks to the enormous amount of money that the Templars lent him to complete the ransom. In the 1260s, he undertook the most important monetary reform of the French Middle Ages. This reform may, *mutatis mutandis*, be compared to our present change in the currencies of the countries of the European Union to the euro: the King decreed a coherent series of measures that redefined the currency units standards. At the same time, he ordered the minting of the first golden ecus and the large silver " tournois ". Louis IX had extended the use of the royal money (that up to then had only prevailed in the private estates of the Capétiens) over the whole kingdom and forced all the French lords to recognise its validity throughout their territories.

This is the first level of reading. To discover the second, one has to know that *istra* is in fact the future tense of two verbs, one being *issir*, to come out of, and the other *istre*, to be. It is the last one that will be taken into account for the moment. In those days being from Egypt meant being Mohammedan, i.e. an enemy of God, an unbeliever, a miscreant. So, on the second level, the meaning of the line changes to: *Il y aura un mécréant (sera d'Egypte) qui voudra détruire (deslier) l'édit qui fixait les monnaies et leurs titres en changeant les pièces et leur taux* (there will be a miscreant who will want to destroy the edict that fixed the money and its standard by changing the coins and their values).

This exploit was undertaken successfully by Philip the Fair – an unbeliever by Templar standards – who, forced by the uncontrollable flight abroad of his royal money and against his better judgement, ruined the monetary stability his grandfather Saint Louis had had so much trouble implementing in 1260 between his two crusades.

Yes, but... Yves de Lessines did not write *istra*; he wrote *histra*. I searched everywhere for this spelling and did not find it anywhere; neither in the in-depth scrutiny of my usual reference material, nor in the numerous lexicons analysing the specific vocabulary of an author. Jumping to conclusions, I decided this must be a little whim on the part of Nostradamus or his first publisher.

On reconsideration however, even if the prophet utterly lacks wit, his few real qualities must be acknowledged. What happens, I wondered, if we assume that Nostradamus copied down exactly what the Old Monk actually wrote? For we must grant Michel what is unquestionably due to him. *Although he never grasped their real meaning, he nevertheless understood that the mistakes and freakish spelling served a purpose.* And so posterity inherited *histra*.

The French use a peculiar kind of wordplay they call "*verlan*", that is "*l'envers*". *Histra* stands for *trahis*. The word is not even disguised; it is simply an inversion of its two syllables to change its meaning. What is now called "*verlan*" was called "*rebours*" during the Middle Ages, and it is the secret language of the Cistercians. Taking into account his background, his personality and the way things were done in those days, it would be perfectly normal for Yves de Lessines to write in the language his convent used in the presence of strangers.

If this particular example of *rebours* stands out here like a beacon, it is almost certainly to remind us to read the text backwards, too.

Furthermore, in the same period, *edict* meant the *written law*, as opposed to *coutume* which is oral law; *monoye* is also monastic life, and *alloy* also refers to the way of life, or the Rule.

Byzantium, for her part, is the new Rome. It is the town's *official name*. The Byzantines throughout the Middle Age were to refer to themselves as "Romans". It was they who were the Roman Empire, Romanie or Romagne; they laid claim to it loud and clear, sometimes even violently. Our Western Emperor was but a vile usurper as far as they were concerned. In 1239,

Arnould d'Audenarde acted as arbiter in a judicial issue to which Baudouin, heir to the Empire of Romanie, was one of the parties. As you are by now getting accustomed to the verbal technique of the Middle Ages, you will have understood that the Old Monk uses the word Byzance to refer to Byzantium as well as Rome.

Let us put all this together and translate quatrain I 40:

> *La trombe fausse dissimulant folie*
> *Fera Byzance un changement de loix*
> *Histra d'Egypte qui veut que l'on deslie*
> *Edict changeant monnoye et alloys*

The hypocritical devastating storm (the so-called crusade) hiding (their) plundering rage will bring a change of obedience in (the new) Rome. (They will be) betrayed by an unbeliever who will want the rule (the written law) to be destroyed by changing a religious state (monoye) and its rule of life (alloy).

An unbeliever destroyed a religious order through betrayal.

Except at the end of the 18th century, no other order than the Order of the Temple was destroyed. This was the doing of Philip the Fair and Pope Clement V in the early years of the 14th century. Clement? Well, well. At the beginning of the 3rd century in Egypt there lived one of the most important Christian theologians and philosophers: Clement of Alexandria. We can only admire the sleight of hand of a medieval poet who points to his contemporary, Pope Clement V, by alluding to Clement of Alexandria. This is subtlety indeed. This is no invention of mine, believe me. The scholars of the 12th century – surpassed even by those of the 13th – were the unchallenged all-time champions of intellectual gymnastics. Nostradamus, on the other hand, was not of this calibre. According to his contemporaries he showed off fatuously, often irrelevantly, what he mistakenly considered to be subtlety, like overripe cheese on a stale piece of bread.

This quatrain that obviously did not spring from a boorish mind, reveals indeed three levels:

1) the fourth crusade, on the one side, and St. Louis on the other;
2) Philip the Fair and his political actions;
3) Philip and Clement V, enemies of the Temple.

Allow me to stress once again that these are *not* three INTERPRETATIONS of the text, but three LITERAL READINGS, word by word, which our forebears called:

- *littera*: the literal sense;
- *sensus*, the meaning for the mind;
- and *significatio*, the moral sense, respectively, proceeding from the fact that they considered the human being as the temporary communion of three different realities: the body, the spirit and the soul.
- Where religious texts are concerned, God must not be forgotten; it is only right and proper to add the theological sense as well.

Throughout the Middle Ages thought, art, the means of expression in general are almost always based on a ternary construction, to which a quaternary order is sometimes added. These are not purely formal rules that might define the concept of beauty in medieval society. It is a complete and coherent system of symbols expressing the medieval contemplation of the world. When they were not living like beasts, our ancestors desperately yearned for knowledge; the slightest detail was a pretext for "teaching". Each and every artistic "product" must be regarded as symbolic religious language.

In this forgotten period, religion was present everywhere. It structured and nurtured all minds, especially those of the monks. Therefore, when he pronounces the word "Byzance" a monk in these times could not help but think of the theological dispute regarding the "filioque", that resulted in the Great Schism in the East on the 15th July, 1054, under the patriarchy of Michel Cérulaire. This monk would of course have been thinking of the Holy Trinity and the number three. And he would also be expecting, quite naturally, another monk to think along the same lines.

The text itself is structured in the image of God, the one-in-three. In order to distinguish between "triple" and "trinitary", I would ask you to meditate on the theological meaning of the "three persons of God". The only clue I will give you is that the word *persona* originally meant the mask of comedians (all the actors wore masks in the Ancient World). And just like in the theatre, where the real person is hidden behind an appearance, the first – apparent – sense of the poem hides the two others. And just like the three *personae* of the one God, the three readings together give us the key to the ultimate truth.

The above summary is only one aspect of the work, namely the construction techniques of the enigma. Yves de Lessines – who indeed was not just a monk, nor an uncultivated man of religion – was the unsurpassed master of this art. However, it is not just the man's intelligence we should admire in this respect, we should also look at the aesthetic quality of the poem, which is further proof of his rare talent. Except for the parts where Nostradamus visibly meddled with the text by adding a personal touch, there is not one single fault in rhyme or rhythm in the whole poem. This is exceptional and probably unique in French medieval literature.

On a first reading of the poem, even superficially, we are simply nonplussed by the plethora of striking images and arresting ellipses. Yves de Lessines has an innate sense for wording and expressive language, granted only to the greatest: no tricks, no recipe, just talent. How many lives does he summarise in a single quatrain? How many cruel and incisive portraits, drawn in two lines? How many characters reduced to nothing in just one line? Everything doused with a ferocious sense of humour that aims right at the heart of things, and strips the Great and Good of all their glitter and glamour to expose their naked truth.

Ah, the delight, the luxury of fearless lucidity that basks in the knowledge, the certainty that it will not be understood. He really was an extraordinary man, this old Cistercian. What a life! What a path to tread! And yet, he only gave the full measure of his immense talent on the last step to eternity, compelled to it by the turn of events.

Chapter Four – The Monk

Yves de Lessines entered the convent late in life and knew well the effects that passions have on people. He knew their vice-tainted souls. Charitable as well as scornful of them, violent and tender, calculating and generous, a man of science as well as a man of religion, architect, estate manager, polyglot, musician or at least a singer, poet and above all someone with a tremendous knowledge of people and things, this was the man who, without wishing to, became one of the actors in the biggest game of deception of all times: pulling the wool over the eyes of a brilliant king, who happened to be a paradigm of ruse himself as well as the most powerful monarch in the Western world.

But he did not stand alone. We have already mentioned one threefold. Now we come upon another threefold. Three men make up this second structure: the Cistercian Abbot of Cambron, a monk called Yves and a Templar-Soldier simply referred to as "the Flemish Templar". On the disputed frontiers of the kingdoms of those days, between France and the Empire, between Flanders and Hainaut, in a small district of the plain, destiny was to bring these three broad-shouldered men together, men who would decide to save the Temple.

It was the Flemish Templar who gave the order to hide the wealth of his Brothers and save it from the rapaciousness of the impure world. The Temple is the *privée mesnie de Deus,* the private army of God. The soldier-monk watched the Army of Christ being destroyed by crude envy, by sheer greed, by the basest feelings that exist in what can hardly be called a soul in those beasts who can hardly be called human. This is not my imagination. The Old Monk spells it out clearly.

The lives of the only three men to share the secret are now locked together, beyond death. In their strong hearts lies the unwavering hope that the Order of the Temple will live again, one day soon, after the rapacious King, the treacherous Pope and their army of vultures have been wiped out by a God-given tempest.

Having saved what needed saving, the Flemish Templar disappeared for seven years, that is during the whole duration of the lawsuit against the Order and the imprisonment of its dignitaries and, says Yves de Lessines, never uttered a word of what he knew. Then, after Jacques de Molay himself died at the stake, and during the weeks and months following this last murder, and God's revenge finally hit all those responsible for the death of the Temple, this Templar came back to hide himself in his native country, and entered the Abbey of Cambron, that played a capital although secret role during the year of 1307.

Being together again at last after all those dark and sombre years must have lifted their spirits almost instantaneously; a stream of hope, freed from the icy, inhibiting hold of adversity, sang like a swollen brook in springtime. Their dreams rushed sky-high; their elation bore them on wings night and day; adventure thrilled their souls. The Flemish Templar had come back...

But he was not the *long-awaited*.

Too old now, veteran of so many fights, broken by too many hardships, survivor of the apocalypse, the man from Flanders waited. He and his fellow conspirators felt they had saved their Order by safeguarding its possessions. They had hoped that on one beautiful morning, after the storm had blown over, a flourish of trumpets would gather the scattered troops. Alas, the sound of trumpets on a graveyard would bring tears to the eyes of the living, but it would not raise the dead. The French had killed off the men; who could have foreseen this fate? And yet, a great dream goes on living as long as the dreamer lives. Is there anything more powerful than hope that borders on despair? Inside their heads, on their lips, in their eyes, the Order's resurrection was imminent. Tomorrow a miracle would happen. A sign would be given. Very soon now, a new man would come...

The old Flemish Templar came back among his own. He probably became a lay brother, which allowed him to remain at Cambronchaux, where the farm belonging to the Abbey of Cambron was. From there, he could watch over the hiding place.

And he waited...

No-one came...

He died.

The Abbot of Cambron was forced to resign. The fact is so extraordinary as to be almost unbelievable. The reason for it remains unknown.

And he waited...

Nobody came...

He died.

And now Yves de Lessines, the old Prior, was the only one left. He waited... He thought about the words of the Gospel: When the time had come...

But what was God waiting for? When would the time come? Would it ever come? If God was deaf, if His Justice was blind, if Providence had fallen asleep then sanctity was a bait, and His Word was nothing but resounding futility.

Yves became angry. He had enough of it. He cursed God, and he did not regret it. How could one love a god who was so very… so… If he were standing there, right in front of him, how he would enjoy giving him a piece of his mind… And then he repented, humbly "Let Thy will be done, not mine".

When the old Prior was at the *barn* of Cambronchaux, he went up to the "Champ de la Mère-Dieu", to the "Croix Philosophe", which in old Picard literally means the crossing of the wise man.

There, at the intersection of two roads, visible from afar, like a beacon guiding the ship bringing salvation, he planted a sign, the tree of the Temple: the weeping willow. That is the place where he went to meditate and wait. His sight swept dreamily over the "Champ des Nuages", up to the hill called "Paradis", but was ever drawn to the "*clere peyne*", the white pointed façade, "*non trop eslongne du ciel*" (not too far away from heaven), over there, past the vineyard, on the other side of the brook, and which he called the secret place or the white shelter. The common people with their good-natured humour soon called him the *philosopher*. The nickname, of which he was well aware, has survived him for seven hundred years, in the topographical name of his resting-place: La Croix Philosophe, the Philosopher's Cross. *The long-awaited will be the new philosopher*; can there be a lovelier sign of emotional as well as spiritual fraternity?

Waiting… endless waiting.

Every morning his hope flared up and then died down with the last ray of the sun.

There is always the certitude that after the storm, things will brighten up again. But one cruelly empty day followed another…

The little white shelter had been the home of a stranger for fifteen years. Someone who knew nothing whatsoever of the story. A brewer. After all these centuries his descendants still inhabit this place haunted by the ghosts of the past whose voices have been stilled forever. Fourteen ghosts… shadows of the men who put their efforts into the undertaking.

Only three of them knew the secret place. Those who walked the last stage of the journey did not survive. And now, only one was left, hope still burning in his heart. On the threshold of eternity, the old man's confidence remained unchanged. Calmly awaiting death at the end of a long lifetime during which he witnessed some of the major events of our millennium, he was torn apart by the despair born of his lucidity and the dead hope springing from his faith. In his narrative, the voice of his suffering cried out louder than his hope, but his suffering was lived religiously and became a godly suffering. When one attains this level of spirituality, one joins the suffering God has had to endure each time our wickedness takes over. In the *Centuries* the "Eli, Eli, lama sabachtani? (My God, My God, why hast thou forsaken me?)" of the Old Monk is heard loud and clear.

Growing old means watching people close to you die. The only thing remaining in the soul of the aged Prior is silence. And cold and dark despair. Every day now he was forced to think of his own death advancing stealthily. He walked towards this mortal appointment carrying a secret in his pouch that he turned over and over in his mind, a secret that crushed him, that drove him to despair. He was desperate because he knew that, apart from him, nobody would be able to resist the power of greed. Nobody would have the strength and willpower to remain a humble guardian watching over immense riches. How often had he been tempted to confide in someone that he deemed worthy of knowing? How often did God have to stop him just in time, and show him the lies hidden inside the heart of men he thought pure?

Desperate because he knew now that no other man would be able to sustain such torment: to be looked down upon, mocked, slandered, disdained by all, when just a little digging would unearth fortune, power, glory and respect. To shoulder the fate of the conquered while being the conqueror. Conquered because one let oneself be conquered, like Christ. To be the humble and proud servant of a victorious God who bore the shame of the conquered. How did he, in fact, manage to keep silent, all those long and lonesome years?

Loneliness! Yes, he bore his solitude, and yet, a little flame never stopped flickering in this solitude: a little flame called hope. The hope that God would intervene, with hope turning into despair because God stayed silent. The same hope would be rekindled in the morning and die out with the last prayers of the day, and awaken again with the first light then vanish in the sunset to reappear once more with the next sunrise.

The Temple would rise again, of that he was sure; but the anguish would not be silenced: how would the Temple rise again, how would the deposit he safeguarded be retrieved when he, the old Prior, would no longer be there to reveal the place? He was the only one who knew, and he could share his knowledge with just one man, the one chosen by God. Why did this destined person not show up? What was keeping him? Where was he now, anyway?

The tremendous secret his heart and his head contained would disappear with his poor mortal body. Was God's Army destined to die forever the moment the old man reached for the Light? Was that God's will? No, He would not permit it. God would surely send someone the next day, in a week, the following year,… or was it maybe the traveller who was hastening towards him in the distance?

And then, one day, it happened that a despair-laden dawn ended in a twilight crowned with glory. A day blessed among all. The old man had seen the light, had heard God's voice. Since no man had been found fit to carry the secret's weight, God himself would guard the secret!

How? Here is how: patient, desperate Yves would write everything down, but in such a way that no human being would ever be able to understand, except the one who had been chosen to resurrect the Order. The only one to whom, after he had proven himself, the Holy Spirit would grant the Tongue of Fire, the insight, the intelligence that would enable him to understand everything and to accomplish his task. Sheer joy! Tears of joy!

During the day, Yves attended divine services and fulfilled his heavy duty as Prior of a large Abbey. The Abbot represents, the Prior administers! At night the old man writes and chants matins. The vain waiting made the time seem longer; and yet, time passed by too quickly: *Des jours seront reduicts par les sepmaines, Puis mois puis ans puis touts defailleront.*

The tension he had endured on the long road of his spiritual ordeal had been almost unbearable. Suddenly freed at last, his mind exploded into a pure and true masterpiece. But a masterpiece of such quality that people, with the text before their eyes, could do nothing but utter lunacies, unable to imagine that such a thing might exist. The work resists all comprehension if one does not know the man who wrote it, if one does not share his emotions, if one does not penetrate his heart, if one does not know his history.

Yves had reached the end of his earthly days. He knew now that his journey had been walked, that he would never again contemplate the Order in all its earthly splendour. But this did not matter any longer! The Spirit had spoken to its servant. A burst of life flared up within his old body. Hope had finally borne fruit.

The year was 1323. The fever of creation pulsating like a source of light in his soul, raged day and night through the man who became the Templars' chanter. By fire and candlelight, this creativity bloomed and blossomed like a water lily in the dark swamp of the successive nights. After the example of John the Baptist, he prepared the road, his was the voice crying in the wilderness. The one who was to hear, would hear. Each night, for someone he would never know, he committed to parchment the lines that had been singing all day in his head: *Estant assis de nuict secrete estude, seul, repose sur la chaire d'airain* (sitting alone at night in secret study on the bronze chair). At Cambron, in his Prior's cell, sitting on his bronze ceremonial chair, by the light of a wick, with only God for a companion, the faithful Cistercian chisels a poem into existence. In his lines, he imprisons the secret that now sings through his head. A song such as had never been written, sung or heard:

the *Centuries*.

Four thousand lines flowed from his fingers onto the parchment; he described it in splendid words: *les voix fremissent par les manches. Splendeur divine! Le divin pres s'assied* (the voices tremble softly through the sleeves. Heavenly splendour! The Divine is sitting close by).

His poem would reveal everything to the envoy, the one who would come to the Croix Philosophe, the one he called the "new sophe", the new adept.

He will understand it all, in one moment of thought: *Le nouveau sophe d'un seul cerveau l'a vu.* The poem will be revelation, but to him alone. The Spirit who showed the Prior the way to conceal the secret and to reveal it at the same time, the same Spirit will grant his Envoy the necessary insight. And so, Prior Yves starts his account: he tells of the perils, he reveals the names of people – of friends and of enemies alike. The paths followed, the stratagems, the indications as to what must be sought after and found, and he lists a number of place names and landmarks, with an unheard of profusion of accurate and detailed information. The old Prior is very much aware of his skills and talent.

He is so sure that no-one will fathom out the secret that often he ridicules openly those who will claim that they know: *Ils sont juste bons a servir a torcher le cul* (they are just good enough to wipe the ass with), he writes literally.

But underneath his derision, we can sense his fear. Doubt tortured him, anxiety tainted his joy. Will the long-awaited one understand and act? How can he not doubt when he knows human nature all too well? He knows that God moves in mysterious ways; the way the Holy Spirit suggests is so unusual, so strange. Of course, doubt caused uneasiness but it also strengthened the old Prior's resolve. He knew that faith had its own demands but that it has grounds in trust; he also knows that believing without ever doubting is an act of stupid foolishness. Even Christ, nailed on his cross, experienced his moment of doubt. On the day the long-awaited one stands on the threshold of Cambron, will Yves have done everything within his power to help the Envoy along the way to his ultimate destination?

His anxiety compelled him on and on relentlessly, but anxious. He went on writing without stopping, always on the same topic. He reformulated the same message in countless different ways, so that the long-awaited one would still know enough to accomplish God's will, even if he only understood a small part.

Yves de Lessines was a tormented soul. Sometimes the burns of his despair made him cry out in pain: *Trop tard viendra l'attendu*, the long awaited has come too late, immediately followed by a soaring hope that took him far ahead into the future: *For 500 years, no-one will mention us, we who were the ornament of our century, but after this the Temple will live again in all its splendour.* Yves de Lessines' words, however, are no prophecy but a cry from the heart. The real work of art is always a pure emotion. And the emotion here is the fear of old Prior Yves kneaded by his talent.

The *Centuries* are unquestionably a work of art, but they are also a work of history. In those troubled days, when the high and mighty provoked one another dangerously, a military Order protecting the humble and modest created unease, and its influence disquieted the Establishment. Its riches fanned the greed of the squanderers. Dark and sinister plans were brewing around Philip the Fair. The Flemish Templar was aware of these. Since he was much more astute than Jacques de Molay, the Master, he decided that the time for security measures had come. He came to Cambron to consult with his relative, Abbot Jacques de Montignies (or Plusquet or Plusquiel after his father's name; the use of patronyms was not rigourously regulated at the beginning of the 14th century). The latter immediately summoned the most intelligent man living in the Abbey, an elderly man who devoted himself to the writing of theological works, a man who was very much acquainted with his fellow men, the world in general, books, science and war. At the Abbey, he was called Brother Yves.

What exactly is Yves de Lessines writing about in the *Centuries*? He writes that the man talking to the two monks reveals the following: from different sources, from Burgundy, from Bruges, from the Papal Curia, from the French Queen, alarming rumours have come to the attention of the Templars. The Temple dignitaries suspected a conspiracy against them, but they did not believe in the imminence of the danger. However, the Templar who came to Cambron and stood right there in the Abbot's quarters had a dissenting opinion.

I am sure that, at this point, you are raising your eyebrows because you, like me, like anybody else, are astonished at what you have just read. I am sure you do not believe one word of what Yves de Lessines affirms in his poem, namely that the Templars had been given warning of the gravity of the danger that threatened them. Like me, you think this is absolutely contrary to historical truth; and if you are as distrustful as I am where historical reports are concerned, you will agree that the matter is worthy of investigation and that, just maybe, we may have stumbled upon the proof, however small, that the whole thing is a mystifying humbug. The history of the Templars has given rise to numerous concoctions and inventions. For us, who seek certainty, being distrustful is a very sane state of mind.

In a situation like this, it is only wise to re-examine our certitudes carefully. Yves de Lessines' text is inconsistent with what we have been told is historical truth. It is commonly agreed that the King's plans had not been disclosed, and it is quite true that, if the Templars were all arrested at day-break on Friday, 13th October 1307, this was due to the fact that they were caught unawares. To assert that they were totally unaware is, therefore, not a proven fact but a deduction that passes off as proven fact.

Before having thought things over again in the light of new information that came to me at exactly the right time, I was convinced that the royal plot had not come to light before the action was taken, due to the profusion of precautions taken by the authorities. Isn't this the story that is found in each book covering the subject? I reflected that, if France had been kept in the dark, it was quite obvious that other foreign countries had been even less informed; and Flanders least of all, since her people were at war with Philip the Fair. Then one day, by the purest of coincidences, I learned that the King of France had summoned Robert de Béthune, the Count of Flanders, to Tours on 26th March 1307, to advise him of his plan and to request his collaboration in this act – more than six months before the arrests! The Templars were duly arrested on 13th October.

At this point we should remember that Robert de Béthune bore the King an immense grudge, if not downright hatred. Following the Peace of Athis, Philip the Fair had seized the southern part of the County of Flanders and imprisoned Robert and his father Gui de Dampierre, who were freed only after the defeat suffered by the French on 11th July 1302 on the plains of Courtrai.

Thus, in the light shed by this anecdote that has never drawn any attention, we may conclude that when Yves de Lessines reveals that the Templars had been warned by Bruges, this fact is plausible. As you see, one can never catch the author of the *Centuries* out; he never makes things up. Whenever the reported facts are thoroughly examined, one must conclude that he is telling the truth.

So far, so good, but how could a warning have come from Burgundy? If it formed part of your French history lessons, or if you have read Maurice Druon's *Les Rois Maudits*, you will remember that Philip the Fair's eldest son, Louis X le Hutin, married Marguerite de Bourgogne, while his third son, Charles IV, was married to her sister. They were both the daughters of the duke of Burgundy, Robert II, and his wife Mahaut d'Artois.

As far as Philip the Fair was concerned, only his second son, Philippe V le Long, was important. He considered the other two to be a pair of no good, idle fools worthy only of his contempt, and King Philippe rarely misjudged people. Fools they may well indeed have been; nevertheless they were the King's sons and as such were constitutionally entitled to attend the King's Council. As attested by numerous sources, good old dumb Louis hurriedly repeated everything to his unfaithful wife, who in turn hastened to keep mum and dad informed. A staunch and forceful supporter of the linen and tapestry industry in the Arrageois region, Mahaut d'Artois enjoyed the best of relations with the Temple bankers…

According to the *Centuries*, a violent row broke out at the top of the Order regarding the advisability of taking security measures: the Temple's hierarchy, its judgement hampered by its vanity, led by a Master blinder than a donkey wearing blinkers, emphatically denied the danger. But someone else, invested with full plenary powers, made the decision to safeguard what needed to be safeguarded, and had this decision carried out by the whole Order.

Yves de Lessines confirms that the Flemish Templar took over command and accused the hierarchy of treason. Nobody argued or disagreed, except one: the bailey of the lower valley of the Rhône ne voulant obeir a l'ordre hesperique (refused to obey the Hesperic order) (Hespérie is the name used by Yves de Lessines to refer to Flanders). This is another of those revealing details stamped with the truth. And the Old Monk enumerates what was preserved from the predators' greed: *documents* (detailed as the rules, the decisions of the chapters, and writs proving the betrayal of the Pope) and also, because they are practical people, *silver* and *gold*, the whole stored in *twenty-one barrels duly greased on the outside* to protect their contents from water damage.

And in fact, Philip the Fair's agents would not find much in the Temple houses, except what had no value, or what was not easily transportable: the cattle, the tools, a few liturgical objects and IOUs. This last item may seem incongruous but is, in itself, a token of the intelligence and the finesse of those who organised the whole thing: if the Order was destroyed, the Templars would have no use for these papers. Indeed, no debtor would be willing to settle his debt and the Temple had no means to force them to do so. They would be the laughing stock of their contemporaries: how would a pursued Order go to court and plead? The moment the King's henchmen launched their attack, all the debtors of the Temple would be overjoyed, believing their debts to have been cancelled in the process, forgetting too easily the avidity of the royal financiers. Our three thoughtful men, however, had taken this into account and had suspected the King would demand pitilessly that all the debts be honoured, and to his own advantage. Our men knew that nothing is more painful than a great hope dashed, especially when this hope was truly dishonest. They expected the King to be hated by the scavengers who applauded the predator on the first day. And so it happened. Unfortunately to no avail as far as the Temple was concerned because Philip the Fair's skilful manoeuvres had given the affair a turn such that the clever scheme became totally useless.

In conclusion, the triumvirate had duly thought over what, from their point of view, was essential to safeguard, after having decided not to be burdened by the unnecessary or the superfluous.

With this in mind, two totally contradictory facts emerge: 1) it is obvious that the King's men did not find what they were looking for – the written reports of the trials are there to prove it – and 2) it is also pretty obvious that the Templars were caught unarmed, which proves that in the Temple houses nothing of the sort had been foreseen, least of all the violence of the attack. If the Templars had not been *surpris nus et sans harnois* (naked and without arms) they would have defended themselves, after the three required summons, as the assailants were Christians, and they would have decimated their aggressors. The sight of the Templars fully dressed and armed would probably have been enough to send their attackers scurrying off like scared rabbits. Without a moment's hesitation; the Templars' reputation as an elite fighting unit was known to all. A Templar never shirked a battle with the odds of one against three. Not because they were boasters, but because it was ordered by their Rule; and moreover they were deemed to obtain victory in such situations.

These two facts combined are clear proof that Yves de Lessines is telling the truth when he says that the safekeeping operation was set up by a few without the others' knowledge.

So, against the advice of the Order's official supreme hierarchy, a few men, or one man, mysteriously invested with the authority needed to issue such an incongruous command, denied moreover by the dignitaries, decided to *ravir le tresor des temples par devant* (to take away the treasure of the temples in advance), to quote the Old Monk. If he is speaking the truth – and the only thing contradicting him is our own fragmentary interpretation of the history, because up to this day all historical and material elements tend to agree with his narrative – then he formally establishes the reality of a mystery within the Temple's organisation.

All those who have ever written about the existence of an occult hierarchy that would have led the Order, have at best rehashed rumours and unfounded "revelations". Never have they shown a serious, verifiable document to substantiate their assertions. This leads us to conclude that either such a document does not exist, or else that the existing documents have never been duly analysed from this point of view. If History is not founded on a credible testimony or a range of convincing indications, it is but a badly written fairy tale. If you take the view that every document someone refuses to show you does not exist, experience will always prove you right.

But, *in tempore non suspecto*, Yves de Lessines states a fact that must have met with complete incredulity even more on the part of his contemporaries than on ours. To the people living in the 1300s, the Temple was an every-day reality, in which authority was held by men known to all, and to whom everybody could turn because they were actively engaged in every area of medieval society. Who could have conceived that within an elite fighting force, upholding unfailingly an iron discipline for two centuries, a few men not even belonging to the official hierarchy had dared to issue such an unusual order and that this order had been ignored by the highest authority? And nobody would have believed that the entire Temple, as one man, obeyed this command down to the letter, without delay and in the deepest secret, no explanations or justifications given or asked.

We must admit we are baffled. The only likely hypothesis, the only possibility, the only realistic explanation is that these men, who were unknown to all, showed a sign familiar to all Templars in order to be obeyed, which gave legitimacy to their absolute power in this moment of major crisis.

In order to grasp the phenomenon clearly, drawing an analogy with today would be very helpful.

The scenario goes like this: imagine that during a period of total peace, an official of middle rank, working in a department that is not even close to the heart of government (for instance an assistant manager in the Department of Pensions, or Forestry, or the administration of Cycle-Tracks) gives an order for all the reserves and cash deposits of the National Bank to be collected, and for all the important documents of the country to be assembled. He then asks that all be handed over to him for hiding in a spot he alone knows of. Imagine that in spite of the formal prohibition of the government and the senior civil service, he is to be obeyed on the spot! Nobody would believe this could ever happen, and yet Yves de Lessines asserts that this is exactly what happened then. Eventually I came to the conclusion that we should trust him. Why? Because he provides an explanation down to the minutest detail, and thus makes the improbable seem plausible.

No-one in their right mind would care to admit that this plan was carried out in haste, and without rigorous preparations. That it consisted, as the dreamers would like us to believe, of a desperate flight during the night preceding the attack with a discrete cavalcade of madly creaking, overloaded carts, which ended in the burial of the fabulous treasure under the castle of Gisors, one of Philip the Fair's prisons, of all places, is quite unbelievable.

Just picture the scene! A thief rings the bell at the remand centre just after he has carried out his crime and he calmly digs a hole in the prison yard to hide his loot. And not a single guard finds anything just a little fishy in the whole business. By far the strangest thing in the Gisors-story would be the IQ of the prison wardens, or of the people who came up with the tale that the Templars selected this place to hide their belongings, in a pit of 36 metres deep; and that this treasure was seen in the 20th century by a man, so guileless he did not even think of taking a picture. He says he saw it. The others scrutinised the bottom of the hole till they were blue in the face, they saw nothing, but nonetheless wrote book upon book stating that the treasure lay there... in 24 coffers each one measuring 3.6 by 2.4 by 1.8 metres, made of pure gold. Without even switching on their common sense and their calculators to do a little mathematics in order to determine the volume of the trifle: 15,552 dm³, and its weight (the man who "saw" them claimed they were filled to the brim with golden coins); the specific gravity (or density) of gold being 19, each of these little coffers weighs 295,488 kilograms. It does not seem to me that in any of all the European harbours, there could be many cranes that could lift such a load. Let us do some more calculations and determine the total weight and value of the Temple treasure (according to the version of Gisors castle): twenty-four coffers of 295,488 kilograms equals 7,091,712 kilograms. At around 10,000 dollar per kilogram, we have 70,917,120,000 dollars worth of treasure. To which must be added a few cartloads of precious stones.

What is more, in spite of what some people have come to imagine, the Order's treasury was not stored in the Temple Tower in Paris. This is a typical example of a French dream. The Order of the Temple was, by far, the largest bank of its time. Money stored in a cellar is totally useless to a banker whose job it is to keep the money working, i.e. in circulation. There is far more money in the branches than in the vault of the building where a bank's headquarters are established. Putting money away behind bars in a dark cellar is the action of a miser, not a banker.

Today, when you need some money and you go to the local branch in the High Street, the branch manager does not rush an armoured car off to the Central Bank to get it for you, while you take your ease and a cup of coffee in the lounge. So there is really no reason to believe that if an Hungarian farmer wanted to borrow six gold coins from the local commanderie, the Templars had to send two armed men to get them from Paris. Banking becomes ruinously expensive if it is conducted that way. To be fruitful, the riches of the Temple must necessarily be spread over the various houses of the Order, in proportion to their specific needs.

Just as in modern banking the accounts of the Temple were of course centralised pyramidally, which has led many people to conclude that the cash was stored in one single place. To draw an analogy with today, it means that in order to verify the cash deposits of all the local branches, all the bank notes and coins would have to be transported first to the district centre, then to the county town, then on to the regional centre, then to the country capital, and then to Chicago or Macao or wherever… since the Temple has been the prototype of the centralised multinational. Once again, the story told by Yves de Lessines is reasonable and logical.

To gather the fortune and the documents of the Temple dispersed all over Europe, to organise their transportation from all corners of the world in the utmost secrecy and then to have them safely delivered at the designated spot and at the right time, would have had no chance of success when done in haste. It makes far more sense for them, long in advance, to have stipulated in detail the roads to be followed, prepared the stopping places, found a safe shelter and, last but certainly not least, given thorough thought as to the means of recovering everything after the storm had blown over.

And the Templars had been prepared and ready for a long time. Throughout the *Centuries*, the Old Monk pursues an *in absentia* relationship by analogy based on the Emperor Frederic II Hohenstaufen (1194-1250). All the while he is in fact targeting Philip the Fair (1268-1314).

 As we have already seen, in 1230 the former had turned the Italian Templars into the scapegoats for his outrageous conduct in the East. He had persecuted the men and stolen their belongings. Thus Yves de Lessines is giving us to understand that the Templars had learned a lesson from the Sicilian episode, that for seventy years the Order had made sure of its ability to cope with a similar return of adversity, and that the decision to start the safeguarding mechanism did not rest with the official hierarchy – too visible and therefore too vulnerable – but with a man unknown to all and occupying the most inconspicuous of functions.

The most simple and effective way to

protect yourself is also the most ordinary: to decide that in the event of a crisis, men no longer obey other men; they obey a sign. No need for a ferocious secret policy to seek out and eliminate the traitors inside the Temple: it is quite impossible to infiltrate efficiently an organisation working on that principle for the simple reason that even a successful infiltration is completely pointless. Even if he were firmly seated in the heart of command, the traitor cannot foresee what decisions will be taken by the man everybody knows he keeps watch over, but nobody knows who he is.

The sign that we are referring to does exist: the Temple dignitaries scratched it on their prison wall; and the photo shows the sign carved into a wooden beam that still remains where it was put at the beginning of the 14th century.

It should be noted that in the *Centuries* Yves de Lessines indicates that the sign is to be found in only two places.

Let us forget for a while the dreams of the Temple treasure seekers who swear by Gisors, Provins and a hundred other places in the French Hexagon. Let us consider similar dilemmas: did the White Russians seek refuge in the outskirts of Moscow? Did the opponents to Nazism hide themselves in Westfalia or Saxony? Did the Pieds-Noirs bury their money in Algeria? To hide your belongings by burying them is not a bad thing in itself, but with the future in mind, you also think about the way to dig them up again. Hiding things in a spot where you will almost certainly be arrested if you show up to recover them does seem to be a rather bizarre idea.

The initiators of the Temple project had analysed the situation thoroughly. Their careful consideration of the countries involved, their appreciation of the men at the top, the great meticulousness in the working out of their plan leave us silent with admiration. The hunters of the Temple gold credit the white soldiers of the Order (never the black!) with extraordinary knowledge and intelligence equalling at least, if not surpassing that of the Holy Spirit. Even if we have to assume they may be one step lower on the ladder of omniscience, does that mean that they dropped off the other extreme, and wittingly threw themselves into the King's claws, within reach of his torturers? All those fairytale dreams are of course delightful, but a little childish. It was reason that dictated the choice of the country where the riches of the Temple were to be hidden. Hence, most certainly not *in* France.

In Italy? While the Pope is your worst enemy? Of course, one could argue that some advantage might have been gained from the fact that rival states ensured division in the peninsula. Nonetheless at the beginning of the 14th century, the Papacy was genuinely powerful south of the Alps. So let us assume the Templars were intelligent and did not choose to hide their little trifles in Italy.

Which leaves the Spanish territories, England and its colonies, and the German state. If you want to protect your belongings, you should try and pre-empt the unwelcome curiosity of the authorities, ensure that you have the time and the possibility to think again when danger rears its head and be assured of a safe and discrete means of escape. You would therefore go and hide your goods in a location where discussion is lawfully possible and where the political situation does not suffer from untimely interference from the powers-that-be. This excluded England because the royal administration was powerful and well organised, as well as the German territories. Although it is quite true that the Emperor carried little weight outside his private estates, his liegemen were very much in control, served by well-informed agents, and at least as rapacious as anyone else. History teaches us that Aragon, Castille, Leon and Portugal liked the Order well, but presumably, they would have liked its riches even better.

To put a fair distance between yourself and your enemy is, of course, an excellent initiative, as long as you do not have to take up residence at the other end of the world, out of touch with your homebase. If travelling is instructive for the young, it is without doubt tiring for the old, and the longer the journey, the more arduous and dangerous it would be, even more so on the return trip than on the outward journey. Besides, how would you go about guarding and, if need be, defending the Order's treasure in a place where it had no army of any consequence nor a dense network of strongholds? Out go Scotland, Ireland and Poland.

And what about America?

Why would they have gone there and what could they have done?

The major shortcoming of all the places proposed is that they result from "before" and "after" points of view which the authors, out of their own lack of wariness, have confused. These authors do not realise that they reason in the light of what happened (or what they think happened) *after* the Order was destroyed, whereas the three men who set things in motion made their decisions, saw to their organisation and acted *beforehand*. It is essential to recognise this and to acknowledge the consequences in order to grasp the logic that swayed in the mind of the Flemish Templar and his companions.

Chapter Five – Refuge and Anticipation

The attack hit them like lightning. There are however no grounds for believing that the safeguarding of the Temple goods resulted in a desperate disorderly flight. According to Yves de Lessines, everything had been safely put away weeks before the fatal Friday, 13th October 1307.

After having meticulously weighed the pros and cons, the three men in charge of evacuating the goods that were to be saved, came to the conclusion that they knew a discreet little location, under no-one's excessive authority, near one of their own most important strongholds, close to the wealthiest place on earth, and where their mortal enemy would never dare to show up because the people of that country had just forced the defeat of the century upon him.

Flanders had always been the region where the Order was the richest, right from the beginning. This was quite normal: two Flemish noblemen were among the founders of the Order, while Flanders itself was the California of the medieval world. What exactly was the situation in Flanders at the onset of the 14th century?

France wanted to appropriate the wealth of the county and Flanders fought for its very life. The French crown and the Flemish people had been engaged for centuries in a terrible battle that had culminated at that particular time in a full-scale war. In his *Histoire de Belgique*, Henri Pirenne describes it as follows: "Cette lutte a été le plus grand spectacle du Moyen Age" (This battle has been the biggest spectacle of the Middle Ages). At the time Philip the Fair started planning his attack on the Temple – and these two facts are obviously interrelated – the men of the Flemish Communes had inflicted its most severe defeat ever upon the French army, killing half of the royal cavalry on the meadows of Groeninge on 11th July 1302; we have already referred to this previously. Philip the Fair did not really feel welcome in the Flat Country, to say the least.

A major consideration in the choice of the Temple refuge was the assessment of the domestic political situation. During the whole of the Middle Ages Flanders had always been a territory where two power bases, the Communes and the Count, kept each other in balance and, *ipso facto*, held arbitrary power in check. But somewhere on the frontier between Flanders and Hainaut lay a small, rather peculiar territory: the *Terre des Débats*.

The Count of Flanders was a vassal of the French King for the largest part of his estates. His county of Alost, however, between the rivers Escaut and Dender, bordering on Royal Flanders, constituted what was called Imperial Flanders and was part of the German empire. *The King of France had no authority whatsoever therein.* This county was owned by the Emperor, a feeble and remote character to whom the Count of Flanders regularly refused to pay his liegeman's homage. Moreover: at that time, the Great Interregnum in Germany had not been over long; the zeal of German suzerainty was purely theoretical and bore no comparison with the total and absolute power Philip the Fair had inflicted upon his vassals, whose authority he curtailed relentlessly.

What exactly was this *Terre des Débats*? A few villages lost on the frontier between Hainaut and Flanders. Never in the whole of medieval history had such an insignificant little stretch of land caused so much commotion. Two families disputed Hainaut and Flanders: the Avesnes and the Dampierre. At the time the Temple was destroyed, the quarrellers had finally come to an agreement, with bad grace and a lot of dark thoughts of revenge: the Avesnes were given Hainaut, the Dampierre Flanders.

But the war raged on for the possession of the *Terre des Débats*.

This *Terre des Débats* (country of disputes) originated from what is called the *tenement d'Inde* (the property of Inde) to which the Old Monk openly refers, for instance in this passage:

> VII 2 *Noir blanc a l'inde dissimule en terre*
> *Sous la feincte ombre traistre verez et sonnez*

What countless dazzling or troubling prophecies have gushed forth from this passage on the land of Inde! And yet, Yves de Lessines said it all. Let us read the first line out loud very carefully: *Noir blanc à l'Inde d'ici mu(e) le en terre* (black white to the Inde of here hide it in the ground). A little bonus: *verez* and *sonnez* must also be understood as: put into verse and song! *Noir blanc?* These are the two colours of the large Temple standard, the one the Templars themselves called *Beaucéant*. The English historian Edith Simon has written an extremely well documented and serious work on the Order of the Temple. She titled her book: *The Piebald Standard*, black and white, like the bird.

There is no question here of the land of the Indians, as is the common belief, but of a rather small imperial gift. Back in 820, the Abbey of Kornelismünster, ten kilometres south of Aix-la-Chapelle, on the road to Trèves, was founded by Louis le Pieux in favour of his friend, Saint Benoît d'Aniane.

At the beginning of the 9th century, Saint Benoît d'Aniane had radically reformed the Order of the Benedictines. He had had a very strong influence on this son of Charlemagne. The said son interlarded his lascivious debauchery with such a theatrical manifestation of repentance that the nickname "the Pious" was bestowed upon him. Since the Abbey needed revenues, Louis the Pious donated a number of domains, among which was the area of land that many years later will be known as the *Terre des Débats*. The church of the Abbey still exists and the small town is worth the detour.

To understand clearly the term "land of Inde" one should know that the Abbey of Kornelismünster was built on the bank of the river Inde, very picturesquely situated on one of its meanders. As a consequence the Abbey was also known as the Abbey of Inde or Ende; the *"terre d'Inde"* is often referred to as the *tenement d'Inde*, and in one of the seven villages of the *Terre des Débats*, called Wodecq, a hamlet is still called *"l'Endemaine"* – pronounced then *Indemaine* – which means: *l'Inde(do)maine*.

During the course of my investigation, certain people offered their assistance; in particular eminent members of an association by the name of CARTI helped out with the study of the place names and the events related by Yves de Lessines. CARTI is the *"Cercle d'Archéologie de Renaix et du Tenement d'Inde"*!

The extract below is from a manuscript dated 1285, i.e. contemporary with Yves de Lessines, to which I will refer a certain number of times (*Viel Rentier d'Audenarde*):

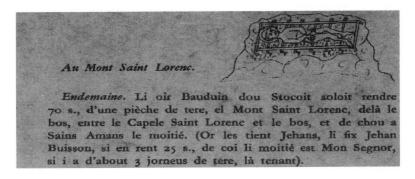

Au Mont Saint Lorenc.

Endemaine. Li oir Bauduin dou Stocoit soloit rendre 70 s., d'une pièche de tere, el Mont Saint Lorenc, delà le bos, entre le Capele Saint Lorenc et le bos, et de chou a Sains Amans le moitié. (Or les tient Jehans, li fix Jehan Buisson, si en rent 25 s., de coi li moitié est Mon Segnor, si i a d'about 3 jorneus de tere, là tenant).

The legal status of the *tenement d'Inde* gets confusing very quickly; with the passing of years and centuries this confusion never stops growing. In the end, having become extremely annoyed with a property costing more than it earned, the Abbey of Kornelismünster got rid of it in the 13th century. But instead of clarifying the situation, the sale resulted in even greater confusion. The seven villages constituting the *Terre des Débats* enjoyed the most incredible mixed up political and legal status in their various aspects, and were considered even then to be the classic example of the imbroglio.

The first question nobody could answer was to whom did this territory belong: to Flanders or to Hainaut? To support their claims, either side with the encouragement or threat of a whole bunch of sordidly interested third parties, appealed to a variety of authorities, each one more incongruous than the other. Everybody had his say: Kings were involved, Emperors and Popes, each being of a different opinion that always found a challenger. Of course, Abbots, Bishops and Archbishops, either entitled to local rights or called upon by friends, also had their stake in the debate.

The village of Wodecq was the *Terre des Debats* in miniature; to quote Gaston Leroy, our best documented historian and my first schoolteacher: "WODECQ ÉTAIT EN LUI-MÊME UNE TERRE DE DÉBAT DANS LA TERRE DES DÉBATS" (Wodecq was itself a region of dispute within the disputed land).

Each judicial procedure invariably started with a long debate attempting to establish which law was to be applied. This in itself was not the easiest thing to determine. As regards the village square of Wodecq, for instance, four different systems, each governed by a different common law, were to be taken into account. To make things more interesting, the jurisdiction boundaries sometimes ran right through the houses. Having to settle a café brawl was a task out of all proportion. The exact spot, to the yard, where it had started and ended had to be defined, and where and by whom the most significant blows were dealt and received. Moreover, there was also a refuge area. To crown it all, some government offices and public functions depended on Flanders, others on Hainaut. Since judges and their sergeants were rewarded *pro rata* the inflicted fines, they each poached the other's territory. Birds of prey know no mercy.

The relish with which the medieval world pursued their legal proceedings is beyond all imagination, as the following will demonstrate. One day a case was opened because two men could not agree on which one of them was entitled to cut the wood on a two hundred metres border to the road. The matter kept the courts busy for some time and was finally settled amicably seventy years later because the judges of Mons, Valenciennes, Ghent, Alost, and also Malines still had not come to an agreement with regard to the preliminary questions.

Even taxes were a brain-wrecking business. The cereals remained in sheaves on the field till the taxman had made his round, after which time they were stacked or stored in barns. Cheating was not all that easy. As far as the other crops are concerned, I am almost certain the same complaint was heard year in year out: what a bad season it had been.

My grandfather used to grow tobacco; I cannot count the times he would complain bitterly in exactly the same words to the excise official who came to collect the tax. It had rained too much, or not enough; the wind had blown from the wrong direction, or there had been a storm. If his plants had not gone rusty, the worms had eaten them; they even suffered both plagues the same year sometimes. Once, in the 1950s, I heard him assert that the chicken dung he used to fertilise his land with had lost its former quality. While, at that time, the largest chicken farm prided itself on a population of two hundred hens, free-range to boot, and fed on grain. Sometimes, as much as he hated it, he had to admit to a perfect, flawless season; he then explained to the taxman with the persuasiveness of a prosecutor that the variety of tobacco he grew was a particularly light-weight sort. In fact he suffered considerable loss and if he went on growing tobacco this was only out of love of the art and the beauty of the plants.

As far as the beneficiaries of the taxes are concerned, almost every field enjoyed its own particular statute; and its revenue had to be split up between different beneficiaries. Quibbling was never far off. The classical example was the following: assuming someone was entitled to one third of the crop, should he receive one third of the total each year, or rather the total amount once every three years? In order to find this out, legal proceedings were started, and the loser... then lodged an appeal. As you can imagine, between the three of them, there was always one who was discontented and who sought compensation in another court.

Even gardens were taxed and as the payers rarely showed enthusiasm in this regard, you can imagine the rest. The fate of a basket of apples or a bag of sugar beet could keep a whole tribe of lawyers in riches. In such a village, if you were asked an annoying question at the age of twenty and you did not totally lack inventiveness, you could be sure your great-grandson would have to give the answer, somewhere around his retirement age. In the end, even there, the law was unified, 500 years after the Old Monk passed away, at the urgent request of Charles V and later on of the Empress Marie-Theresa of Austria.

In Wodecq, the only authority of any clout, which was not challenged, (at least, not too much), was Cambronchaux, the Cistercian "barn", i.e. the very large farm belonging to the Abbey of Cambron, that, by papal privilege, enjoyed general exemption from all civil and religious jurisdiction. Even the bishop had no authority to excommunicate a monk of Cambron for any reason whatsoever. The Pope had extended this immunity to all the people working for the Abbey, as well as its suppliers and customers. This meant that, if you were a monk from Cambron and happened to be in Wodecq, it would have been surprising if anyone had asked you about what you were up to. The opportunity offered the Templars to finalise their project was nearly ideal. In those days Wodecq was the answer to all their problems.

In 1307, at the time the Temple was destroyed, the *Terre des Débats* was at the centre of the war. Shortly before, the town of Renaix had been devastated; the town of Lessines had been under a heavy siege and finally burnt down in April and May 1303. Armed troops were marauding everywhere. In those circumstances, who would have wondered at the sight of a few Templars engaged in the ordinary act of transporting hay on a cart and stacking it in a barn? That the wagon was escorted was a very ordinary precaution given the bandits stalking roads and fields, and the soldiers foraging. "Where shall we hide a pebble", asked Father Brown. "On the beach", the wise Flambeau answered.

And so, on the decision of one single man of lower rank, the Order of the Temple, having been warned of the impending catastrophe, was able to put its long-thought-out operation into execution in time, which was to protect its means of survival from the grasping fingers of the century's villains. Unfortunately, after the storm had blown over, the favourable circumstances that they needed and hoped for never arose. When the wind stopped raging, the Order was no more. The only thing that was left was hope, hope that God would send a messenger, a sort of Messiah. But the man of Providence never showed up. And what could he have done anyway? All was to no avail.

A few astute men – very well acquainted with politics – had "cracked" the King's mind and seen through the intrigues of his entourage. The persecution staged by Frederic II had taught them that kings must be dreaded; however, the implacable will of the French monarchy to diminish the Pope's power had led them to believe the latter was their ally against a common fiend, Philip the Fair.

The audacious ride of Guillaume de Nogaret and his troops to Anagni, where the Pope had been arrested, was the French reply to the Bull *Unam Sanctum* of 18th November 1302. This raid had probably caused Boniface VIII's death in October 1303, but most of all it revealed the vulnerability of spiritual authority without the military might to underpin it. The most obtuse intelligence could see where the Pope's interest lay. A firm stand in favour of the Temple was the only thing that could support his ambitions, protect him against the worldly powers that tried to bring him to submission and maybe even – who was to know what could happen in those troublesome days – guarantee his very existence. Therefore to fend off the attack of their enemy of the moment, the Templars had counted on the rivalry between Paris and the Pope, and trusted that the Pope would be unwaveringly on their side, threatening the King and his whole kingdom with excommunication and anathema. At the same time this would allow the Templars to seize their weapons, as the aggressors would no longer be considered Christians.

This was a disastrous mistake! Benoit XI, the successor of Boniface

VIII, although virtuously accommodating and not at all inclined to challenge Philip the Fair's edicts, but probably lacking the right submissiveness, was not to be Pope for long. He died of indigestion, eating figs, so the story goes. Cleverly anticipating the ignominious desires of the Princes of the Church and the multiple grudges the factions of Cardinals bore against one another, Philip the Fair succeeded in placing his own favourite on St Peter's throne. Pope Clement V, that highly un-commendable creature of Philip, called "the Fair", betrayed the soldiers of Christ, out of vile self-interest, whatever is said to the contrary. Consequently, things did not turn out as foreseen: the Order could not survive the ordeal.

The full measure of the "Holy Father" can be seen when it is known that he wasted no time bestowing upon his family the properties of the Order, even before its abolition had been officially ordered, in order to be the first one at the kill and confront the other vultures with a *fait accompli*. Neither his nephews, nor his mistress, nor his adulterous son felt the slightest inclination to make good their malevolently acquired new fortune. This is what the Old Monk calls "le fait Gothique", the false trick of the Goth, the barbarian, in this case being Pope Clement V whose secular name was Bernard de Goth. Another of those little pieces of evidences that go unnoticed. But for those who have eyes…

But let us return to the *Centuries*. As well as the routes of those who escorted the "treasures" of the Temple, on land or by sea, Yves de Lessines also describes the places where messages were waiting to be read and understood by the long-awaited one, so that he would discover the secret spot where for so many years now the precious load had been resting. He writes, among other things, that the keys to the secret are engraved on a wall, near a door, at Chinon.

This is indeed correct. But how did the Cistercian know that the Temple dignitaries had put signs on their prison wall? How did he know these engravings were not very far from a door? Because I am convinced that Yves de Lessines never set foot in the Coudray tower of the castle of Chinon. Where did he get his information from? Geneviève Mouligneau suggested that he may have been told by the Flemish Templar, the man who went underground for seven years and then came back to Cambron. We are left in no doubt, however, that these drawings are irrefutable proof of the fact that, without ever realising it, the henchmen had a Templar knight fully aware of the secret at hand.

So, messages there were: a message at Chinon, a message at Wodecq, messages in the *Centuries*, maybe a message at Lampernesse, a message at Moustier. These messages are coded in such a way that only the addressee will be able to understand. The engravings of the Chinon prison remain totally obscure to anyone who is ignorant of the fact that the only thing they indicate is a spot to be found.

So does the message of Moustier. The Tables of Moustier are and remain a mess of consonants if one does not know the Latin text from which the vowels are taken. The *Centuries* look like a text in pidgin French at best, until we capture Yves de Lessines' spirit, understand his purpose and identify the literary means he puts to work. He who is "initiated" to use the Templar vocabulary, immediately guesses the meaning and finds the road; the others are hopelessly lost because the diversionary lures increase exponentially. Well, there is only one path to be followed step by careful step, moving forward from place to place as indicated by the guide.

Whether it be outlined in brick or charcoal, hewn in stone or carved on a wooden beam, painted on a altar, written in a poem of four thousand lines, it makes no difference. The awaited one will always understand the message and will, following Tom Thumb's pebbles, finally arrive in a small forgotten village of the *Terre des Débats*.

This was the plan thought out by a few acute and resolute Templars; this was their plan of safeguard. A system set up on that basis is one hundred percent fool-proof. No need to cudgel your brains to break a code, no need to search for a mysterious map, no need (as proven by Philip the Fair himself) to bribe a traitor: one must follow a road.

Discovering a passage by ruse or by sheer luck leads nowhere, because at each step you need a guide to show you the next step. And if this guide happens to be a coded poem, good luck to you!

The purpose of the measures taken was to safeguard the financial power of the Order pending the next political upheaval. That is the meaning that must be given to their hiding of the treasure: they thought that as long as they could keep a part of their wealth, they would quickly recover their previous glory and power. They failed only because they had to contend with the political genius of the most intelligent King in European history. The Iron King understood this better than any other man, and directed his attack where it was the least anticipated: he had the *judicial* existence of the Order annulled. Being no longer a legal body, the Temple lost its power and its existence in one single blow. Jacques de Montignies, Yves de Lessines and the Flemish Templar had succeeded brilliantly in warding off any attack on the material possessions; they had not foreseen that Philip the Fair would lay violent hands upon the men of the Temple.

Genuine Templars no longer exist. As the Old Monk states: "I am the last one to survive, I have seen the others die." I think we may believe him. The Temple died in 1329, leaving as sole legacy an enigmatic cenotaph: a text written in the 1320s by an old Cistercian monk of the Abbey of Cambron, called Yves de Lessines.

Yves was a scientist with an Aristotelian logic. He must have expected what logic dictated in the given circumstances, namely that his message would remain buried in the Abbey's library until the day the awaited one would arrive at Cambron at the end of the first leg of his long journey. And there the *Centuries* would lie, waiting to reveal the ultimate destination. This whole approach is thoroughly medieval: knowledge lies at the end of an initiatic path. Yet this knowledge must remain hidden to the eyes of the impure. Please note that once again we come across a three-fold thought-structure, that a medieval person would visualise as an equilateral triangle, the symbol of the Holy Trinity, the sides of which would be knowledge – a secret – and two men. The first man delivers the knowledge in the form of a very long enigma; the second one fathoms the secret and accedes to the knowledge. Understanding the message is a question of Revelation and not of confidence. It no longer matters that Prior Yves would not be there to welcome the man who was to come; enlightenment was deposited in a book, just as the light that exists in a candle waits for the hand that will light the wick.

To Yves de Lessines it was very clear that the future of his work would be counted in years, in months maybe, but certainly not in centuries.

What made it possible for this poem to survive a reasonably foreseeable time? In all likelihood, the brother-librarians must have watched over this strange manuscript resting in the Abbey library and obeyed an order for generation after generation, without knowing the reason why. Whatever the reason, it seems as if after Yves de Lessines' death in 1330 of our calendar, history came to a standstill, as if time passed without really existing.

Then – either by coincidence or the work of Providence – almost 220 years after the Old Monk passed away, a very strange character showed up at the Abbey. A man from Provence, speaking broken French, who claimed to have been staying at the Abbey of Orval, and who seemed to be moving from one Cistercian Abbey to the next. He already boasted of being a sooth-sayer because, having been invited one day by the Lord of Florenville, he cleverly solved a problem related to the colour of a pig.

He caught sight of the book. Since it was written in the future tense, in what seemed to be very old French, and the text successfully resisted any attempt at explanation, Michel Nostradamus was convinced that he had laid his hands on prophecies. Or, and this is also possible, the librarian showed the book to Nostradamus hoping to take advantage of the presence of a soothsayer to finally try and find out the meaning of that mysterious book that had been lying there for ages. It is not at all impossible that having become Abbot, Yves de Lessines, to protect his work, duped his monks and made them believe in mysterious prophecies.

During the period in which he lived, and indeed throughout the following centuries, a book of prayers, of devotion or of prophecies was almost a sacred object. I have myself witnessed this superstition to be very much alive as far as the older people were concerned. In a resurgence of the old magic from prehistoric times resulting in a somewhat guilty fear of the vengeance of mistreated dark powers, the respect for the text was extended to the support on which it was written. Yves de Lessines knew perfectly well of course that he had never written prophecies, and we may rest assured of this because he asserts it himself, but he was also very much aware of human nature. There is of course no proof of him having used this stratagem, and I have no intention whatsoever of assuming a non-proven fact to be the reality.

However, one may wonder if there is not more than first meets the eye to his denial that the *Centuries* are prophecies, together with the vigour and even the roughness of the words he uses to insist on this denial.

Towards the end of the 1540s, Michel Nostradamus came to ask for hospitality at Cambron, as he had done a short while before at Orval. Maybe he was a travelling *agent provocateur* in the service of the Inquisition in those years; his contemporary Théodore de Bèze and the Protestants from Geneva made this accusation against him. This may be slander, but they were very much convinced of it and must have had their reasons. We have no right to ignore the opinion of the victims. These small trifles may be ignored or swept under the rug by his protagonists. What they should remember is that the man did claim to be a good Catholic when in the company of Catholics; the opinions he expressed in the Papist milieu were far from moderate. Quite the contrary in fact, and he took an intransigent and fanatical stand more often than was justified by the raging religious storms that blinded whole populations. Yet, in a letter to a Protestant client, this same man hinted in prudent words that he was in favour of the Reformation. It may of course have been just the clever ploy of a horoscope seller to get into the good books of said Protestant client. I simply mention the fact because I lack precise and verified elements to form an opinion. It is up to each one to draw his own conclusions…

In the 16th century, even more than today, to set up a doctor's practice, one needed a substantial amount of money. One needed to have a large house, the rental or purchase cost of which was proportionally much more expensive than today. One needed to acquire some material that also cost a small fortune; one needed to show off beautiful and expensive attire; one needed to hire at least two servants. On top of that, one needed to pay for other things such as: a patent, various permits, suitable gifts for the established authorities, elaborate banquets to entertain the worthies, a few bribes, a few loafers to sing your praises from house to house, etc. Finally, once set up, the doctor's fee was settled at the end of the year. In the heart of the *Terre des Débats* that custom still existed when I was young. So money was definitely needed.

And when he returned to Provence, Nostradamus had money. He had sufficient money to buy a large house, set up a doctor's practice and get married. The bride was a widow and contributed a dowry. Nostradamus, however, was already settled as a doctor before the ceremony, and usually widows with dowry have enough experience not to get involved with someone who is penniless. Moreover, the merry widow from Salon did not enter into matrimony with a passionate young beau in search of an easy life. She moved in with an old man. Nostradamus was nearing fifty at the time, the age of Seigneur Anselme, the old goat with a taste for green leaves in Molière's comedy. These are unquestionable facts and not the life of Saint Nostradamus as glorified by the same. If he had just been on the road all those years as he tries to make us believe, where did his pockets get filled with money? It did not rain gold coins in those days anymore than it does today. In all truth, nothing related to this character is clear. From whatever side his personal history is approached, whatever he or his son Caesar relate always has the taste of a lie.

The man could not have chosen a better opportunity to commit his theft. These regions were going through a very troubled period, one of the worst in their history: the war with France was not yet over when the religious war broke out, and Cambron also shared in the violence and disaster. In a short while, thanks to the combined efforts of the Inquisition and the Spanish Fury, the land that had been the pride of the West for five hundred years, was turned into a desert. One third of the population was slaughtered, one third fled the country with no hope of return. The rest roamed and plundered, stealing what could be stolen and raping who could be raped. The Abbey had to be evacuated continually and the monks had to flee to Ath, Mons, Soignies, Brussels and even Bruges. The order of the books in their library was not their top priority, nor was the fact that a manuscript might have disappeared.

On his return to the Midi, Michel Nostradamus prudently tested the water. Then, in 1555, he made his big move and published in his own name

300-odd quatrains of the stolen manuscript. Nobody reacted by denouncing the deception and the plagiary. Maybe the theft had not been noticed yet at Cambron. Or maybe they thought that it was not worth their while to start inquiring about such a meaningless manuscript. In short, Nostradamus took the plunge!

Moreover, an extraordinary stroke of luck propelled him to the pinnacle of astrological glory, he who had no knowledge of astrology, as was demonstrated masterfully by his contemporary, Laurent Videl, astronomer and astrologer.

To tell this adventure, we will revert to the story Caesar Nostradamus, the son of our Michel, came up with fifty years after the facts. It would appear from a recent study that lies are profuse once more in this particular case. However, pending any formal exposure of Caesar's concoctions, we will give him the benefit of the doubt and just take his word for it, with reservations.

In fact, Nostradamus owed his luck to an accident. While they were joyfully jousting in Paris, Montgomery inadvertently stabbed his lance in Henri II's eye. The King's final agony lasted for nine days. God knows why, but amidst the weeping and wailing, the Constable of France, Anne de Montmorency suddenly remembered having read a book of prophecies written by the already renowned Nostradamus, and, in which so he claimed, four lines in this book prophesied this event. A servant was hastily sent to fetch the book and, flabbergasted and babbling with admiration, he showed the following lines to the assembled court:

I 35 *Le Lyon jeune le vieux surmontera*
En champ bellique par singulier duelle
Dans cage d'or les yeux lui crevera
Deux classe une puis mourir mort cruelle

Proud as a peacock he hurriedly explained: the young lion is of course young Montgomery who unfortunately wounded the King. The old lion is Henri II (the fact that the King was still young being conveniently overlooked). *Champ bellique*, the battlefield: the tournament ground; *singulier duelle* needs no further explanation; the golden cage is the King's helmet. As for the gouged out eye, that is quite obvious: even while the Constable was speaking, a part of the lance was still protruding from the King's eye. They all marvelled, cried out and admired. The Queen herself took charge of the publicity campaign. The Great Prophet's career was launched.

And so this quatrain of which, at the beginning of this chapter, I gave you the three levels of understanding according to the coherent system of

Yves de Lessines, can also lead to the most fanciful interpretations by decoders who come under the spell of mirages of all sorts. Nonetheless, it is also this quatrain that saved the *Centuries* from total oblivion, just as Nostradamus' larceny had saved them from probable destruction; without any of the actors ever understanding anything of its content: not the letter of the text, nor its Temple-related character, nor the concurrence of circumstances. It is the faulty explanation of this quatrain that cemented the prophetic renown of Nostradamus for centuries to come. The destiny of the *Centuries*, i.e. the preservation of the text, itself, depended on this: Anne de Montmorency had the right idea, he did exactly what he had to do, spoke exactly the right words at the right place and exactly the right time, totally ignorant of the role he was playing. He was but a pawn on the chessboard of the *Centuries'* destiny, like Nostradamus before him, and the numerous people who came after them to squeeze all (im)possible prophecies from this text.

But today we are on the threshold of a new stage in this story. The poem will at last be allowed to reveal what it has been wanting to disclose for such a long time. Whether the story told by Caesar is correct or not is of anecdotical importance only when considered in view of the genesis and the destiny of the *Centuries*. What really matters is that this quatrain has made the text immortal.

There remains one mystery to solve, of small importance no doubt: one quatrain of the *Centuries* was probably not written by the Old Monk: Nostradamus published it as "prediction" for the month of November 1567 in the *"Présages"* of his last almanac.

Naively quoting the inventions made up by Caesar, the "proposers" unanimously contend that the Great Prophet prophesied his own death. They extol it profusely as the bejewelled crown on the prophetic powers of the Great Visionary, the only man to have predicted his own death. A peer to Jesus-Christ, no less! What a bizarre thing to do! Why should he have done that? If we may assume that for once in his life Caesar has not been telling outrageous stories, then it seems at least incongruous that the prophet announces the event in his almanac relating to November of the year 1567, whereas he died in 1566. I have a hunch though, that clarifies all these mystifications: it is Nostradamus' ultimate joke on us, planned a long time in advance.

> *De retour d'ambassade don du Roy mis au lieu*
> *Plus n'en sera sera alle a Dieu*
> *Parans plus proches amis freres de sang*

You will notice that the first line counts twelve feet, cesured 6-6, in a decasyllabic poem. Let us applaud the performance. The word "ambassade" placed there is as shocking as a scar on the face of any Miss World. The *Dictionnaire Etymologique* by Albert Dauzat will help us solve this problem; it tells us that the word: "ambassade *appearing in 1387 was taken from the Italian* ambasciata." This of course clearly favours all those who continue to claim that Nostradamus is the true author of the Centuries. I will be the first to admit that Yves de Lessines, who died in 1329 or 1330 depending on whether one adopts the Easter or January system, cannot possibly have used it. But let us read on Dauzat: "(ambassade)... *of which* ambassee *used from the 13th to the 16th century by italianising authors (Brunetto Latini) was a former gallicising. It is a typically migrating word. The Italian borrowed it from the Provençal* ambaissada, *derived from the vulgar Latin* ambactia, *representing the Gothic* andbahti *"service, function"; the latter was in turn taken from the Gallic* "ambactos" *(client, servant) latinised by Cesar to* "ambactus".

This word *ambactia* is the source of the old Picard word *anbey*, used frequently until the 19th century. When I was a young boy, the older generation still used it. *Aller à l'anbey* meant that one was undertaking delicate negotiations, in theory on account of someone else. When my great-grandfather, Augustin Cambier, intended to get married, the matrimonial arrangements were made by one of his aunts *d'allée à l'anbey* (gone on a mission) to two uncles of my great-grandmother Aimée Papegnies. By crossing, the word then generated *abiy,* which means quickly. Moreover, it is certainly possible that Yves de Lessines also had the Flemish word *ambacht* (craft, trade) in mind.

A last point to note is that the line, put in old Picard, reads

Retour d'anbey don du Roy mis au lieu

and that it is perfectly decasyllabic, cesured 4-6, the work of Yves de Lessines.

With regard to the second line, I am sure you will have raised at least one eyebrow reading *sera* twice. When used by any smooth-voiced popular singer, it is just about acceptable. But to use such an obvious trick to get to the required number of verse feet is a rather low practice. However, the corresponding Picard word is *sara,* and *sara* is the future tense of two verbs: to be and to know. *Plus n'en sara, sara dalle a Dieu* means: Plus n'en saura (on n'en saura pas plus – we will not know more), il sera allé à Dieu (he will have gone to God) (the future tense expressing hope).

This quatrain may refer to two of the people who played a key-role in this story. The first one is the Abbot Jacques de Montignies, who had, very strangely, resigned from office in 1308, a few months after the Temple affair, and who died upon his return from a mission. His tombstone bears the following inscription "... *Dant Jacquemes de Montigni qui trespassa l'an de grace 1315, le jour de ste Julienne... et fut jadis XIIe abbé de Cambron,...* ". He was buried – and this is an absolutely unique occurrence – south of the chapter, between his father and his mother. Is it possible to have *parans plus proches* (closer parents). If the quatrain refers to him, then it was surely written by Yves de Lessines.

But it so happens that Yves de Lessines himself died upon his return from a mission he conducted in Paris, during which he met the King of France who bestowed a large gift on him. The proof of this can be found in the Belgian royal archives. If, a short while after the Old Monk's death, another hand has written these four lines as a conclusion to the epic, it will probably remain unknown forever. The reason I think this quatrain was not written by Yves de Lessines is the following: it is the only one in which the rhymes are not crossed (aabb as opposed to abab). This formal element can be regarded as a discrete sign of an unknown man who pays an ultimate homage to the fifteenth Abbot of Cambron.

I have warned you right from the start that the *Centuries* is an extraordinary, unusual work, a unique product, a many sided oeuvre, a trap of illusions. Placed in its proper epoch, and explained according to the spirit, the standards, the religious and secular habits of the Middle Ages, read with the knowledge of Latin as well as ancient Picard and Thiois, this masterpiece, in its unfailing coherence that will become clearer and clearer throughout these pages, emerges from the darkness of ages long gone and from the mist in which soothsayers with howling voices and eyes tightly shut still fuss around.

The destiny of the *Centuries* is indeed the proof that the future, like the wind, is unpredictable.

What extraordinary prophet could have predicted the destiny of the *Centuries*? What madly inventive novelist could have thought up this story?

The search
for a
manuscript

Chapter Six – Disguising the evidence

At the outset, I did not think that there was the slightest chance of ever finding the original text of the *Centuries*. There were many good reasons to bear out my feeling. At the top of the list was Nostradamus' own avowal. In the foreword to the first partial edition of the *Centuries* in 1555, the "prophet" admits to having burned old manuscripts. There is no proof whatsoever, which might lead us to believe that this assertion was forced upon him. Quite the contrary: it discloses what happens frequently and typically to the liar who, by answering a question that crossed nobody's mind, reveals in spite of himself a truth that no-one suspected. This compares to the criminal returning for no good reason to the scene of his crime.

On the other hand, the question arises as to why should Nostradamus have to burn manuscripts that he is publishing? It is improbable and stupid. To believe that he may have uttered a lie under constraint is highly unlikely. On the contrary, reason suggests that we are facing an awkwardly disguised truth, and that the *auto da fé* served only one purpose: the destruction of evidence.

Our minds now being constantly alert, we have no problem avoiding the lies contained in the words, and disclosing the truth hidden between the lines of the foreword.

There is a most curious fact to take into account: although posterity preserved sheaves of manuscripts of the "prophet" of Provence, no-one has ever found one single line of the *Centuries* written in the hand of either Nostradamus or his secretary.

You might object by saying that no manuscript of Molière or Shakespeare has survived. However, this is quite different. A play belonged totally and completely to the theatre or to the "producer" who bought it. They were the only ones who could decide on the advisability of reselling it to a publisher, sometimes after scandalously mucking it up. The long history of philological scholarship as regards Shakespearean theatre gives ideal instruction on the matter. The fact in itself, namely the disappearance of the manuscripts of the *Centuries*, would be nothing extraordinary considering the time, except for one peculiarity of Nostradamus': he kept a copy of most of his writings, he sliced and cut them up, and served the pieces on another table later on. He even resold them in slightly modified form to an editor competing with the initial buyer. This is not the first time that this has happened and it stands to prove that the man was a born plagiarist, who did not hesitate to plagiarise himself. This character trait reveals a twisted spirit but a poor creative talent.

However, as far as the *Centuries* are concerned, there is not a single trace of its origin, no manuscript, not even a draft or a piece of rough paper. Odder still: it seems that the *Centuries* is Nostradamus' only work of some importance that has not been copied out by his scribe. Four thousand lines is no small feat. Watching them emerge from nowhere, knowing they are floating in emptiness, without the slightest reference or allusion to the blood, sweat and tears that their elaboration must have cost, all this must trigger our vigilance. If we keep in mind that the *Centuries* were published in three episodes, it is not one but three manuscripts that go mysteriously missing.

We have just taken the first step on the path we will be following in this chapter, and we are already forced to point out one of the many anomalies the nostraddicts modestly cover over with a veil of silence. Everyone must play his own part in the debate: mine will be to reveal the facts that offend against either the truth or reason. With this in mind, the nostraddicts might be persuaded to answer this question: why did Nostradamus feel compelled to erase the smallest trace of his personal work with an unprecedented meticulousness whilst he left copious remains of the rest of his bulky, but none the less mediocre, productions?

The subject of our enquiries is part of the foreword Michel Nostradamus felt compelled to produce when he took the risk of publishing the first part of the text he stole from the Abbey of Cambron, all the while claiming to be its rightful author. This foreword is known by the name of *"Letter to Caesar"*, i.e a letter to his son, Caesar Nostradamus. May I ask you to read it carefully, bearing in mind what Buffon said in 1753 in the *Discours sur le Style* pronounced by him when he was admitted to the French Academy: more specifically the well-known aphorism: "Le style est l'homme même" (the style reflects the man himself). This will allow you to appraise the hotchpotch the prophet serves up and then to answer the key question: is it conceivable that one and the same man wrote the pure piece of art that are the *Centuries*, and committed this stylistic crime?

"… Mais la parfaicte des causes notice ne se peult aquerir sans la divine inspiration: veu que toutes inspiration prophetique recoit prenant son principal principe mouvant de Dieu le createur; puis de l'heur et de nature. Par quoy estant les causes indifferantes, indifferentement produictes en non produictes, le presage partie advient ou a este predict. Car l'entendement cree intellectuellement ne peult voyr occultement, sinon par la voix faicte au lymbe moyennant la exigue flamme en quelle partie les causes futures se viendront a incliner. Et aussi, mon fils, je te supplie que jamais tu ne veuilles emploier ton entendement a telles resveries et vanites qui seichent le corps et mettent a perdition l'ame, donnant trouble au foyble sens: mesme la vanite de la plus qu'execrable magie reprouvee jadis par les sacrees escritures et par les divins canons: au chef duquel est excepte le jugement de l'astrologie judicielle: par laquelle et moyennant inspiration et revelation divine, par continuelles veilles et supputations, avons nos propheties redigees par escript. Et combien que cette occulte Philosophie ne fusse reprouvee, n'ay onques voulu presenter leurs effrenees persuasions: combien que plusieurs volumes qui ont este caches par longs siecles me sont este manifestes. Mais doutant ce qui adviendroit en ay faict, apres lecture, present a Vulcan, que pendant qu'il les venoit a devorer, la flamme leschant l'air rendoit une clarte insolite, plus claire que naturelle flamme, comme lumiere de feu de clystre fulgurant, illuminant subit la maison, comme si elle fust este en subite conflagration. Parquoy affin que a l'advenir ni feusses abuse perscrutant la parfaicte transformation tant selme que solaire, et soubz terre metaux incorruptibles et aux undes occultes, les ay en cendres convertis. […] Mais estant surprins par foy la sepmaine lymphatiquant, et par longue calculation rendant les estudes nocturnes de souesve odeur, j'ai compose Livre de propheties, contenant chacun cent quatrains astronomiques de propheties, lesquelles j'ay un peu voulu rabouter obscurement: et sont perpetuelles vaticinations, pour d'yci a l'annee 3797. Que possible fera retirer le front a quelques-uns en voyant si longue extension et par souz toute la concavité de la lune aura lieu et intelligence et ce entendant universellement les causes, mon fils — que si tu vis l'age naturel et humain, tu verras devers ton climat, au propre ciel de ta nativité, les futures adventures prévoir. Combien que le seul Dieu éternel soit celui qui connait l'éternité de sa lumière, procédant de luy mesme: et je dis franchement queà ceulx à qui sa magnitude immense qui est sans mesure et incompréhensible, a voulu révéler…"

What you have just read – or did you skip it? – is the true Nostradamus. Putting this and the Old Monk's admirable lines side by side should certainly set the alarm bells ringing. Let us take an up-to-date example: could someone in his right mind imagine Marguerite Yourcenar, having written the *Mémoires d'Hadrien*, destroying her reputation as a writer and degrading her masterpiece by prefacing it by such a nonsensical foreword? Of course not! The true wordsmith does not need to wallow in a cloying style, whereas the scribbler will never reach the summits of literary art. A mediocre author *believes* he writes elegantly because he puts words down on paper. A good writer *knows* when his writing is good, and he also knows the price to pay in terms of doubt and effort.

Having written this foreword was Nostradamus' greatest mistake: it gives us an irrefutable example of his own lack of talent; he proves himself that he is but an artful scribbler. "Le style est l'homme même."

What seems odd and off-putting is only the strangeness of the spelling and the richness of the vocabulary, unfortunately lost during the 17th century. These two distorting mirrors, though, do not justify the promotion of Nostradamus' to the level of author of genius. There have been nostraddicts who did not hesitate to compare their hero to François Rabelais, the Rabelais considered by authors of all languages and all places as one of the giants of world literature. This must be on the strength of his verses, not on the strength of the foreword. But why these experts have never seen the discrepancy between both is amazing, to say the least. And, of course, when talking about the verses, these are not Nostradamus' at all…

Let us not be blinded by the lures of immediate appearances, however, thereby supposing that now, having ascertained the literary mediocrity of the artist, the incident is closed. Not all has been said yet. This dreadful style is not just the result of Nostradamus' absence of talent. It also reflect a tactic, which may or may not have been accidental at the start, but which was very soon deliberately applied due to its proven efficiency: the systematic use of a voluntarily de-structured and erratic discourse. To this end he uses all the most vulgar as well as common tricks of nonsense; on top of the verbal swamp float a small amount of slightly structured islets. Eluding all criticism and examination, these unwittingly and treacherously invade our memory, and we give them a meaning.

This is Nostradamus' subtlety: the only purpose of his sentences is for them to have no meaning at all, so that we feel compelled to find a meaning in them at all costs, one that suits us, pleases us or makes us feel important. As the significance that emerges from the words is our own doing, the result of our own astuteness, our petty vanity is tickled and we will cling to it and defend our findings as the bees do their honey. They are like a mirror, in itself immaterial and merely reflecting the image of the one staring in it. The mirror is not the judge of beauty; the person is. So are the verses, which is precisely the "prophet's" goal. In this way, Nostradamus is always right, not when measured against reality, but because disavowing the prophet also means a disavowal of oneself, a judgement of our hopes and a condemnation of our souls. The man is a megalithic monument of ruse who uses his intellectual shortcomings and infirmities as a means to attain his financial aims. This would have easily been understood, or at least suspected, if someone, just once, had been curious enough to read his correspondence without being blinded by the Nostradamian myth and with a clear intention of tracking the truth in the bushes of illusion.

The Nostradamus phenomenon is easily summarised in one sentence: the man became the most celebrated prophet not because his texts were the most arduous to read, the most obscure, the most difficult to understand, but because they were by far the most un-structured. Once his numerous failures have been carefully buried in the cemetery of oblivion, there is no limit to interpretation, and fantasy can roam freely till it finds a semblance of correlation with any particular historical happening. It is like producing the best text which needs decrypting: the best text is indeed a random sequence of letters, with no meaning, but which will, however, keep all decipherers busy until the end of their days, trying to find a meaning and each failing, hence proclaiming the ingenuity of the cipher.

A full stylistic analysis will clearly show that Nostradamus produced worst things than the text quoted above. For instance, the last part of his "*Letter to Caesar*" is a soup of words picked out of the old poem, mixed and blended into an absurd text, whereby Nostradamus tries to establish his authorship of the poem by luring us into believing that the vocabulary is identical. However, the total incoherence of his sentences belies the procedure.

Finding the same words in the splendid song that are the *Centuries*, where they are in the right place, where they are meaningful, where they are at the heart of poignant images, and then finding these same words in the foreword, mashed up in a sort of tasteless, sticky sausage, generates a contrast that does not exactly work in favour of Nostradamus. As Buffon said: a man and his style. And the lack of talent exposes the liar.

When this foreword is analysed lucidly, the even slightly critical reader cannot fail to see that the Great Nostradamus thinks we are nothing but complete fools, and that his whole system is based on the confidence he has in this conviction.

In the "Prophet's" whole voluminous production nothing can be, even vaguely, compared to the *Centuries*, whether it be the quality of the style or the brilliance of the imagery, or whatever defines the author of a text better than the name printed on the front page.

Nostradamus' bluff is not unique, and more than one poacher – indeed even some geniuses – have become famous by the fraudulent appropriation of some poor unknown wretch's work. We all know that some of the most successful writers never put a pen to paper, or nowadays a finger on the keyboard. Sometimes, unfortunately, advertising having missed its target, sales are low and profits next-to-naught. Hunger being a fierce master, some of these artistic slave drivers forget all prudence and do their own writing. The discrepancy in quality always affects the scribbler's public image dramatically. As far as Nostradamus is concerned, the crevice becomes an enormous chasm.

This question of style is of the utmost importance. The nostraddicts have failed to notice that the *Centuries* are a stylistic jewel, a golden crown studded with the most beautiful literary diamonds. I will never be able to describe the joy I felt when I recently discovered that I was neither the first nor the only one to have been touched by the strange beauty emanating from the *Centuries*. It seems that Robert Sabatier mentioned it about twenty years ago; at least this transpired from indirect evidence heard on the radio. When one has been preaching in the desert for a long time, one feels comforted when one discovers unexpected allies, even if their words have been smothered in a lot of witless talking.

Of course, one must be sensitive to style in order to notice its inimitable characteristics straight away: words are colours and music; sentences become paintings and patterns. This sensitivity is so much a part of my own being that for more than half a century I was convinced it was something our Lord had generously distributed to one and all. The course of years, however, tarnishes the sweetest illusions. I finally had to admit that people really capable of identifying a writer's style were as scarce as those who can recognise a painter's brush strokes. The obvious became inescapable: this aptitude is an offshoot of the aesthetic sensibility. It is an innate art that must be cultivated each day, it cannot be taught or learned.

On the other hand, I also met people who had a "stylistic ear" without even being aware of it, just as painters who discover their gift late in life and start attending the academy at the age of fifty. One has to make a try. Identifying a style requires sensitivity that is on a par with the ability of some people to take the measure of others at first sight, or almost, and who can "feel" the personality of their interlocutor, generally with more accuracy than a graduate in psychology.

This being said, I would like to invite those who are challenged by literary style, to compare the *Centuries* with any other text (*prognostications, almanacs, horoscopes, jam recipes*) written by the prophet from Salon-de-Provence. They will not fail to conclude very rapidly that it is quite impossible for one and the same person to have written them both.

Let us now turn our attention to another passage where Nostradamus instead of covering his rear, unwittingly betrays himself again:

"...*Combien que* plusieurs volumes qui ont este caches par longs siecles *me sont este manifestes. Mais doutant de ce que adviendroit en ay faict, après lecture,* present a Vulcan, *que pendant qu'il les venoit devorer, la flamme leschant l'air, comme lumiere de feu de clystre fulgurant, illuminant subit la maison, comme si elle fust este en subite conflagration. [...]* les ay en cendres convertis. "

Free translation: various volumes that remained hidden for many centuries came to my attention. However, fearing what may happen, I read them and then burned them. The flame produced an unholy light and they (the volumes) were reduced to ashes

With the bombastic, obscure and saturnine mishmash that is the trademark of his own writings, our prophet uses this pretentious malarky just to say: I do not know what may happen. I burned the old books. (By the way, a prophet? not knowing their future value?) What man of sound mind would treat precious and ancient revelations as if they were mere firewood? Moreover, such a reaction clashes with the man's inborn avarice. I would not dare criticise his thriftiness – I, for one, abhor inconsiderate and extravagant throwing around of money – I simply record the inconsistency. You either keep old books, or you sell them. Whatever forced him, at that moment, "to sacrifice them to Vulcan"? Were the revelations they contained so terrifying that to make them known to the common people would lead inevitably to unheard-off damages? This sounds like undisguised vanity lightly covered over by a cloak of concern.

Let us not be mistaken and make sure we know the exact meaning of the words: the terrible knowledge is given to no-one but Nostradamus himself. Once the text is purged of his apparent humility, the author's feeling lies crudely bare: no-one other than himself is worthy of sharing the knowledge. As if he were a living image of God, he remains alone and aloof, enjoying his immense grandeur. Thus it follows that all men without exception, do not reach up to his knees. Let us quickly and devoutly light the largest candle we can find in front of this holy man's statue. Imagine the fate of poor mankind if the good Michel, helped by the big fire in his hearth, had not saved us from the horror and terror of these revelations!

In order to end once and for all the story that these cabalistic manuscripts were allegedly inherited from his forebears (who were not doctors as he implies, but grain merchants as we know), let us admit that these books did exist and really were hyper-apocalyptic. Why would Nostradamus feel obliged to publish his books and by spreading them Urbi et Orbi assuring them a stupendous publicity? Why did he not keep silent? What made the previous possessors so courageous that they were not terrorised by the contents of these magical books? Why did they keep anything that dangerous?

No, all the oddities that are found throughout the three partial publications of the quatrains are easily explained when one knows that the manuscript was stolen.

To claim that the *Centuries* were nurtured by the study of papyri that by the most opportune of opportunities emerged out of the blue or out of a grain trader's attic, is in fact a clever move made by the thief of Cambron to counter possible annoying consequences of his crime. With the prudence of a rat stalking a hunk of cheese, he seeks the best way of benefiting from his theft, dodging foreseeable risks.

The most immediate danger was that the manuscript was missed as soon as he left the Abbey. Here luck was his only ally. In common with all his contemporaries, Nostradamus knew that the monks had established a re-markable communications network over the centuries, which was opera-tional between all abbeys whether they belong to their own order or to other orders. If and when the theft was discovered, all the abbeys of Europe would be warned to look out for him. At the time, monasteries were also used as hostelries with a rightfully earned excellent reputation. Therefore every trav-eller lodges at least as often in a monastery as in a tavern. Information spreading in all direction, news running as fast as the wind, an identified robber had little or no chance of getting away. Consequently, if the monks at Cambron linked the disappearance of a manuscript from their library to Nostradamus' presence in the abbey at the same period, he was done for, wherever he tried to hide.

The second hazardous moment would arise as soon as he started pub-lishing Yves de Lessines' text under the name of Nostradamus. On the whole his luck had been almost limitless. One should never tempt the Devil, how-ever, and provoke him by being overly intrepid. Audacity will do for fid-dling, there is no place for imprudence. To test his luck, he published a few quatrains disguised as "*Présages*" in modest almanacs. His luck still held. No reaction, no accusation to blemish the success of the new almanachor.

He discarded all hesitation and in 1555 he brazenly published not the whole poem but some 300-odd quatrains – and he made the stupid mistake of entitling the publication "*Les Centuries*".

Indeed, who would have the tortuous idea of calling a poem of 353 quatrains or 1412 lines "Centuries"? Of course Nostradamus claimed his writing was progressive, depending on the dictation of the Holy Ghost. How was he to know, in 1555, that the Holy Spirit would dictate precisely 2588 more lines, unless of course he was convinced of being in control of "the Holy Spirit". The title of the poem makes no sense unless he simply copied it from a work of a thousand quatrains, grouped by hundreds, which he happened to possess?

But the whole of the ten *Centuries* as published by Nostradamus contains only 948 quatrains. Stylistic analysis proves that twenty of them were undeniably by his hand. Furthermore, Nostradamus actually tried to have one thousand quatrains published under the title of "Les Centuries" but by deceiving the publisher. The latter turned down 52 of the four hundred quatrains offered by Nostradamus for the second partial edition of the poem, arguing that "the author" tried to sell as new material some quatrains that had already been published in almanacs, i.e. sold to and paid for by his competitors. This explains the strange incompleteness of the 7th *centurie*.

Is it credible that Nostradamus unwittingly re-wrote word for word poems he had written three years earlier and which he had already sold for a handsome price? More likely he just tried to sell them again, and make a profit along the way. Or it might merely have been forgetfulness. After all, we do not argue that he was creating new material each time, merely that he lifted portions out of a longer, stolen document. And perhaps he merely forgot what was new and what he had already used.

We have not yet reached the end of the strangeness. The *"Présages"* consist of 141 quatrains, 72 of which are indubitably of the same make and inspiration as the *Centuries*. And now a little mathematics comes in handy: subtract from the 948 quatrains of the *Centuries*, the twenty of more than doubtful origin. This leaves us with 928 quatrains to which we add the 72 quatrains of the *"Présages"*. You will already have done the sum: one thousand or ten complete *Centuries*. Surprising, isn't it? But it does suggest a pick 'n' mix approach rather than an act of creation on the part of Nostradamus.

During this whole enterprise, Michel Nostradamus certainly did not bask in heavenly serenity. Fraud has a nasty tendency of casting a shadow over your peace of mind. Even if the Cistercians showed no reaction, people who knew him would certainly start to wonder and question his suddenly blooming talent and his torrential prophetic output. The facts as well as his correspondence all show that Nostradamus knew that scepticism, or even the incredulity of some people, might trigger disaster.

If cool-headed thinking led him to believe that no well-read man from Cambron would stoop so low as to glance at an ordinary almanac printed somewhere in the south of France, the book of the *Centuries* however might well raise suspicion. What would he do the day someone knocked on his door and gently told him: "Sir Doctor, forgive my audacity; I know I am guilty of importuning you for such a small trifle but my brother at Cambron told me that, a long time ago, he entrusted you with a book that due to an annoying force of circumstance, you have not been able to return to him yet. He charged me with inquiring about your health as well as your prosperity, extremely deserved he said, and… well, being here and all, maybe unburden you of this manuscript, that is if you have no further use for it?"

Nostradamus did not doubt his denials would not stand up to the monks' word. And anyway, any question, any astonishment is detrimental to a thief. As long as he is in the driving seat, a car thief knows no fear. Danger starts when the first question is asked. The best thing to do is to be prepared a long time in advance so as not to be caught unawares. And that is what our man did, very skilfully indeed.

The opaque story he tells in the foreword to the first partial edition of Yves de Lessines' *Centuries*, about the books being burned, is in fact his anticipated reply to the following possible scenario:

- It is true, I must admit I have not written everything myself but I did not steal your book. I took inspiration from various books which, as luck would have it, all covered the same subject.
- *Where did you get them from?*
- I found them in my father's attic. They have always belonged to the family.
- *Where are they? Show them to us?*
- I burned them so that no-one could make improper use of them. I considered them to be much too dangerous for poor mankind.

In the course of time I have learned that, whatever sauce is used to cover up the story, the destruction of proof is always the hasty doing of a criminal; the honest man keeps the evidence.

This is then followed by Nostradamus' account of the inevitable nightly scene of diabolical magic, flames and bright flashes included. Contrary to what you may think, this is probably quite correct; the so-called astrologer from Salon-de-Provence may have had the fright of his life. The parchment used in manuscripts was made of the skin of stillborn lambs or calves treated in a special way: the Pergame method. It is highly unlikely that any Prophetic Revelation warned Nostradamus of the fact that the parchment tanning salts contained a good deal of nitre (i.e. saltpetre KNO_3), a substance also used in making gunpowder. Hence the hell-fire in poor dumbfounded Michel's hearth.

Racing from one mistake to the next, the Great Prophet gaily continues to give himself away when he admits to having mixed up the quatrains and the lines:

"… Mais estant surprins par foy la sepmaine lymphatiquant, et par longue calculation rendant les estudes nocturnes de souesue odeur, j'ay composé Livre de prophéties, contenant chacun cent quatrains astronomiques de prophéties, lesquelles j'ay un peu voulu rabouter obscurément: *et ce sont perpétuelles vaticinations, pour d'yci à l'année 3797."* (*rabouter sans ordre* according to some editions)

"Rabouter" is a carpenter's word. It means joining two bevelled pieces of wood end to end, when the timber at your disposal is not long enough to span the arch in single lengths. More than thirty years ago, I remade the roof of our cattle sheds with a friend of my father. I was the helpmate of the carpenter, a man belonging to times when a beautiful piece of work was appreciated. I watched him "rabouter" without the help of an adze, without markings, just from sight. It was an artist's performance. The poor man, full of illusions – or was it merry mischief that made his eyes twinkle? – hoped to teach me the technique! At the time we were on the roof he had been at it for over fifty years and done at least one hundred thousand "joinings". I, before those days, had never even seen a man using that tool. But I certainly learned the meaning of "raboute dè kewett".

Nostradamus' use of the word therefore is not innocent. It defines exactly the trick he used to mask the stolen object. We have already touched upon it, but since *bis repetita placent,* it will not hurt to mention once again that he stuck parts together, parts that originally did not relate to each other. There are various ways of doing this procedure: interchange of two whole lines, is one; take the beginning of one line and the end of a second, is another. The process is simplistic, even primitive, perhaps. It is also stupid and uninspired. That, however, is the least of Nostradamus' worries: it causes the text to be sufficiently destructured. Of course, he wants to scramble the meaning; his first objective though, his fundamental concern is to fake an alibi and an ex causa! As these fantasies are literally drowned in a long and obscure text, they go unnoticed if the attention is not already kindled by the sparks of suspicion. But their effects persist.

In the good old days of intellectual craftsmanship, systematically detecting this fraud would have worn out God himself. Nowadays, I dare say that Nostradamus' cutting, mixing and sticking together differently would very soon yield to the sagacity of the first person to instruct his computer to sort out the quatrains in cascade.

To ensure myself of an easy escape, I must confess that, during the first months of my study, I was very secretive about what I was doing. When I finally decided to tell my son I was actually working on Nostradamus, he burst out laughing. Up to then he had thought his father to be of sound mental health To him the information struck him, whose main interests are mathematics and physics, like lightning. It seemed I had left the quiet waters in which he and I usually swam. Or maybe some disease had got its claws in me: in my case, such an intellectual collapse could only be caused by a severe case of poisoning or a four-days' fever.

I spent whole days trying to explain what I had discovered. His scepticism was certainly not overcome at an Olympic speed but, finally, bored out of his wits by my preaching, he decided he might as well humour me a bit and read the *Centuries* in the way I told him to. How? From a purely aesthetical point of view, seeing nothing but the images depicted, hearing nothing but the music of the sentences. This was not an easy exercise and most of the time he did not grasp the meaning. This is absolutely normal, the text being very difficult. To tell the truth, it is the most difficult text I have ever seen. However his lack of understanding was of no consequence because the primary goal was quite different. Whenever he thought he understood or simply guessed the meaning, I wanted him to sense the literary qualities of the oeuvre.

After he devoted himself to what I might begin to call attentive reading, he had to confess that I was right. This is indeed a very great poet. Up to now the *Centuries* have always been read with the mind switched off for anything except digging up revelations strewn about as nuggets. As a consequence the goldwasher's sieve only contains the gravel of nonsense. Of course, tracking prophecies with the aggressiveness of a ratter pursuing a hare is not likely to make for clear judgement.

On the other hand, he disagreed with me absolutely on the subject of the manuscript itself. He very soon became convinced that Yves de Lessines, being the intelligent, logical and careful man he was, would have guaranteed his work against the risks of fortune and the stupidity and silliness of men, by making a back-up copy. I told him over and over again that I was sure the monks had no idea what the whole poem was about and hence, that there would have been no grounds for the security measure he was suggesting.

However, he did not relent.

For three years, I refused to believe him although I agreed, reluctantly, that it would have been a "Templar" attitude: everything went by two in their world.

Now I am reconsidering my harsh point of view of those days: he may have been right, for the following reason. At the beginning of 1998, a friend of mine, Soeur Alice, who is a nun of the "Congrégation des Soeurs de Notre-Dame" and librarian at the Episcopal Seminary of Tournai, told me that this library had an inventory of the manuscripts that were kept at Cambron around 1740. It appeared this list was made by a Bollandist, and was therefore extremely well done. Each work is carefully identified with titulus, incipit, excipit, a summary of its contents, etc. One of these works, however, is simply noted: "*Ignoti liber in forma psalterii*" with no other detail, i.e. the book of an unknown writer in the form of a poem. This seems to mean that no-one, neither the person drawing up the catalogue, nor anybody in his neighbourhood, had any idea about the meaning of the text. Circumstances concur to confirm my feeling that this manuscript could be the second copy of Yves de Lessines' *oeuvre*.

That this manuscript still existed in the 1740s is a small wonder in itself. Beside theft, loss, fire and mould, the existence of manuscripts was also threatened by the monks' sense of economy and their modernistic tendencies. We know that making parchment took a long time and was very expensive; therefore, once a book was not considered interesting anymore or no longer appealed, the text was scraped off and the basic material re-employed. The new book is called a palimpsest; and thanks to modern technology the original text can often be reconstituted, at least partly. This is what should have happened to the *Centuries*.

Moreover, during the first century following the invention of printing, most owners of manuscripts often reacted as the 1950s country housewife who eagerly exchanged a three centuries old carved wooden cabinet for a formica one, and thought it the best bargain of her life. Preference was given to brand new printed books, all the more so, as a constant attitude of the Renaissance was to consider previous centuries – contemptuously baptised the Middle Ages – to be a period of barbarism. New technology brought in a new state of mind. The style of the day was strengthened and legitimated even more by the elegance of the characters, the perfection of the engravings, the silkiness or the glossiness of the paper of the printed articles and the 16th century opuses in general. Whoever has had the chance to leaf through books printed by Estienne, Plantin, Elzevier, Alde Manuce, Froben… is left forever with a feeling of pure wonderment. It was normal therefore that manuscripts, the making of which was not exceptionally good, should be held in disdain and considered barely suitable to stuff the bindings of printed books!

Every connoisseur knows that when he has the extraordinary luck of coming across a book which still has its original binding, he must unglue and unstitch the cover very carefully: in this manner a considerable number of interesting works were discovered. It is a procedure like this that finally furnished the proof that the *Roman de Renard* was derived from a Flemish work:

Reinhart (literally pure heart, in Dutch) *de Vos.*

For a manuscript bearing a text as odd as the *Centuries* still to be present at Cambron in the 18th century, and even in the middle of the 16th century, only one explanation is plausible: during hundreds of years, through generations, from one brother librarian to the next, the strict instruction to preserve that particular manuscript must have survived.

Chapter Seven – The Safeguard

Fate took a turn for the worse again with Joseph II, because his progressiveness, although sincere, barely concealed a proven, quibbling cesaropapism. He issued an edict suppressing the so-called contemplative orders, but having no aptitude for governing, he neglected to submit the course of events to a strategy that would have limited subsequent excesses. As it was, Vienna opened the door to overexcited, shameless profiteering, and took not one single sensible and practical measure. As a result, the plundering was heinous and uncontrollable chaos ensued.

The situation was still completely out of control when the France of the Revolution sent in its soldiers of fortune to join the pillage. In a speech to the Convention, Condorcet – though a great and honest man – defined the export of Freedom *"à la mode française"* succinctly as "Belgium must be emptied". And Belgium was emptied.

Using the rabble as a pack of hounds, worked up before being sent in for the kill, the smart ones brandished the words of Justice and Equality as banners, with the clear intention of keeping the booty for themselves. The brigands and general scum of the earth began the job by plundering the abbeys of all their movable goods. When the French bourgeois state decided to put the religious properties on sale, it acted exactly in line with its own institution. Instead of allowing ordinary people to acquire property by selling off small plots, it did quite the opposite. Thus it was only the upper middle class (notaries, lawyers, bailiffs, judges, bankers, merchants, inn-keepers) already largely endowed with gold reaped from previous years' speculations but not shy of adding some more, who acquired the lands, buildings, material and cattle and at small cost.

Within the year they re-couped the cost of the land by re-speculating on food. Being experts on "famine pacts" they knew from experience that this practice was sure to provide them with a substantial income. Hence, they organised famine and then sold their grain at usurious prices on the black market. The buildings too were quickly turned into profit in their own way. They had them demolished and sold the wood and the stones as second-hand building material. Most of these architectural marvels were acquired for a lesser price than the profit made on the sale of zinc, copper and lead of the roofs to the armament factories. The needs of the conquering Republic armies arose to such unheard-of heights that the price of metals defied imagination. Sometimes though, it was considered more fruitful to turn them into the bourgeois version of a prison, i.e. a factory. Or, at strategic places, they served as lodgings for the troops, who often wrecked the place out of sheer boredom.

As luck would have it, the religious orders were stripped of their belongings right at the moment the *"commende"* system had one foot in its grave. For centuries, the lords had ruined the religious institutions by a typically medieval racket, i.e. they called themselves "avoués", that is protectors in the sense Al Capone gave to this word. Or else by imposing the favourites of Kings and Queens as false parasitic Abbots who were not satisfied with less than three-quarters of the income. This time, however, the favourites of the new regime moved in to claim their share. Copiously and definitely: they were no longer content merely to enjoy the use of the Church's property, they became the owners, denying the Church the right of possession. They made their own adage : for the wise man, ownership is the only sure way of making a momentary favour hereditary while guaranteeing it against the temper of the powerful. The wisdom of the rich was not lost on them either. The large inheritance has always been, is and will be the shortest, surest and most used path to fortune.

Having become rich just for the sake of it, the purchasers of "national property" were heartless, soulless, no-nonsense owners exempting themselves, in the name of Progress, from taking on all the charitable work of the monks. The French revolutionaries knew their way around. Seldom have people been more adroit at burying such mountains of greed, brutality and vice under an avalanche of idealistic and grandiloquent bombast. Beforehand, under the "Directory", they openly admitted to, and even flattered themselves on their greed, brutality and vice. And yet, the Revolution was more than necessary. Nothing is simple!

Not surprisingly these storms also hit Cambron and dispersed the manuscripts: some are found in Tournai, Mons, Brussels, Ghent, Bruges, others in Paris, Florence, England, America and elsewhere. Philippe Demets launched a true manuscript-hunt in order to unearth the *Centuries* of Cambron so that we may have it published. Although we risk the one eternal, skilful, snaky and well-placed rascal shouting out of the blue: "I found it, I will publish it", raffling the fruit of someone else's quest. Twice in my life I have come across this kind of person who, unable to build their own reputation, became famous by plundering others. I would not like this to happen a third time. At present, we know that the manuscript is neither in Tournai nor Mons or Brussels. At least, it is not mentioned in the lists of Cambron that have been examined. Perhaps it is not even indexed at all.

But, after a bit of a set back, I made an unexpected discovery of the utmost importance. Consulting the index of the manuscripts of Cambron at the Séminaire de Tournai, and then examining those that were more readily accessible, I have been able to collect a series of external proofs that all lead in the same direction. They add weight to the idea that the *Centuries* originate in Cambron, and allow conjecture, without much risk of error, and notwithstanding Nostradamus' pollution, that the true author of the poem is a Cistercian Picard monk living at the beginning of the 14th century; and most definitely not someone living in the Provence around 1550.

When I first started analysing the *Centuries*, I noticed that Yves de Lessines used some beautiful expressions drawn from writings of St Bernard. The opus of Clairvaux' first Abbot was immense. In those days the saying went that it could cover the whole surface of the earth. That, at the very least, is large-scale flattery. No abbey could pride itself on possessing St Bernard's whole production; it is a normal tendency for people to refer more easily to books they are familiar with.

The quotations from Bernard de Clairvaux that are scattered throughout the *Centuries* are *all* drawn from hand-written copies dating from the 13th to the beginning of the 14th century. There can be no doubt as to their physical presence at Cambron since every second or third page carries the mention: "de Camberone" or "de Sancta Marie de Camberone", which is the abbey's official name. The Old Monk, writing between 1323 and 1329, had them close at hand. Conversely – and this fact firmly supports the previous one – there are no quotations from works that were not part of the library at Cambron. The author of the *Centuries* lived at Cambron and nowhere else.

A second element that has been highlighted is the following: I have said that the stories told by the author all happened in the period from the end of the 11th until the beginning of the 14th century. Most of them are small anecdotes, little known even then. Yet they are all mentioned in historical works which he had at his disposal, including, among others, Vincent de Beauvais' *Speculum Historiale*, a work that had been copied at Cambron by Jean de Rebaix at the time when Yves de Lessines had just taken holy orders.

Thirdly, when he speaks about Blanche de Castille, the mother of St Louis, our Cistercian gets the details of his narrative from a letter sent to the Queen by her sister, a letter that is entitled: "*Berengeriae regine Legionis* ad *Blancam reginam Francorum*", in other words: "from Berengeria, Queen of Leon, to Blanche, Queen of the French". The library of Cambron held a copy of this letter dated from the 13th century! In the same manner his evocation of Baudouin de Constantinople, or his brother and successor Henri d'Ancre, Count of Hainaut and Flanders, who became Emperor of Byzantium, is based on original letters and writs preserved at the Abbey.

Whereas one will probably be quite surprised by this beautiful complex of disconcerting elements, one is likely to be disconcerted in the same measure – but in a very different way – by the one and only, true, dated "prophecy" that is to be found in the *Centuries*:

> X 72 *L'an mil neuf cens nonante neuf sept mois*
> *Du ciel viendra un grand Roy d'effrayeur*

> (The year one thousand nine hundred ninety-nine seven month
> From the sky will come a great King of fright)

This prophecy which, to be strictly accurate, is not a prophecy, is simply the announcement of the solar eclipse which was visible in our regions on the 11th August, 1999.

To predict, in 1325, an eclipse that will occur 675 years later is not something that everyone was able to do so. The astronomical table that made it possible to calculate the moment of the appearance of this *grand Roy d'effrayeur* was at Cambron in Yves de Lessines' time, and it still exists.

This whole matter, on the other hand, sheds a light on the mentality of the nostraddicts. About three years before the fateful date, as the Millennium drew near and gurus of all kind heaped foolery upon delirious foolery explaining these two terrifying lines, I tried to make clear, as well as I could, that these lines were not a catastrophic prophecy at all. They simply referred to an eclipse in which only the astronomical milieu had been interested so far. In those days, the event had not yet earned the later media coverage and no-one had linked the Nostradamian "prophecy" with the earth-moon-sun rendez-vous. My prediction is on record since my remarks were published and broadcast on the radio.

The answer of the guru tribe was one of sarcastic contempt. One of them even told me, in no uncertain terms, that there were laws "protecting names". I guessed he probably referred to something like the protection of privacy. But I was to understand quite clearly that this meant his name could only be cited flatteringly, and that he did not wish anyone to contradict or challenge what he stated and published. Cruel dilemma: must I keep silent or issue a panegyric that would be a gigantic lie from its beginning to its end? Should I appear to be in agreement with stupidity by not denouncing it or to be an imbecile by praising it? What the poor man had not realised clearly is that no-one can make me hold my peace once I have decided to honour somebody. I will therefore sing his praises, while respecting his wish for humility: I will call him the Anonymous Author, Mr. AA, to make my life easier.

Mr. AA then, who had quite a lot to say about this date of which he is particularly fond, wrote somewhere in the 1980s that this quatrain prophesied (this is a literal quotation):

L'an mil neuf cens nonante neuf sept mois
Du Ciel viendra un grand Roy d'effrayeur

"L'INVASTION DE LA FRANCE EN JUILLET 1999.
INVASION AERIENNE.
Traduction: En juillet 1999, un grand chef terrifiant viendra par la voie des airs pour faire revivre le grand conquérant de l'Angoûmois (sic). *Avant et après la guerre régnera* (resic) *heureusement. L'Angoûmois* (re-resic) *fut conquis par les Wisigoths et bientôt menacé par les Huns, race mongole sous le commandement d'Attila."*

Invasion of France in July 1999. Invasion by air. Translation (sic). In July 1999 a terrifying leader will come by air to bring back to life the great conqueror of the Angoûmois (the region of Angoûlème, in France). Before and afterwards war will blissfully reign. The Angoûmois was conquered by the Visigoths and pretty soon threatened by the Huns, a Mongol race under the command of Attila.

It would seem that Mr. AA's comprehension of facts and his interest can only be shaken out of hibernation by the loud noise of the media. This explains why, when I spoke of Yves de Lessines and his astronomical table a long time before the actual event, Mr. AA in a few choice words told me I was out of my mind with my eclipse of the eighth month (11th August, 1999). Did I not know Nostradamus clearly said "ninety-nine *seven* months"?

Such ignorance! Professing to be the prophet of the prophet, knowing perfectly the life story of the magus, explaining Michel's announcements to the admiring crowd, and then ignoring the fact that the calendar had been changed in the meantime! It really gives the full measure of the expounder's scientific approach.

And yet, my statement had been duly documented. I explained that the expression *"un grand roy d'effrayeur"* was a poetic image inspired by the Bible as well as the millennial and apocalyptic writings that were profuse at the time. The image was frequently used in the Middle Ages to indicate any imposing astronomical phenomenon. I also said that, although foreseen for July, the event must nevertheless have been the eclipse of August because in the author's time his reference would have been the Julian calendar, whereas we now live under the Gregorian calendar. I went so far as to explain that, due to the fact that the period of the solar year, during which the Earth makes one complete revolution around the Sun, in 365.25 days, before the leap year system of adding one day every 4 years was imposed, the relationship of the physical year to the calendar year was seriously out of line. In order to resolve this, Pope Gregory XIII deferred to the wish of the Council of Trent and declared that the day following October 4th 1582 would not be October 5th but October 15th. I also explained that Thérèse d'Avila had passed away during this curious night and that the difference with our calendar would be thirteen days between the 29th of February 1900 and the 28th February 2100. Hence, an astronomer writing in the period 1500-1582 would inevitably have dated the 29th of July 1999, whereas Yves de Lessines in the beginning of the 14th century would have set on the 27th of July of his calendar, the eclipse we were given to admire on the 11th of August of our calendar.

When the eclipse materialised but not the disaster, they realised they could still get more sales mileage out of the "prophecy" by assuring their audience that the event had been postponed until July the following year – or maybe September…

Let the crowds rest assured: the superb catastrophes of that fateful summer of 1999 were postponed to July 2000, or maybe, so it might seem, to September. Anyway, Mr. AA overlooking his successive failures, announced that the summer of 2000 would witness a terrifying war of the Western world against China. I must admit that I still fail to understand the obvious reason why it has now become necessary to add 12 or 14 months to July 1999. However, there is more to come.

A very recently sprouted nostraddicted exponent has started his career by calling all the others damned old… (you know what), for having thought that the King of France "Henri V" would reign and lead his troops to the war in July or August 1999. The announced event did not occur, which proves sufficiently that he is right, except of course if the battle was fought discreetly below the threshold of noise. But what our smart little newcomer has understood, which all of us stupid people missed out on, was that Nostradamus' Great Revelation of 11th August 1999 was the birth of Henri V. Let us not crucify him: at least, it is an innovation, but let us hope the revealer dies before the revealed, living his life in unharmed blissful certitude until his very end.

One of the great fantasies that prevail in French nostraddict writings, concerns Henri V. As you may know, there have been only four Kings of France called Henri, three of whom were killed, the last one stabbed by Ravaillac on 14th May 1610. All the nostraddicts basing their interpretations on the Great Prophet's revelations, have announced the restoration of the monarchy in France for about 150 years, with the Bourbons on the throne again.

> VIII 54   *Sous la couleur du traite mariage*
> *Fait magnanime du grand Chyren selin*
> *Quintin Arras recouvrez au voyage*
> *D'Espagnols faict second ban macelin*

Of course, the event is always to take place in the years that follow the publication of the book one is reading at the moment... Pushing the ridiculousness to stratospheric heights, they are divided into Legitimist and Orleanist nostraddicts, each accusing the other of vile heresy, more hateful than the crime of lese-majesty of the godless Republicans. Since the publication of *Gargantua*, never a more comic tale has been imagined than the misadventures of this Henri-still-to-come. Let us recall, even if it is just an anecdote, that caught up in the spring fever of May 1968 and convinced that the eve had finally come, they innocently asked De Gaulle to resign in favour of the Count of Paris. I am sure de Gaulle would not have accommodated them.

One nostraddict announced for the 1980s, or the next decade at the latest, before the war of the Antichrist in 1999, and in addition to the assassination of Pope John Paul II in Lyons, the arrival of Henri V as a Bourbon Emperor who, in a hundred different places in France, would crush hundreds of Mongolian divisions, who had had the curious idea of invading France by making use of the Swiss tunnels. On his awakening and before starting to write, he should have stopped and realised that, for an army marching towards the enemy, no place is more dangerous than a tunnel. Even a one-eyed squinter cannot miss his target when shooting a rifle, and a man on a bicycle can easily stop and roast a whole tank division.

It is a fact that the same man, Mr. AA that is, also claimed that Nostradamus predicted that during the same war, before the air invasion of France, the Belgian King at the head of his troops, probably as in 1914, would drive back the Libyan aggressor from Hungary to Gibraltar. I hope the man realises great things lay ahead of him...

All this based on two words: "Chiren selin". It is quite extraordinary how two words can lead one such a merry dance. They translated them by "Henri de la lune" (Henry of the moon)! Thank heavens they failed to notice that these words are also the anagram of "nicher l(e) sein" (cup the breast). Hence their famous Henri V would be working one hand in the open and the other God knows where.

There has never been any question whatsoever about the next King of France, the always-to-come Henri V. But that the quatrain refers to the marriage of Philippe-Auguste (1165-1223) to Isabelle de Hainaut in April 1180. Since there is indeed a Henri, let us introduce the right one. Known as Henri de Hainaut, or de Flandres, or d'Ancre, or de Sele, Selle, Cele, Celles, or Zele, he is of course: selinus or celinus, the two spellings are used by Yves de Lessines. In everyone's opinion, he was the most remarkable of the Latin Emperors of Constantinople. He succeeded his brother Baudouin, first as Regent from April 1205 till August 1206, later as Emperor from 20th August 1206 up to his death on 11th June 1216.

On 13th January 1213 (or 1212 depending on whether one follows the new year cycle of January or of Easter) he sent a letter from Pergame to his friends in Hainaut and Flanders to keep them informed of his expeditions and the victories he had won during 1211 and 1212 over his principal adversaries: Michael I Doukas, despot of Epire; Strèz, lord of Prosêk; Theodore I Laskaris, Emperor of Nicée (or Nisse, or Nice); and Boril, Czar of the Bulgarians. This letter is included in manuscript 21,887, held at the Belgian National Library in Brussels, the so-called Albertine. It goes from the back of page 191 to the back of page 194.

Its titulus is: *De quatuor imperii hostibus a se pervictis.*

Its incipit reads: *Henricus Dei gratia fidelissimus in Christo imperator a Deo coronatus, Romanie moderator et semper augustus, universis amicis suis, ad quod tenor presentium litterarum pervenerit, salutem in Domino dominorum. Quoniam dilecto vestra de statu nostro...*

And its excipit:... *Nichel autem nobis deesse sciatis ad habendam plenam victoriam et possidendum imperium, nisi Latinorum copiam, quibus possimus dare terram, quam acquirimus, immo quam iam acquisivimus, cum sicut scitis parum sit acquirere, nisi fuerint qui conservent. Apud Pergamum in octavis Epiphanie anno Domini MCCXII.*

When my quest comes to an end, when the manuscript of Yves de Lessines is discovered, how many more surprises will lie in wait for us? The only thing I am sure of is that the *Centuries* are, and will be even more so tomorrow, a vast domain of philological and historical studies. Having been the one to open the gate leading to this immense treasure is the only thing I am really proud of.

The
Templars'
Road

Chapter Eight – Too Many Twins

As Johan Wolfgang von Goethe once said: *in dem Anfang war die Tat.* This somewhat watered down aphorism after St John's Gospel means to its author: in the beginning was the Deed. We might also translate it as: in the beginning was the action, and even in the beginning was the Feat.

Indeed, what generated the *Centuries* was the successful performance of three intelligent, resolute and disinterested men, but it was the utter futility of their very success and an old man's despair that finally gave birth to the poem.

The end of the Temple was like a shipwreck, the *Centuries* the bottle thrown into the sea. Yves de Lessines disguised the story he had to tell beneath other stories. By means of itineraries to be followed, he indicated a precise location and he covered in enigmas a progress that, following the example of a pilgrimage, he intended to be spiritual as well as real.

This complex intellectual and literary construction, a true network of meanings and suggestions, proceeds directly from the medieval canons of aesthetics, as already briefly mentioned in the preceding pages. The same rules apply to every form of art and we find them even in the heart of the labyrinths laid out on the floors of many cathedrals. The labyrinths are now claimed to be part of an initiation ritual, whereas in fact they were a guideline for prayer and meditation. When followed correctly, i.e. in the direction of the sun and always on the inner side of the path, they will fasten the attentive eye on the spots where religious symbols, deemed the most important by the builders, were hidden. The same strategy governs the writing of the *Centuries*. They must be read with this clearly in mind if one does not want to get lost beyond recall.

When medieval clerks wrote in the vernacular, they called this "mettre en roman", putting it into Romance language. The term "roman" indicates a kind of *koîné*, i.e. a common language, generally spoken, in which the regional vernacular expressions were blended and in which the Francian was to play the part of the cuckoo.

If one has something to say, one's major concern is to be heard and listened to; to talk is to request attention and understanding. To the people of the medieval era, the principal property of the Romance resided in the fact that it was supposed to be understood by a large number of people living on a sizeable stretch of land. It was not a strictly coded language as we know them now. It was essentially the language of the people, of almost spontaneous generation and taught in no school. Each and every person created his own *koîné*. This resulted in a large number of vigorous and colourful expressions from each author's region of origin, and made up the exceptional richness of the Romance. According to Ferdinand Brunot, the modern language may have lost up to ninety percent of the vocabulary of the ancient language. From this point of view, Classicism was a real disaster.

The episode of the Crusades was decisive for the promotion of the Romance. The *lingua franca* was all but the official language of all the Oriental Latin States (the Kingdom of Jerusalem, the Principality of Antioche, the County of Tripoli, the Kingdom of Cyprus, etc.). During the 12th and 13th centuries it was the English or Malay of the Mediterranean. Evidence of its sphere of influence is ample. Marco Polo's book in its version called *Le Million* starts with the Venetian traveller justifying the dictation of his opus in Romance as follows: *"pour ce que parol des franceis est plus comunement entendu."* (because the speech of the franca is the most commonly understood.) Bruno Latini, Dante's master, wrote his "Trésor de sapience" (Treasure of Knowledge) in Romance; his explanation is warmer and gentler: *"la parleüre la plus delitable et la plus comune a toutes gens."* (the speech that is the most delightful and yet most common to all people."'

The *Centuries* were therefore quite unsurprisingly written in a Romance language with a Franco-Picard basis, i.e. the language spoken in the north of France, resembling the language of Jehan Froissart's *Chroniques* (but older by seventy years) and identical to the language of the *Viel Rentier d'Audenarde*. This is a splendid manuscript from 1285 decorated with 160 humorous drawings. It contains 187 recto-verso pages and lists the endless litany of the revenues of the lords of Oudenaarde-Pamele, naming each location and its occupant. This treasure from our past is an incomparable source of linguistic and historical information.

Fortunately Nostradamus, who was never accused by his contemporaries of being a humanist or even a civilised person, left a lot of rubbish and waste in his modernising and forging enterprise. Archaeologists have recently come to the conclusion that the study of waste pits is the most reliable source of information regarding the daily life of ancient communities. In the same manner with regards to the *Centuries*, the errors, mistakes and stupidities, read in their original language, will explain a great many quatrains that have defied all understanding up to now.

We will now get down to the root of the matter and as you will have gathered from the heading of this chapter, we are going on a journey.

Throughout the *Centuries*, Yves de Lessines alludes to a great number of stories, all happening in a period starting at the end of the 11th and ending at the beginning of the 14th century. More specifically, he sticks to a time frame that commences with the Investiture Quarrel and the perils of the first crusade, and finishes with the immediate consequences of the peace treaty signed in Paris in 1322 by Louis de Nevers, Count of Flanders, and Guillaume le Bon, Count of Hainaut, Holland, Zeeland and Friesland. This unusual historic treatise is interlarded with numerous annotations that, when put together, determine a number of itineraries. Let me take you to the discovery of just a part of one of these itineraries, by far the most detailed of them.

My procedure is not a piece of fantasy, nor is it haphazard. My goal is to shed a light on the Old Monk's way of proceeding. His poem reveals the roads travelled by the Templars obeying the *ordre hesperique*, but all the place names mentioned also serve another purpose: they are *landmarks* that are intended as a first stage to catch the attention of the long-awaited one, and then mark out his route.

On closer scrutiny, it strikes us that none of the topographical annotations refers to one particular place, *in abstracto*, but they all come in twos, threes or fours, defining a direction or naming the next stage. The subtlety in the composition method of these annotations is such that, once understood, each place name mentioned in the 4000 lines can be used as an entry, on the condition, however, that it is quite clear in one's mind that a marked-out road must be followed. One's step will always be guided to a predetermined place. It seems logical therefore that we should walk a part of this road, for a mile or three, as a practical exercise.

The general movement of the poem carries one towards a centre. On the first reading level we start with an old story that acts as a slip road to a contemporary fact, finally to end up with a Templar message. The more the narrative present comes closer, the closer we are brought to the meaning: in stages. The same logic governs the description of the itineraries. In the departure zones they are sketched out very roughly; they become more and more detailed as the journey goes on and finally reach the incredible meticulousness of the miniature as if, standing on the point of arrival, we watch them coming to us from the far distance. It is the increasing density of the place names as guide posts that structures the direction by determining the perspective of the author, who is viewing the scene from the centre of a vortex.

The accumulation of details finally becomes so overwhelming that we have to limit our study by making often frustrating choices, otherwise there would be no end to the book. In passing, we can point out that this way of working in perspective has a lot in common with the paintings of the so-called Flemish Primitives. Their process is totally different from the geometrical drawings of the Italian style, because it is based essentially on working with colours and light, in perfect synergy with the lines of equilibrium of the composition.

Whatever word of the *Centuries* struck the spark, long before arriving at our starting point, the long-awaited one would already know that the Templars came from Germany, England, the south of Europe and the east of France to Ypres, the head *commanderie* of the Flemish *baylie* (province). They then proceeded to St Léger, still on Flemish territory, where their route converged with that of the Parisians. The next stage led them on to Moustier, after crossing the river Scheldt at Herne (called Hérinnes nowadays), at the exact confluence of that stream and the Espierre, the river flowing at the foot of the *commanderie* an hour upstream.

I suggest that we follow our old guide starting at Moustier, a small village bordering on Frasnes-lez-Buissenal in the west of Hainaut, in what is now known as the "Pays des Collines".

> I 95   *Devant Moustier trouve enfans besson*
> *D'heroiq sang de moine vetustique*
> *Son bruit par secte langue et puissance son*
> *Qu'on dira fort esleve le Vopisque*

A *moustier* is a monastery, an abbey and sometimes a church, although this is an improper use. According to Geneviève Mouigneau, in this incorrect use, *moustier* relates to a church situated outside the abbey, but with the services being conducted by monks. *Besson* means twin; at present this word is considered archaic or dialectic. The first line literally means: *Devant le monastère (ou l'église) on trouvera un enfant jumeau* (In front of the monastery (or the church) one will find a twin child).

A twin of what? Which child?

Here you have the classic example of the line that serves as fuel to light the spark for the miscellaneous ravings. Let us not blame them for overlooking Moustier, such a small trifle compared to the immense joy derived from reading their explanations, as varied as there are exponents. It is, separately or in combination, an anecdote about the finding of two abandoned babies, the story of two brothers living on opposite sides of a church square, the tomb of twins in a cemetery (the sepulchre of course, that hides a fabulous treasure), or the Gemini constellation, or two alchemy symbols, a sculpture even, or possibly… On account of necessary and inevitable secrecy, the spot where the marvel in question lies is never stated and the description of the thing itself remains vague. In short, it is a jungle, a swamp, a jumble. Which goes to prove that as long as one does not know exactly what pair one is looking for, the door is wide open to all kind of fantastic speculations regarding any pair of any thing.

If we listen carefully to the old hands of the medieval clergy, if we empathise with the outlook of the Middle Ages, the key will turn without a hitch in the mystery's lock. Because then, before running here and there and chasing illusionary twins, we will start by looking for a monastery, as suggested by the order of the words. Because maybe – and we should always have this question in the back of our heads – it is not a pure coincidence if the word Moustier is found at the beginning of the line, or even the quatrain. The place of things is rarely left to chance or fancy; quite to the contrary, it is carefully chosen to draw attention to itself and to be meaningful, in line with the holistic way of thinking of the medieval people. We add the *double entendre* and we know at once that, in the present case, we must also look for a "moustier" that is *different* from a monastery or a church.

Now, if you had the good fortune to be born and raised in Wodecq, you would be sure to know of the existence of a village called Moustier. A peculiar Moustier, by the way, since in this village that goes by the name of Monastery, there has never been one, as far back as memory can reach. Whatever the origin of this incongruous fact, it must have been quite conspicuous in the Middle Ages. The word was indeed very much alive and referred to buildings present everywhere and visible to all. According to medieval standards, a place without a monastery would be abnormal, the more so if the place in question was called monastery by one and all. It should be noted that in some older publications of the *Centuries*, the word is written with a capital letter, which is totally illogical if it is not a place name. Therefore it is not impossible that the Old Monk originally spelt it that way and that Michel Nostradamus dutifully copied it.

Unfortunately, the name Moustier rings no bells historically or geographically in the heads of the nostraddicts. The existence of a place by that name has never occurred to them, and their comic productions provide much fun for the reader. They read Paris, Lyon, or Nancy, etc. and within seconds there follows an event predicted by Nostradamus. If they stumble upon Luchon, Luçon, Montluçon, Ecoman, Vieille-Brioude, Mydit-Le-Joli-

Village (in the Vexin) that do not sound too familiar, they will rack their brains and conjure up the memory of a near-battle that might have taken place if by misfortune the wind had not blown or the rain poured down, more or less somewhere in the neighbourhood. But what if the toponym does not suit them at all? Still, no fear. A small change here, a little modification there, and the problem becomes non-existent. Mr. AA succeeded in transforming a Picard *grande vague* (a billow) into an Italian *grande vache* (a big cow). This somewhat astonishing topographic result was achieved by pure ignorance, by mixing up two languages, by believing a Spanish word to be an Italian one. The whole is ceremoniously presented as the discovery of the century, written in a more serious tone than the Papal Bull on the use of contraceptives.

Subject the past of Moustier to microscopic scrutiny as they may, there is no trace of the slightest battle, no shadow of a fight. And thus, as far as the exponents are concerned, Moustier might as well not exist, or be somewhere in the wastelands of Siberia.

The first time I ever set foot in Moustier, a very long time ago, was with my bugle to encourage my village team that had to play a decisive ball game against Moustier's team: a matter of life and death, of course. Three hours later I was running for my life through the fields, being chased by a bunch of raving mad locals, in pursuit of me and my instrument. I must say that at the crucial moment, when one of the opponents was preparing to catch the decisive ball, I happened to be at the right spot to blow a formidable blast on my bugle into his ear. Totally paralysed, he failed to catch it. Possibly as a result, our team won the championship and Moustier lost, for which we were given no thanks. That particular Sunday afternoon, the enemy's supporters were not in a very good mood...

And yet, the afternoon had started in peace and bucolic serenity. Even before leaving my Vespa against the wall of the local pub, my eyes were drawn irresistibly to the two churches standing there side by side, in what can only be described as a rural backwater. The fact had struck me as being abnormal, to say the least. A good thirty years later, spurred on by the words *Moustier* and *besson*, I decided to go back to that dangerous place, hoping that the erstwhile hotheads blessed with a good memory and a long life, would not recognise me.

From the tiny car park, grandly called "La Place" by the locals, I walked over to the parochial temple, not to worship God but in search of something in a pair. But great disappointment awaited me. Try as I might, there was not one pair of anything except the two churches in the whole of Moustier.

Whereupon I decided to turn my back on that village that could not inspire me and go home. At the very last, and therefore most favourable moment, I remembered that in Picard "devant" (in front of) is pronounced [*devan*] and "dedans" (inside of) is pronounced [*devẽ*]. Written in the script of the 14th century, the only difference between the two words is a tilde on the "e". To someone whose palaeographical knowledge is minimal and who moreover is not truly familiar with Picard, the difference may go unnoticed. I thought about a number of lines of the *Centuries* featuring "dedans" and "devant", and concluded that pending an in-depth examination, it seemed as if Nostradamus had been stumbling around in front and inside. It was not much, but then even God himself did not have much before he embarked upon the Creation. At least, it was a start and it enabled me to conjecture that the line Nostradamus copied may as well have been speaking about a twin child found "deDans" (inside) the church as "deVant" (in front of).

A sudden revelation of that kind demanded that, standing in front of the church, I should take a few more steps and go inside. Which I did. As soon as I entered the porch, I understood. The object of the line is not *enfAns besson* but *enfOns besson*, a misreading of *un fons*.

Let me explain. From a stylistic point of view, that "twin child" had always bothered me: we usually speak of a twin or twins. The heaviness of "twin child" is inconsistent with Yves de Lessines' otherwise brilliant style. Although it has happened; in Pierre Bersuire's translation of Titus-Livius in the 14th century we find even worse: "*les deux enfants bessons ou jumeaux*" (the two twin children or twins). The man's syrupy style is well known, but you must admit that saying three times almost the same thing in three successive words is a rare performance. Maybe he feared being misunderstood. But the final "s" of *enfans* bothered me even more. It seems to indicate a plural while *besson* is singular.

A few words on declension are appropriate, I am afraid. Many among us know what it is, especially people having studied German, Latin, Greek or Russian. I am therefore more specifically addressing those among you who took English, Italian, Portuguese or Chinese, so that you may thank Heaven on your bare knees for having been spared the torture.

Conjugation is known to all: in French, to conjugate is to add an extra meaning to a verb by varying its ending. The forms "matelasseront", "matelassassiez" or "ayant été matelassé" add a particular sense to the verb "matelasser". These added senses are called: form (active or passive), mode, tense (past, present or future), number and person.

In the Indo-European languages, the declension is the same linguistic technique applied to nouns and their adjectives, determiners and pronouns. The variation in ending will indicate the gender, the number, the function and, for some languages, the category. In Latin, these variations are known as "cases" of the declension and they indicate simultaneously the gender, number and function of the word or the logical group within the complete sentence. The subject function will be expressed by the nominative case, the direct object by the accusative case, the indirect object by the dative case, the determiner or possessive complement by the genitive case and the adverbial complement by the ablative case.

To explain the development of the Latin into the Romance languages, what we must remember from this is that, as time go by, the tools of a language tend to flake off, the vigour imperceptibly turns to languor, juicy expressions become blander and blander.

If we add to this the shift of meaning, the emergence of new things (objects, thoughts, feelings, moral and religious values), social and political upheavals, the passing of generations, and last but not least: fashion, then we can easily conceive that a language is not a self-existing reality, locked up in a dictionary, sealed in its grammar, and descended as manna from heaven on the desert of the uncultivated mind. A language lives; like peat: it dies back at one end, and regenerates at the other, and lives in between. A language is in permanent unstable development, and testifies to the unremitting addition of novelties that revitalise what has become hackneyed or weakened, and to new words that are created simultaneously with the things they refer to.

So, fatigued by centuries of toil, the Latin declensions were at long last consigned to the home of dead languages. Homo loquens quickly came up with his new favourites: prepositions, which each have their own special case. The immediate consequence on the structure of the sentence is a weakening of the direct system (verb (or noun) plus declined nouns) in favour of the indirect system (verb (or noun) plus prepositions plus nouns). We all know what distinguishes a masculine singular from a feminine plural (each one guaranteeing the happiness of the other) but do we also know that these are the fossilised remains of the Latin declensions?

Vulgar Latin went through a near-earthquake between the 4th and the 7th centuries: the spread of muting and diphtongs was such that the vowel system underwent an in-depth change. Some unstressed syllables were no longer pronounced and the declensions were reduced to two cases: the nominative and the accusative (plus some traces of the genitive). In the end, the accusative triumphed over the nominative – almost all our nouns today are accusatives – but the total victory only occurred in the 14th century. Up to then, an end-declension remained in two cases: the subject-case and the object-case. The *singular* subject-case and the *plural* object-case of most of the masculine nouns were written with an end "s".

Let me give you an example to try and make things easier to understand. We will take this from a French popular tale entitled "Des Vilains ou des .XXIII. menieres de vilains".

"*Li vilains apensez si est uns vilains traitres qui flate la gent tant qu'il en a fait son preu*" (the cautious (with an underlying meaning of cunning, sly, sneaky) crook is an hypocrite who flatters people as long as it is profitable to him). As you can see, the first two verbs, *est* and *flate*, are singular whereas the two groups, subject and subject complement, *li vilains apensez* and *uns vilains traites* total five final "s"-es.

In passing, a short word on the medieval way of thinking. This simple sentence contains two wordplays, the first on *apensez*, the second on *traitre*. *Apensez* comes from the similarly spelt verb *apenser* which means: to think (over) on the one hand, and on the other: to suspend, to hang. "*Li vilains apensez*" is the one who thinks carefully as well as the one who deserves to hang. The word *traitre* comes from two homophone verbs that mean *trahir* (to betray) (deriving from the Latin *tradere*: to deliver) on one side, and *tirer*, *obtenir* (to get from) (with a strong pejorative sense, bordering on *traire* (to milk), a development of the vulgar Latin *tragere*: to draw from, on the other side). *Uns vilains traitres* is the one who betrays and also the one who milks people.

The combination of the two wordplays provides us with four different meanings for the same sentence!

"*Li vilains chenins si est cil qui siet devant son huis a la feste et moque chascun qui va par devant lui et dit, s'il voit venir .i. gentil home qui porte un esprivier sus son poig: " Ha! Fait il, cil huas mangera enquenuit une geline et mi anfant en fussent tuit saoul.*" The vile "dog grape" (raisin de chien -sic) (acid that irritates the mouth) is he who sits in front of his door (on the day of) the feast and makes fun of everyone passing by and who says when he sees a noble man approaching carrying a sparrowhawk on his fist: Ah! says he, that owl will eat a chicken tonight and my children will all have their fill.

Note the unwitting double entendre in the sentence *cil huas mangera enquenuit une geline et mi anfant en fussent tuit saoul.*

Li vilains chenins si est cil…, cil huas mangera: the verbs *est* and *mangera* are singular, but the subject groups *vilains chenins* and *huas* carry an "s". (…) *et mi anfant en fussent tuit saoul:* the verb *fussent* is plural but the subject *anfant* and the subject complement *saoul* are singular. This is sufficient proof that the subject case is characterised by a use exactly the opposite of ours today, i.e. they attached "s" to the end in the singular form, but no "s" in the plural form.

If we revert to our line: *Devant Moustier trouve enfans besson,* the group *enfans besson* is a direct object; it must therefore be in the object-case and *besson* is undeniably a singular object-case. And yet, the spelling *enfans* can only be either a SINGULAR SUBJECT-CASE or a PLURAL OBJECT-CASE. *Both cases are wrong.* And it is not a peccadillo either. The final "s" of *enfans* is a gross mistake, not so much a spelling mistake as one might be led to believe on first glance, but a grammatical error. However, I cannot believe that the Old Monk may have blundered so badly. Would Shakespeare or Hemingway or Steinbeck write something like one children or three child? The above mistake is one of the same kind.

Printer's error, scribe's gross negligence, or a mistake that reveals fraud? The nostraddicts' usual saying in a case like this is: "The printer did it." Let us not be misled into believing that printers were an inferior race. Rather, to do right by them, their spelling was usually far better than most of the authors'. It seems therefore most unlikely that they would have printed a blunder of this kind, even if Nostradamus had inadvertently written it. What we should also keep in mind is that during the 16th century, at least half of the books printed were Latin. Printing a Latin book is not a job for the village idiot. I am not saying that printers were infallible, but systematically laying the sins of Nostradamus on their shoulders is exaggerated and dishonest. The nostraddicts' explanation has one big advantage: it is so easy.

But the ease of some is not necessarily the truth of the others. Reason, balanced judgement and common sense would rather suggest that if the error was maintained, it was done so of Nostradamus' own volition. I think this hypothesis is built on firmer grounds than discourteous contempt for professional printers. I mentioned before that our self-appointed astrologer was not stupid. Very often he shows that he understood perfectly that nothing in this poem is without sense or meaning. Granted, he sold off the *Centuries* under the guise of prophecies, and we will demonstrate when the occasion arises, that he himself was unable to decipher their meaning. Nevertheless, a great many elements point to the fact that he was convinced it was a prophetic poem of divine inspiration. This touch of superstition incited him to treat some text elements with great respect, probably not so much out of sensible reasoning, but as an homage to the prophecy he was plundering, a propitiatory genuflection. I do not know why but the man reminds me of the sanctimonious bigots of my childhood. Insensitive and narrow-minded, they specialised in favour-haggling prayers that were supposed to increase the chances and merits, that they considered were due to them by the Godly Power who, as is commonly known, is a great purveyor of piously earned successes, paid for in cash by weekly confessions and posthumous masses, and who strictly honours His part of the bargain by rewarding the public virtues of the Good Christians, as well He should.

But back to the original mistake. There is always a logic to be found in errors. As with any other mistake, the bad spelling arises from the blending of the writer's knowledge and ignorance. As such, a mistake is an image of the mental universe of its perpetrator. Spelling mistakes never proceed from an intellectual void, in which nothing is to be found except the mists of primal awareness. Consider the following: the strange or unexpected aspect of spelling mistakes makes us laugh. As always, the comical result is caused by deviation from the standard norm. This means that a scribe's errors are, *ipso facto*, firmly rooted in what is conceivable in his own period of time; they will never bring out the inconceivable from the culprit's mind, but are on the contrary, in accordance with his own logic that is not necessarily deficient but simply ignorant of the norm. *Enfans besson,* however, utterly lacks logic. In order to explain the mistake within the Nostradamian context, we must presuppose the existence of other mistakes of the same nature, which quite obviously the scribe did not make.

It would seem to me that Nostradamus would have been hard put to commit the reported mistake (*enfans besson*): in his days the subject-case had disappeared for two-hundred years, nobody had a need for it and even its memory had almost fallen into oblivion. It is hard to imagine someone suddenly starting to write and using subject and object-cases, without any reason at all and incorrectly on top of it. And finally, the Renaissance prided itself on its Latin culture, took its example from Antiquity and ruthlessly rejected the legacy from former centuries, the more so when its language was that barbaric French from the "Dark Ages". In short, the whole set-up creaks and cracks.

Even supposing that Nostradamus intended to cover up a prophetic message under this grammatical jumble, what inscrutable subtlety would he have been conveying by using a declined form that would, at the most, have looked strange to the eyes of his contemporaries for want of sounding strange to their ears? Its expressive value is non-existent because of its obsolescence; that has no value with regard to the meaning of the line; that has no effect on its form; and that, moreover, is incorrect.

The clearest lesson that emerges from the above is the following: as long as one doggedly insists the *Centuries* were written by Nostradamus in the middle of the 16th century, one drowns in a hotchpotch of improbabilities, contradictions, impossibilities and errors. It is not as if these intellectual flowers are of an exceptional nature. They are as dense as nettles on an untended grass verge. They leap at us from every word. To express them with great aplomb is the only way of putting a veneer of reasonableness upon the prophetic discourse. The self-confident tone of the sentences polishes the stupidity of the contents and makes us believe that the author is not what he is: namely a servant of the folly. This status is enjoyed by all the nostraddicts, of their own volition, because, like many, they prefer being foolish in the limelight to being wise in obscurity.

If, on the contrary, at the end of an in-depth critical analysis of the poem one agrees to the various proofs and indications that show this opus was written by a man who explicitly refers to the Abbey of Cambron, who states he is Prior and is called Yves, then a simple enlightened reading of the *Centuries* will suffice to reveal that Yves de Lessines's blunders are as scarce as dew on a red rose growing on the North pole. In his time, *énfons* is a Picard form, it is correct and the word makes sense.

In fact, Nostradamus never understood the word as it was spelled; his mind automatically transformed it into the word to which it looked the most alike. He replaced the O by an A but kept the end "s", though it is not justified in the word "*enfant*". This is not at all exceptional and we cannot blame him: anyone reading old manuscripts will make mistakes; some of the greater have done worse. Of slighter literary stature, I, too, am guilty. Experience has taught me that it is terribly difficult to revert to the simple truth once our mind has created a problem where in fact there is none. We will forgive whole-heartedly this particular Nostradamian error, for it has been a bright spot on a long road.

But even knowing everything I explained above, knowing that the word would have been spelled *enfanz* if there were really children involved because this is the only phonetically correct spelling, and knowing that the "s" must logically have been written on the original parchment, none of this simplifies the problem and we are not one half of an inch closer to the solution. How are we to discover the original word – a singular object-case with the appearance of a plural? We can start guessing and go on guessing till we are blue in the face and our brains have dried up.

Before Yves de Lessines' revelation invited me to take a trip to Moustier, I had not had the slightest idea about the true meaning of this line. That it might be purely physical had not even crossed my mind. Looking back, I realise now that without the obliging help from the Providential stroke of luck, it was impossible to fathom out the meaning. To understand the word, one had to see the object. And that is why, as soon as I recognised the object, I understood simultaneously the word and the reason for the linguistic anomaly, that had been gnawing at my subconscious. I realised that it was not the word *enfAns*, "child", that had been written in the Old Monk's manuscript, but *enfOns*, now pronounced *é fon* or *in fon* in Picard, and *∂n'fons* in ancient Picard, i.e. the receptacle containing the holy water, a small font. The word is derived from the Latin *fons* meaning fountain. The plural *fontes* gave the French "fonts baptismaux" which during the Middle Ages was spelled either "le *font*" or "le *fons*". The latter word is a singular form assuming the appearance of a plural, hence *un fons*. In modern Picard we still say: *el fon batismô = le fonts baptismaux.*

Let us pick another relevant example from our "Vilains": *Li vilains purs est cil qui onc ne mist franchise en son cuer des l'eure qu'il vint de fons: Le vilain pur est celui qui jamais ne mit franchise en son coeur depuis l'heure où il revint du baptême* (the pure rascal is he who never puts openness in his heart from the moment he came back from Baptism).

The above gibe is quite indeterminate as four different and contradictory meanings can be discerned:

- the pure rascal (vilain pur) is he who never put *sincerity* (franchise) in his heart from the moment he came back from Baptism;
- the pure rascal is he who never put *freedom* (a very common sense of franchise) in his heart from the moment he came back from Baptism;
- the *mean villain* (*vil impur*) is he who never put sincerity in his heart from the moment he came back from Baptism;
- the *mean villain* is he who never put freedom in his heart from the moment he came back from Baptism.

To these four meanings must be added a word play on "fons", which has an anatomically precise meaning. Decency, however, forbids my detailing this any further. This is a good example of the way in which the *Centuries* should be read though.

Let us bid our "Vilains" farewell and devote ourselves to more exalted subjects.

I must admit that I had a good reason suddenly to understand the *fons besson*. The twin font, the exact duplicate of the one standing there before my eyes, in the porch, is at my home.

Or rather, it should be there, because a short while ago someone took the trouble to remove it.

My grandmother has told me the story time and again. Since days long past, more or less up to the last war, around 1937–1938, our dogs used to drink out of a stone container left on purpose near the water pump. Anyone drawing water from the well automatically replenished the container so that the dogs always had fresh water at their disposal. Then, one day, a stranger happened to walk by and offered my grandmother a pretty sum for this stone pot. My grandmother was poor and the amount proposed was really a fortune for her. Nonetheless she refused, saying: "This is quite a lot of money, but if that pot is worth so much to you, it is worth the same to us." My grandmother has never known what this thing was exactly, but as of that day, it was kept inside and served as an ornamental flowerpot. My grandmother had always stipulated, in the presence of witnesses to boot, that upon her death the pot was to be given to me. My grandmother, without having any idea of its true nature and signification, out of pure instinctive appreciation of the spiritual meaning, sensed that this object needed to remain where it had been for 700 years: in our house. I finally understood that through her words she was relaying a message that went quite beyond her understanding. I was but a boy then and could not have cared less. Those ideas were the least of my worries.

As to the line in question, it takes on an obvious meaning and refers to a specific object that still exists.

I cannot understand, or rather I cannot begin to try to imagine what went on in the brains of those people who managed to ascribe another meaning than the logical and literal one to the second line:

D'heroiq sang de moine vetustique

Five words, as clear as the purest water. To try and discover something that needs a lot of explaining requires a real effort. Like the temporarily dried-up scriptwriter of your favourite soap, I am reduced to writing that will not convey much. The first *de* means belonging to; the second *de* introduces a determiner complement; *sang* (blood) indicates the family or the descendants; and *vetustique* is the barely frenchified Latin word for old, ancient, with a notion of venerable, used especially during the Middle Ages. The two lines together translate as follows: *In Moustier will be found the twin font belonging to the heroic descendants of an old monk.*

I will add immediately, in order to keep your mind from taking the wrong turn, that we are not talking about the noisy and audacious brood of a passionate monk who would, in his old days, have copulated without restraint and without taking elementary precautions. That is not where the heroes are found. During the whole lifetime of their Order, the audacity, the superhuman courage of the Templars was never denied or questioned. As for the *moine vetustique*, in the 12th–13th centuries, even the least of men knew perfectly well that this referred to St Bernard, one of the greatest of the western monks, and who gave the Temple its rules.

Those who devote their lives to hair-splitting and nit-picking love to pass themselves off as the ultimate connoisseurs and they will no doubt be getting ready to expose the gross error of the above sentence. Of course, I know that from the supercritical historic point of view, the fact is disputable since there is no official report stating that on that particular day of the year of Our Lord 1128, St Bernard seated himself at his Louis the Umpteenth desk, to lay down on the spot and in one gracious movement of his pen, the rules of the Order of the Temple.

The Order of the Temple was officially established by a council especially convened for that purpose and they drew up its rules based on a project submitted by Hugues de Payens, who was inspired by the rules of the Order of the Holy Sepulchre. The rule of the Temple, as with each human undertaking, is like a brook being fed from different sources. It is absolutely correct that several men contributed to the work, one of them was St Bernard whose hand left numerous and obvious traces. The man living in the 13th century however had no use for the supercritical historian of the end of the 20th century; he could not care less whether a certain word of the Temple rules had been written by the Abbot of Clairvaux or by the Papal Nuncio, Cardinal d'Albano. For our ancestors, the reference to Bernard had no philological or historical import but a *spiritual* one. In order to be correctly understood, it has to be viewed in the light of the medieval frame of mind. The only justification for this reference is to confer a Christian foundation to an order of monk-soldiers.

Chapter Nine – A Thorn and some Tablets

What is the reason for referring to St Bernard? In those days, each man had his place in the line of succeeding generations; each man was the legatee of his forebears, charged with passing the legacy down to his descendants. To have ancestors was of the utmost importance; it was their value that determined the rank of the descendants. The kinship legalised the present status. The man who could not point out his ancestors was suspect; if he did not speak about them, he was reputed to be odd; if he did not praise them, he was despised. Everyone's forefathers had to be known; he who lacked them, invented them. Institutions, crafts even, did not escape the rule. The growth of genealogical trees was particularly luxuriant in the course of the 12th century. These were real marvels of calligraphy and illumination, as well as of an inexhaustible imagination: after the example of Julius Caesar, many of the great families claimed to be the direct descendants of Priam, the legendary Trojan King living in the 13th century BC!

The Templars for their part relate back to St Bernard and Godefroid de Bouillon, to whom they would add his mythical ancestor, the Knight of the Swan. They boasted about this in such a way that nobody could ignore it, even if they desperately wanted to. They proclaimed themselves the sons, or rather "the beloved children" of St Bernard. Even under the most horrible tortures that took the life of so many, forced upon them by the royal and papal inquisitors who tried to make them confess to heretical beliefs and Satanic practices, they called out to the brutes: "How can you accuse us of heresy, we, the sons of St Bernard!" Who, more than a Templar, deserved to be called the "heroic descendants of an old monk"?

But *sang* (blood) also refers to the family, even the siblings; therefore the line also translates: *the twin font belonging to the heroic brother of an old monk*. This gives three different meanings to the line, and I am unable to choose between them. However, they must probably all be accepted simultaneously anyway:

The old monk is St Bernard and the heroic blood stands for the Templars as a whole.

The old monk is Yves de Lessines who considers himself to be the Templars' brother.

The old monk is Abbot Jacques de Montignies whose brother played a crucial role in this story and may have deposited the font personally at Moustier.

But is not the most important thing in the end, the fact that this line is a sign of recognition, put there to show the way?

On reading the third line, *Son bruit par secte langue et puissance son*, we should refrain from jumping to conclusions and pointing at the Protestants as do most of the nostraddicts, who only focus on the word "secte". If you think of a sect, you will soon realise the line has no meaning, neither common, nor symbolic, nor esoteric. The word "secte" is so natural for the time of the Reformation and the Religious Wars that today nobody questions the word or its use in the *Centuries*. As if it had not existed before Martin Luther! In fact, the 12th and 13th centuries saw more sects of all kinds than the 16th, all under the cloak of religion. There even flourished sects that, quite successfully, extolled the virtues of general and sacred fornication: one for all, at any time and place.

The sect of the *Centuries* yields up its secret only to those who analyse the value of each and every word. And naturally, the "secte" is no sect... but the abbreviation of the word *secrète*.

Almost every medieval text is generously interlarded with abbreviations. I have chosen the following example for two reasons. The first one is that it is written in the Caroline lower case letters, the medieval handwriting that is, by far, the easiest to decipher, so that it will not be too difficult for you to identify the words. This Caroline lower case, hewn out by the engravers of Italian characters at the Renaissance, became the Roman lettertype, i.e. the one you are reading now. The second reason for my choice is that these few lines are the first and modest witnesses of the existence of our "Romance". They are an extract from a history book written in Latin, in which the author cites two texts in Romance and the same two texts in Tudesque. They concern the famous Oath of Strasbourg sworn in front of their respective troops by two grandsons of Carolus Magnus (Charlemagne or Charles the Great), Louis the German and Charles the Bald, thereafter taken by the soldiers of each camp, one year before the signature of the Treaty of Verdun that split up the Caroline empire. The historian Nithard, one of the numerous fruits of the countless mistakes of Charlemagne, born around 800 and deceased in 844, wrote an "History of the sons of Louis the Pious" (his illegitimate cousins), wherein he reports that

On the 16th day of the March calendes (14th February 842) Louis and Charles met in a town formerly called Argentaria and now commonly Strasbourg. Louis in the Romance language and Charles in the Tudesque language swore the following oaths [...] Louis, being the eldest, swore first to remain faithful to them:

For the love of God and of the Christian people and our common protection, as

of now, insofar as God knowledge and ability gives me, I will by this assist this my brother Charles, and in help and in each cause, as of rights one must assist one's brother, insofar as he will do the same for me, and from Lothar never take any agreement that by my will this my brother Charles will harm.

Pro dõ amur & xpian poblo & nro comun
saluament. dist di in auant. in quant ds
sauir & podir me dunat. si saluarai eo.
cist meon fradre karlo. & in ad iudha.
& in cad huna cosa. sicu om p dreit son
fradra saluar dist. Ino quid il mi altre
si fazet. Et ab ludher nul plaid nunqua
prindrai. qui meon uol cist meon fradre
karle in damno sit. | Quod cu lodhuuic

This famous text contains but a small number of abbreviations (words or parts thereof that have been underlined) for an obvious reason. With a hitherto exceptional concern for authenticity, Nithard wrote down a new language, and of necessity used the alphabet of another, i.e. an inadequate and approximate tool. His prime worry was to reproduce the sounds in the most realistic way. If he abbreviated words at all cost, he would be counterproductive. Therefore, the abbreviated notations (words marked with a tilde would be more correct) are limited to those words the pronunciation of which leaves no room to doubt. The fact of actually finding a few is the most remarkable feature.

A small anecdote will show how widespread the use of abbreviations in medieval texts was; it even influences modern medievalists. Let us revert to the 6th line of the little poem cited above: *Temp[est]e les vilains tout outre.* I noted *temp(est)e* while the spelling in the manuscript is undoubtedly *tũpe*, pronounced tempe. Why? Because carried away by the habit of seeing the spelling *tũpũ* for "tempeste", a certain number of medievalists automatically considered *tũpe* to be a wrong spelling of *tũpũ*, i.e. an omission of the second tilde by the scribe. A rather inaccurate interpretation to my mind, since the verb temper, tempter or tempier does exist and its meaning (to touch, to reach, to shake, to torment) fits in the line. The misreading by these philologists strengthens our position in the sense that it clearly proves that the spelling *se∂te* for "secrète" is certainly neither unusual nor odd. To remove all doubt as to the uselessness of chasing heretical Calvinists, I would recommend the reader to peruse Jacques Stiennon's palaeographic manual often considered to be a classic of its kind. It clearly states that *se∂te* is simply the abbreviation of "secrète".

The second *son* of this line means the song or the poem, the ancient word for "sonnet". You will also note the Old Monk's extreme refinement: the first and the last words of this line are identical, *son*, twin words as well as the anagram of *nos*: we or our.

The fourth line: Qu'on dira fort esleve le Vopisque. *Vopisque* is another word for twin. The use of this particular word is very revealing with regard to the Old Monk's state of mind. The *vopisque* is, indeed, the twin but in a very restricted sense. It is the literal phonetic transcription of the Latin *vopiscus*, used exclusively to designate the surviving twin.

We are now in a position to understand what we can read: *His splendour through the secret language and the strength of the song (will be such that) the surviving twin will be very highly said (praised).*

Let us now examine the apparently incorrect rhyme of the words *vetustique* and *vopisque*. When a poem is recited, or better still when it is chanted – and indeed until the 14th century when the words were separated from the melody, all poetry was sung – the rhyme is almost automatically corrected. Indeed, although it has still been written up to the modern times, the "s" preceding a mute consonant had not been pronounced since the end of the 12th century.

The allusive power of a word such as *vopisque* is enormous when one thinks of the Latin (= learned) meaning; it is even more revealing when considered in Picard. In our language *∂n'pik* or *é piko* is a thorn. Sometimes a thorn-bearing species (hawthorn, sloe, gorse, more usually called *∂n'spèn* however), sometimes a wild rose or a bramble (which we prefer to call *"rinche"*), but preferably the prickle: *i n'a nî d'rôs san piko*: there is no rose without a thorn, or *dou fi darkô a piko*: barbed wire. The word "pique" also refers to any kind of pointed weapon, especially the lance. *Vopi(s)que* is literally: "your thorn" or "your lance", *vo pik*.

The Templars seem to be very closely connected to the thorn; a fact that has been remarked upon by almost everybody. A few ancient texts are revealing and modern studies indicate irrefutably that one hawthorn bush, or several, were always to be found in the vicinity of the Temple houses, however small. Within the scope of our study, the important feature is that, in the Temple milieu, alluding to a thorn is a sign of identification and connivance, and would be considered as a summons. In my opinion, a Templar reading *Vopisque* would quite naturally think of a twin if he knew Latin, but even if he did not, he could not miss out on the reference to his Order contained in the fourth line: *That your thorn will be said highly.* As a consequence it will surprise no-one that veiled allusions to "pikos" are legion in the *Centuries*. How otherwise are we to explain Nostradamus' obsession for the pointed thing?

In the same moment, we can also easily understand the basic idea behind this way of revealing a secret. The secret is visible to everyone, just like a stone on a pebble beach. He who knows exactly which stone he is looking for, will find it. The more so, as the Old Monk, really gifted where laying of traps is concerned, inserts a crude allusion, slightly or not at all disguised, to a man with an erection. The best way is to divert the attention and perspicacity of the enemy by making him laugh out loud. The sceptics who are amazed by the delicacy of the manoeuvre betray how little knowledge they have of the great medieval authors; only he who is not familiar with the medieval clerical world will take offence at the licentious writing of a man of the Church. I would urgently advise the unbelievers to read a few of the letters Saint Hildegarde de Bingen sent to Saint Bernard and to the Venerable Pierre, Abbot of Cluny. Very, very edifying and... surprising.

But we are not finished yet with the many meanings of this very rich line.

The next one could only have been thought up by a Picard, and only someone who can speak this language will be able to understand it. It proceeds from the fact that, in Picard, the form *dira* is the future tense of the verb *dire* (to say), as well as of the verb *aller* (to go). Therefore *"dira fort esleve le Vopisque"* means: *the surviving twin will be said very high*, as well as: *the surviving twin will be raised very high*. Moreover, when read out loud, it also contains an indication as to a certain place. There are many other references in the *Centuries* to this same place – to which we will return later.

Let us read the whole quatrain again and conclude:

> I 95 *Devant Moustier trouve enfans besson*
> *D'heroiq sang de moine vetustique*
> *Son bruit par secte langue et puissance son*
> *Qu'on dira fort esleve le Vopisque*

The *Vopisque* designates the Temple, whether one bases it on the La-

The texts on the altar of St Martin and the texts on the altar of the Virgin Mary

tin or the Picard meaning, and is "innocently" written with a capital letter to draw a Templar's attention. The double use of the word *son* just as "innocently" placed at the beginning and the end of the line with two different meanings which make sense when put together: son son = sa chanson (his song). The use of two words meaning twin refined by their subtle difference; the sacred nature of the twin object: a font is a purifying, protective fountain, a shell of cleansing water; the material: the stone, a direct reference to the leader of the Apostles. Everything in this quatrain is summons and sign. Within the Order of the Temple everything concerning the human being went in twos. The only seal of the Order as such representing a human figure, shows two Templars seated on one horse. We must also grasp the non-spoken meaning, sense the emotional charge discreetly transpiring from the quatrain that outlines, as if going against the tide, Yves de Lessines's hope to see the rise of a new Templar Order after the disappearance of the first "twin".

You are beginning to understand the mechanism of the enigma, from the inside, when it has been put together by the adroit fingers of Yves de Lessines. But why, for heaven's sake, did the author use the word "twin" twice in the same quatrain?

Back in Moustier, the day being very hot, I felt exhausted and had some doubts about finding fresher air in the local pub. I decided to push on and explore the church for a while, and thereby recover my breath. I took fifteen steps and nearly fell over backwards. There, in front of me, at the end of the right aisle and engraved on the front of the altar, two Tablets of the Law were beckoning me. Slightly recovering from my stupefaction, I stepped forward to read them. It was but an incoherent series of letters.

I unearthed a long-forgotten receipt from the depth of my pocket and carefully started copying the cryptogram. Somewhere in the back of my head I resolved to decipher it one of these days, whenever I had ten minutes to spare. My decision made, I felt quite serene and refreshed by the coolness inside the church, and resumed my tour. I crossed the nave along the communion bench as local people say here. At the top of the left side aisle, there was of course another side altar, and there again were two Tablets of the Law. I must admit my composure took another knock.

The depiction of Moses carrying two Tablets of the Law in his hand is fairly common in the Christian imagery. I had never yet seen any engraved on the front of an altar, but... why not?

Twice two tablets must probably be viewed as an allusion to Moses' anger. Moses came down Mount Sinai carrying two tablets engraved by God's hand and found himself among the Hebrews dancing around the – still standing – golden calf, chanting its power throughout the camp, wallowing in the blood and the mud wherein the ardent metal lay shining, and Satan leading the ball. Venting his rage on the first debauchees that he came across, Moses threw the Tablets at them. Too overcome with surprise, the sinners lacked the reflex to catch the stone Tablets. Yawheh's work hit the ground and broke.

Bearing in mind the importance of the mess, Moses dealt out harsh punishments. Helped along by the tremendous beating for their irreligious behaviour, the bruised souls regretted and repented. Full of remorse, the chosen people found it improper to put the bits and pieces into the Ark of the Covenant: after all, two whole Tables would not weigh an ounce more that two broken up ones. So, on account of his impetuous demolition job, Moses found himself condemned for lack of cement, to switch over to the job of stone carver and punished so it seems as he had offended, without the right to complain.

If my "Ten-Commandments hypothesis" was correct, logic and reason would have ordered either the engraving of the same text on either side, or else that the two pairs put together should result in a coherent text. My first idea was that the second pair was an exact copy of the first. A glance at my receipt instantaneously proved me wrong.

You will find below a transcription of the Moustier Tables to the best of the computer's ability:

LΓEGKRVQ   NCLXBPDW
YPZHNRLBD   RNCCHZRP
MΓΛNVD C   MDXRΛPLN
NΛPVJHMΛ   HΓALDNXW
LΓNΛCBKP   ENLVNDΛPN

JNLKBΓPR   PΓVBLPMR
VMGHWEC   RACGKTD
QLSBNΓHP   BNDΓJVRW
MGCKHVR   LUBΓPNID
ΛLRNΓSXV   CCTRLQM

Rather crazy, to say the least… What on earth is it supposed to mean? Holding this in my hand, what else could I have done at Moustier-the-Two-Churches? Nothing., so I went home.

First of all, I gave myself firm instructions not to think. I am not inclined to see the wonderful in each hole in the ground and I am not easily carried away. I usually keep cool. Excitement and pretty wrappings do not agree with me. Once the veils are shed and the masks removed, if the subject is really very, very, very… interesting, yes, then… I let myself be seduced.

Fortunately, verifying the "Ten Commandments hypothesis" should not be too hard a task. Contrary to popular belief, the coding procedures in the Middle Ages were not elaborate at all. In truth, they were quite simple. The systems are based upon the substitution of letters, leaving their number unaltered. What makes our assumption even easier to confirm or refute is that the ten rules and regulations are all worded in the same aphoristic way. One more serious difficulty remained to be considered: the possible use of abbreviations. And thus I started working on the text of the Ten Commandments, taking the usual abbreviation into account.

In Latin and in Greek, the commandments consist of short, terse formulae. In consequence, the relative frequency of the letters is a hallmark, well known to everyone studying the Holy Scriptures, and easily recognisable given some practice. In Latin, for instance, the group "ne" should have occurred a great number of times; in Greek it would have been "ouk". It did not work. Then I tried the same text in its French, Flemish, Picard, German and Italian versions, languages I know a little. I thought that English as well as Spanish could be left aside without any problem.

In our modern languages, the Commandments are conveyed in various ways. It is however quite obvious this requires many more letters than those provided by the Moustier tables. Which might mean that each letter stands for a group of letters, always the same, otherwise the code would have no sense, and become utterly and totally indecipherable and hence lose all usefulness. In short, it would be stupid. And, worst of all, we would have too many letters instead of not enough in that case. Whichever group of letters was tested, the result was always the same: nothing sensible ever showed up. We did not take one problem-solving step. So, this did not work either.

Anyway, I had a pressing motive for doubt even before I scrutinised the tables closely: the religious outlook. These tables are engraved on the altar and moreover not far from the abyss, that is the spot were relics are sealed into the stone, the most sacred area of a church, apart from the taber-nacle. Leaving a coded message at that particular place, even a religious one, or a dedication, borders on sacrilege. Malevolent minds, at the devil's instigation, would soon have transformed it into disrespectful sentences giving rise to derision and vulgarity. At the same time, the sacred stone would become a stumbling block, the stone that brings you down, in Greek skandaleion, the scandal, which according to Christ himself, condemns its author to everlasting damnation: "Woe to the world due to the stumbling blocks! Of course, the stumbling blocks must of necessity come, but woe to the man through whom the stumbling blocks comes." (Matthew 18:7) (New World Bible Translation Committee 1984).In those long forgotten days, no-one would have dared to make such a provocation! This, as far as a religious and sincere message is concerned.

No priest would allow such a donation formula be engraved on an altar in his church, to say nothing of a cryptic profane message of which nobody could be sure that it was not a diabolic incantation. No bishop would tolerate in his bishopric. That would constitute a profanation in the most literal sense. But the fact also proves that the message must have been of the highest importance to those who had it carved originally and that in addition they had sufficient authority to impose its placement.

What is probable, however, does not lead us to a sensible solution. Therefore we will have to remind ourselves of Sherlock Holmes' timely advice from his adventure, The Sign of Four: "When you have eliminated the impossible, whatever remains, however improbable, must be the truth." Tracking the truth down requires the mind to be cleansed of all the remnants of vain cogitations, to return to a virginal state to which the Holy Spirit, at long last moved to pity, might grant some insight and understanding.

Resolutely banning Moustier, its tables, its stone pot and its ballgame from my memory, I set about the dual drudgery of the moment, carried out simultaneously so that one might relieve the boredom of the other. This consisted on the one hand of the linguistic, etymological and semantic analysis of each and every word of the *Centuries*, the only method to avoid the entanglements of the numerous contradictory meanings wherein those who explain things too self-confidently regularly get caught. They all tend to forget that the meanings, the nuances, the emotional charge and even the sound of a word vary with the passing of time.

The second job consisted of a comparison, word by word, letter by letter, of eight old editions of the *Centuries*, compulsory toil because Nostradamus' text is reproduced by his enthusiastic commentators with such fantastic approximations, that when not deliberately deceitful and fraudulent, may easily be compared to a surrealistic rendition. When referring to a text, common sense, if not simple civility, requires that one cites what has been written. At least, this is my opinion, although it is of little or no importance as far as the nostraddicts are concerned. When I had gathered 1100 pages of notes on this subject, I felt I could trust the results and decided to put an end to it.

I was busily engaged in part one of the drudgery when all of a sudden I happened to see the following line:

Au marbre escrits prescripts interjetes

The sense of which leaves no room for doubt: *On the marble are written the mixed-up orders (things to be done).*

The complete quatrain follows:

VIII 28   *Les simulachres d'or et d'argent enflez*
           Qu'apres le rapt lac au feu furent jettez
           Au descouvert estaincts tous et troublez
           Au marbre escripts prescripts interjettez

What must be mentioned at once – as an echo of the 4th line of quatrain 28 above – is a quatrain from the sixth *Centurie* that clearly alludes to indications allegedly engraved by the Temple dignitaries on the wall of their prison in the Coudray tower of the castle of Chinon.

VI 73   *En cite grande un moyne et artisan*
         Pres de la porte logez et aux murailles
         Contre Modene secret cave disant
         Trahis pour faire sous couleur d'espousailles

I am sure you can all see the monk; but do you also see the *artisan* (craftsman)? Of course, the *artisan* is no such thing. *Art* is a form of the verb *ardoir*, to burn, be on fire. *Isant* comes from the verb *issir*, to come out of. *Artisan* is a blaze. Can you see the flames?

Could it just be possible that the Moustier tables are a piece of this sort of Temple puzzle? If this was the case and if, in the *Centuries*, the "marbre" with the "escripts prescripts" refers to these tables, then the Old Monk's text must necessarily give the key to their transcription.

And indeed it did! So, on three winter evenings in December 1995, with a little effort and a little skill, the whole thing was deciphered. Which goes to show that nothing is expensive when it is given to you. Paradoxically, explaining the whole procedure is much more difficult and complicated than actually doing the job. The Moustier tables indicate – in a very concise way, to be sure – to the long-awaited one, to him who will be capable of decipher- ing them, the secret place where the Temple belongings lie hidden.

I was locked solidly in the dilemma: on the one hand, since our part of the trip started in Moustier, I felt compelled to mention its tables. On the other hand, there was not enough room to prove irrefutably and exhaustively that these tables were indeed a Temple sign.

How did the *Centuries* allow me to read the tables from the church of Moustier? In an article by François Descy published in "Le Courrier de l'Escaut", I have given a small beginning of an explanation – that, I have been told, stirred up some curiosity. Incredible as it may seem, François ac- tually succeeded in summarising the lengthy explanations that took me a whole evening to compose, in such a way that all is made quite clear for the first-time reader. It is worth anyone's while to read it.

A complete demonstration would occupy a whole chapter. It is too long to detail here. You will grasp the reason for such a long exposition immediately once I have told you that Yves de Lessines devoted more than 200 – two hundred! – lines to the subject. I am sure you remember the number of pages needed to clarify *enfans besson*; you will agree with me that, propor- tionally, sixty-odd pages are a strict minimum to tackle a task of this scope.

Nevertheless let me give a few keys here so that the reader may at least glimpse the general line of reasoning in this work of decoding that has a sheer stroke of luck to thank for its execution. And what hesitations on my part before disclosing even such a small amount!

The *Centuries* illuminate the Moustier Tables like a chandelier: which lamp to choose from the profusion at our disposal? My choice is one that indicates that there is more to come but as yet gives no proof. And always keep in mind two fundamental things: medieval writing is *suggestive*, and Yves de Lessines *hides* his information; we should never expect to find it in the usual places, expressed in simple terms.

> VI 9 *Au temple sainct seront faits grands scandales*
> *Comptes seront pour honneurs et louanges*
> *D'un que l'on grave d'or d'argent les medales*
> *La fin sera en tourments bien estranges*

To understand the first line, we should remember that the Greek *skandaléion* designates simultaneously a *trap* and a *stumbling block*; the allusion becomes very clear: *in the church will be put large stones that will be traps. It will be thought (that these stones) are homage and praise of someone (whose name or portrait is) engraved on gold or silver medals*. The word *"médaille"* from the Latin *metallia*, means small metal discs, primarily coins. Since the Merovingian period and all through the Middle Ages, the largest mint of the Western World was always at Tours, in the annexes of St Martin's Abbey. The Tours coins enjoyed the highest esteem and were considered to be the best reference. Their distinctive feature was either the effigy of St Martin or the acronym SMT (*Sancti Martini Turon(en)sis*). As already mentioned, the tables are set out on the altar dedicated to St Martin. Who can be more subtle?

Yves de Lessines, of course, in his fourth line.

"La fin" is the end, the goal, refinement, and... financing. *"Menter"* is to think, to remember; *"ment"* means a thought, consciousness, an idea. We should not be too surprised that Tours should also appear in this line. It is one of Yves de Lessines' favourite, almost obsessive, procedures: he will slip an element into a line, a syllable or a word that is a key to the foregoing line. As far as the two last words are concerned, all you need to do is to think of the double-entendre and speak them out loud; you will hear *"bien étrange"* (very strange, peculiar) as well as *"bien est rangé"* (is well put away, put in the right place).

The meaning of the line: *la fin est en pensant à Tours* (et St Martin) (the end is in thinking of Tours and St Martin), as well as: *la fin est en tours de pensées mis dans le bon ordre* (the end is in a train of thoughts put in the right order).

Very quickly another example:

> *Tout transmue ormis le viel langage*

"Le viel langage" (the old language) in question is Latin. We may rightly wonder what the use is of this rather odd line in the *Centuries*. Well, it so

happens that among the thousand quatrains in "roman", there is one quatrain plus title-sentence in Latin. These five lines are most definitely not Nostradamus' contribution, since I had already read them more than twenty years ago in the form of a quotation, in a text from the 13th century; this is slightly more than 300 years before the prophet of Salon-de-Provence was ever heard of.

Here they are:

> *Legis cautio contra ineptos criticos*
> *Quid legent hosce versu nature censunto*
> *Prophanum vulgu et inscium ne attrectato*
> *Omnesque Astrologi Blenni Barbari procul sunto*
> *Qui aliter faxit is rite sacer esto*

I am not going to expand here on the line of reasoning that finally led me to the correct idea. The fact remains that the Tablets abound with consonants, and, as I decided not to search too far and wide, I wondered if by any chance Yves de Lessines might not have provided the vowels – through a well-known cryptographic expedient – enabling us to read the Moustier cryptogram. Well, it actually appeared to be the case, and this is what may be considered quite simply a stroke of luck.

I must however close this topic, although it leaves me with a feeling of frustration; discovering the Old Monk's intelligence and finesse in the matter is a real pleasure.

Chapter Ten – A Nut Tree, a Garden and some Oil

Moustier was only a stage. Will the long-awaited be able to find the rest of the way?

Yves de Lessines is an exceptional guide. Ever since we left the commanderie of St Léger in our approach from the west, and from each spot to which he has led us, we could see the next: the road is clearly marked out. During the last kilometres the indications follow one another closely, at two or three hundred meters intervals. We would have noticed the same if we had come from the east, from Cambron; or from the south, from Quiévrain, the birthplace of Yves de Lessines' father. On the northern road, the landmarks become denser from two towns onwards: on the one hand Oudenaarde, on the other Ninove (by following the river Dendre up to the Abbey of St Andrie, in Grammont).

The reader who has realised that the *Centuries* describe an itinerary can no longer go astray. Whatever point of the last stage he may have arrived at, all he has to do is look around him and do a little thinking to discover the next place to reach. If, by misfortune, he takes the direction leading him away from his final destination, he will no longer be walking from point to point once he starts upon the third stage. The distance between the successive landmarks increases with a clearly calculated regularity. Like the long-awaited, he will soon be aware of his mistake.

Standing on the little square in front of the church of Moustier, his back turned on the way he has just been walking, the long-awaited would see this:

> V 57 *Istra le mont Gaulsier et Aventine*
> *Qui par le trou advertira l'armee*
> *Entre deux rocs sera pris le butin*
> *De SEXT Mansol faillir la renommee*

Almost all the nostraddicts I have read translate *istra* by *entre* (between). This is a mistake. Historical phonetics demonstrate that it is absolutely impossible that imperial Latin *inter* or low Latin *intra* could evolve into any other word than *entre* (plus its regional variants) and most certainly never into *istra*. There is no link whatsoever with the Picard *étér* or *intér*. The mistake is as stupid as it is unnecessary: *istra* is a word that does indeed exist in both French and Picard, and causes no problem. It is the future tense of two verbs: *istre* equals *estre* equals *être* (to be), and *istre* equals *issir* equals *sortir* (to come out of)

Totally ignorant of the Picard spoken in Wodecq, the nostraddicts have concluded once more that the spelling *Gaulsier* was the umpteenth printing error. Then, doggedly following the course they had set, and applying the brand-new and rather peculiar philological rules intended to serve their own purposes, they decided the correct word had to be *GauTHier*. And off they went, looking for a mountain called *Gauthier*.

There are a certain number of mountains by that name, spread all over the world. Each nostraddict therefore has his own favourite one. Alas, whichever one they choose, it never gives any meaning to the verse. Ah, if only they had been able to unearth a *Gauthier* somewhere in the vicinity of the Roman *Aventin*, triumph, victory and success would have been their rightful award. But up to now, despite continuous research, the peak of that particular Gauthier has not emerged yet. Not that the nostraddicts regret it. A mysterious Gauthier resisting discovery is an unending source of varied pseudo-astrological-apocalyptic interpretations. A few even imply Mount Gauthier may have an esoteric sense.

In Picard, however, it is so simple. A nut (the fruit!) is called a *gauque*, sometimes a *gausse* or a *gaille*. The word is derived directly from the ancient name: nux Gallica, Gallic nut. The tree yielding the fruit is of course the *gauquier, galgier, gaugier* or *gaussier*. What is more, I am sure Nostradamus never imagined it also meant a small hamlet situated in the Pays des Collines. Since he was unable to attach a meaning to the word, no image came into his mind when reading it and he had no sense of its reality. As a consequence, he copied what he thought he read and he read "ls" instead of the "k" that was actually written: *gaulsier* instead of *gaukier*. The latter spelling was normal in the Roman-Picard of Yves de Lessines' days, as seen in the extract from the *Viel Rentier d'Audenarde* shown below. Whoever is familiar with the handwriting of the end of the 13th century and the beginning of the 14th knows this is a common misreading.

The *Terre des Débats* has a splendid mount Gauquier that is simply dying to be noticed: it is the hill separating Frasnes-lez-Buissenal from Ellezelles. Seen from Moustier, it forms the northern horizon. To round it off, this Gauquier is not too distant from Aventin, meaning the mountain of the winds, where all four of them harass the summit: the Quatre-Vents (the Four Winds).

This line, considered to be so obscure and prophetic, simply means: *Il y aura le Mont Gauquier et les Quatre-Vents* (there will be Mount Gauquier and the Four-Winds); and: *On sortira du Mont Gauquier* (we will come out of Mount Gauquier).

What a pity our friends never consulted the *Dictionnaire de l'Ancienne Langue Française et de Tous ses Dialectes*, by Frédéric Godefroid! They would even have learned that *Gauquier is the name of a hamlet of the municipality of Ellezelles*, with a vintage example, to boot. Anyway, here is the proof that the nut did not fall from the tree yesterday:

> *Elesielle.*
>
> C'est entre le tere dou Nuef Bourc et le Gaukier.
>
> Li feme Thiri de Haneton Masure, 8 s., de 5 quartiers de tere, en le couture del Nuef Bourc.
>
> Gossars li Fèvres, demi bonier de tere, là joindant, 10 s.
>
> Li oir Robert de Haneton Masure, 18 s., de 3 jorneus de tere et 26 verghes, ki gisent là joindant, après le tere le feme Thiri de Haneton Masure.
>
> Pieres li Kiens et Gérars Hélias, 10 s., de demi bonier de tere, joindant à le tere Williaume Barbe.

Let us take a look at the second line:

Qui par le trou advertira l'armee

Qui: it is useless to rack our brains to try and find out who is who. The medieval usage of relative pronouns is very loose. A distinction between *qui* (who) and *que* (what) is rarely made; *ou* (or) is used instead of *où* (where), and

which one is meant exactly … I am sure you see the point.

Advertir is not the modern word *avertir* (to warn, to notify); it kept the meaning: to turn to, to turn off; in Latin *vertere* means to turn. To pay attention, for instance, is *animavertere*, literally to turn his mind to. As for the *trou*, the hole, even now, today, in Picard, it also designates a sunken road. So the meaning of the line is: *où par le chemin creux tournera l'armée* (where in the sunken road the army will turn off). You can walk the Templars' route yourself; you will notice that at the exact point where the path turns off towards the mount Gauquier, it really disappears into a hole, a sunken road.

Entre deux rocs sera pris le butin

First let us analyse the meaning of the words. *Prendre* is to grab hold, to press or to capture. As for the meaning of stealing, the medieval word was *rober*, Swiss verb that is still in use. Moreover, there is a very similar verb which is probably the one actually used by the Old Monk: *préer*, to have (something) returned, and more specifically to have booty brought back (*préer* is related to the English word "*prey*"). The word disappeared in the course of the 14th century. Nostradamus, writing 200 years later, cannot possibly have known it. Reading manuscripts is not an easy task, even though today palaeography is done scientifically with the best possible tools. It should not surprise us that Nostradamus believed the word *pree*, totally unknown to him, was a form of *pris*.

The word "*roc*" has three different meanings that must be considered simultaneously:

1) the two *woods and fields of "La Roque"* shown on the map, the existence of which during the Middle Ages is duly attested.

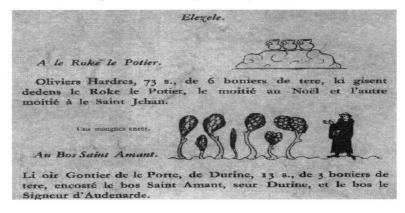

2) The *roc* is also the monk's habit, called "froc" today. As I will explain later on, in connection with the famous Varennes, the combined habits of the Cistercian and Benedictine monks were the symbol of the village of Wodecq, already in the 13th century.

My paternal house, by the way, is located almost exactly in front of the boundary between the Cistercian and Benedictine estates, the memory of which lives on in place names such as: le *camp de Lablay* = le champ de l'abbaye (the field of the Abbey), or *l'Endemaine* = le domaine d'Inde (the domain of Inde).

3) Finally, the *roc* or *rocher* also means a wall.

A few words regarding the ends of lines one and three, where *Aventine* rhymes with *butin*. In the 16th century, this rhyme is impossible: you will never encounter it in the work of Pontus de Tyard, Olivier de Magny or Georgette de Montenay. If, on the other hand, the line has been written before the nasal pronunciation had come into use, the rhyme is correct. At the beginning of the 14th century, *butin* was still pronounced [butine] just as *pin* was pronounced [pine]. Those who still want to cling to the Nostradamian myth, must admit once more to a printing error, which in this case is most unlikely.

The fourth line is quite transparent! Nothing is hidden, nothing is coded: a sentence in the indicative mode saying exactly what the words and letters mean:

De SEXT Mansol faillir la renommee

SEXT, of course, is the acronym for *Sacer EXercitus Templi*: the holy or sacred army of the Temple. When the words *SEX* or *SEXE* are used elsewhere in the *Centuries*, quite naturally, the nostraddicts thought what you may be thinking right now…

Those of you who think that abbreviations are a modern invention, are in for a surprise. For different reasons, the European Middle Ages made an even more abundant use of it. Abbreviations were everywhere, in books as well as in short, stone-carved inscriptions; even the name of God was abbreviated. The acronym SEXT is not wrapped in mystery and was used primarily by the Templars themselves, along with a few others. In one of the quatrains, Yves de Lessines writes: Quand l'écriture D.M. sera trouvée. D.M. = *Domini Militia*: "Our Lord's Troops". This was one of the titles of the Order of the Temple, which is also found in Dante's writings, or on seals: *Sigillum Militum Domini*, seal of the Lord's soldiers. With their tunnel vision, none of the nostraddicts ever thought of the *Domini Militia*, or understood the evidence: these two letters are one of the acronyms of the Temple. It is exactly as if in the year 2700, the USA being history, serious people would teach that once, long ago, these three letters meant Union of Silly Amateurs.

This *Domini Militia* is not shrouded in esoterism or secrecy. The expression, abbreviated or not, appears literally everywhere, even on the main seal of the Master of the Temple! How could it ever be rendered more official and more public?

As a matter of fact, there are quite a few acronyms referring to the Temple:

SEX	*Sacer Exercitus*: the Sacred Army
LIX	*Legio Iesu Xristi*: the Legion of Jesus Christ
HTM	*Hierosolymitani Templi Militia*: the Troops of the Temple of Jerusalem
PCXTS	*Pauperes Commilitones Xristi Templique Salomonis* the Poor Companions of Christ and of the Temple of Solomon

KQL   in Greek: ιριου Θεου Λεγεεῶν: KTHL: the Legion of the Lord God

We also begin to understand why the Old Monk called his poem *Centuries*: just by reading or hearing the title, any Templar would think of the legion, *his* legion. Yves de Lessines expected the word to ring out like a flourish of trumpets, beckoning to a monk-soldier, who may perhaps be the long-awaited. What inventiveness is revealed by the very general structure of the opus! A literary tour de force to construct a poem after the organisation of an army! This, in itself, deserves an in-depth study because it is all done with a purpose: four thousand lines, a thousand quatrains, the lines grouped in fours, ten centuries. The admirers of the prophet from Salon-de-Provence thought, each and every one of them, that the title reflected the fact that the quatrains are arranged in groups of hundreds; the word never stirred the mists hovering over their intellectual morass. The word "*Centuries*" never called soldiers to mind, the only soldiers who, since Roman times, called their army: the legion! How did they manage to overlook this evidence?

The meaning of the line: *Par l'armée sacrée du Temple, la gloire de Mausol est tombée* (owing to the sacred army of the Temple, Mausol's glory has fallen). Who is Mausol? There are two different spellings of this coded surname in the *Centuries*: Mausol and Mansol(e); the latter results from a reading error of the former. We will not go into the details of proof at this time; suffice to say it was a person of Philip the Fair's entourage, Jacques de Châtillon, the governor-executioner appointed by the King of France to torture Flanders. Elsewhere in the poem the Old Monk says: *Pol Mansole mourra a trois lieues du rosne*: the man in question was indeed killed at Groeninge, on 11th July 1302. His full name was Jacques de Châtillon-Saint-Pol.

Let us regroup the whole line:

> V 57   *Istra le mont Gaulsier et Aventine*
>   *Qui par le trou advertira l'armee*
>   *Entre deux rocs sera pris le butin*
>   *De SEXT Mansol faillir la renommee*

There will be the   )
They will come out of   ) *mount Gauquier and the Aventine*
Where in the sunken road the army turned off
Between two   *Roque (fields)...*
                 monks' habits...

walls…   the booty will be returned
Owing to the Holy Army of the Temple the glory of Mausol has fallen.

Once the mount Gauquier is crossed, we are invited to go into a garden for a stroll:

> X 49 *Jardin du monde aupres de cite neuve*
> *Dans le chemin des montagnes cavees*
> *Sera saisi et plonge dans la cuve*
> *Buvant par force eau souphre envenimee*

This garden, of course, is more than just a garden. Probably the manuscript had the Picard spelling *gardin* frenchified by the Provençal astrologer, whose poetic failings are shown up once more at the end of the same line, where the word *neuve* does not rhyme with *cuve*. The 16th century authors made fun of his pretensions to poetry; the saying went that he could neither count metrical feet, nor rhyme two lines. The authentic Nostradamian writings, those he was unwise enough to write personally, are full of bombastic drivel and mistakes. They are, in short, the tasteless fruit of the (divine, he says) inspiration of the Very Great Prophet: his own decasyllabic quatrains (four times ten syllables) consist of lines counting 9, 10, 11, 12 and even once 4, 8 and 13 syllables! The Holy Spirit is a truly fantastic poet…

But is the Holy Spirit really the mediocre poet that we can pin this particular rhyming error on? Or rather should we consider that the Old Monk has rattled through his homework? Of course not. The whole problem disappears magically when the wrongfully frenchified word is given back its rightful Picard form: *neuve* becomes *nuve* again, and the rhyme of the two lines is correct once more.

What we are doing here is simple: we are catching Nostradamus *in flagrant delicto*, in the act of disguising a text. What liberties does he take? Just a few trifles: he modernises the spelling of the words, he frenchifies the text within the range of his intellectual ability, he changes place names to attract the Southern French clientele, and he completely disrupts the sequence of the lines and the quatrains. But his ignorance betrays him: having no knowledge of Picard, he was bound to make *the* mistake, and this mistake – following upon so many others – is his undoing.

The Old Monk is better company and we will return to him. With the Picard *gardin* as point of departure, he teases the language, indulging in games based on Gothic writing as well as the spelling of his times. If we had the leisure, we could examine in detail the spelling of the following words. In less than three seconds it would be obvious that a slight change modifies the sense of the word: *gardin* (the garden), *gardon* (the present, the reward, or the Little Gard), *gardur* (the place were things are kept, are put aside), *garide* (the shelter, the refuge). We should take it as a significant fact that only a tilde makes the difference between *gardin* (the garden) and *gardi(e)*, a variant of *garide* meaning the refuge. So much for the "*jardin*". *Monde* also means pure, unblemished *(immonde* = unclean, repulsive). The "*jardin du monde*" therefore means *the refuge of the pure.*

The *cite neuve* is a new dwelling, but not always a new city. Far from it. Now, at the end of the 13th century the manor of Hubertmont had been founded, where archaeological digs were undertaken by Michel de Waha. The results were published in an issue of the *Annales du Cercle d'Archéologie et d'Histoire d'Ath*. It was a large building set in the midst of "montagnes cavées" (hollow mountains).

Even if the long-awaited gets the wrong impression, even if he considers the "cite neuve" to be a new village, he will not be lost. Reading the next quatrain will convince us thoroughly of this, because it allows us to put our finger on the unexpected potential of the cleverly managed allusive language, that has been sufficiently changed to deceive, and which has been kept sufficiently precise to avoid confusion and misunderstanding. You will not be able to help doing what I did: bow your head humbly in admiration of Yves de Lessines' uncommon abilities.

Caver means to dig out. A *cave* or *cavée* is a depressed area, a sunken road, a cave… and even, sometimes, a cellar. The sunken road described in the *Centuries* as the "*trou du mont Gauquier*" follows the heights of the "Cavée de Frasnes". And thus, over a distance of a few hundred meters, the road skirts two "*cavées*", certainly an uncommon phenomenon and one which explains Yves de Lessines' use of a plural. These words would strike home with the reader or listener as they would have been heard by medieval ears which are accustomed to expecting and seeing signs and symbols in each and every object. They would have been responded to both the name of the hamlet and the relief of the hollowed mountain in this way.

By using the expression *cite neuve* the Old Monk clearly indicates that he was writing for one of his contemporaries from the 14th century and not for the glory of an AA living in the year 1985 AD. Referring to a place by calling it simply a new building makes no sense if it is intended for a reader coming into the world 450 years later. If, by a miracle, something survives men's destructiveness and the ravages of time, one would expect the building to have suffered at least some wear and tear.

> *Sera saisi et plonge dans la cuve*
> *Buvant par force eau souphre envenimee*

Saisir is to seize, but also to hand something over. *Souphre* is the smell that emanates from marsh-mud, from the bottom of a cesspit.

> X 49 *Jardin du monde aupres de cite neuve*
> *Dans le chemin des montagnes cavees*
> *Sera saisi et plonge dans la cuve*
> *Buvant par force eau souphre envenimee*

The refuge of the pure will be near to the new building, set on the edge of the road in the hollowed mountains. Something will be handed over to someone and plunged into a barrel, drowned (buvant par force = forced to drink) *in a disgusting and poisonous* (envenimee) *liquid* (eau souphre = sulphuric water).

The long-awaited now descends the other side of mount Gauquier, in the vicinity of Hubertmont. He knows he is following the right road and feels satisfied. Where is he headed for now?

Here follows another landmark that can only be understood by a reader living in the Old Cistercian's time:

> IX 18 *Le lys Daussois portera dans Nansi*
> *Jusques en Flandre Electeur de l'empire*
> *Neuve obtenue au grand Montmorency*
> *Hors lieux prouves delivre a clere peyne*

The word *lys* makes no sense in this context and its spelling is unlikely in the 14th century. The "lis" (lily) of the virginal brides (one of the many species threatened by extinction) [the virgin brides, of course. Denise] is in fact a plural, a tardy remake of *fleur de li*. In heraldic jargon, well-known for its archaic language, the word is still pronounced that way. The *li* derives directly either from the Latin *lilium*, or from the Flemish *lelie* – this is a matter of discussion – and designates the flower of the marsh iris, *iris pseudacorus*. In the Middle Ages this was also called *fleur de glais* (fleur de glaive – sword flower) in a direct reference to the form of its leaves, exactly as the "glaïeul" (gladiolus). This explains why the emblem of the French royalty, in spite of its name, has no resemblance whatsoever with the *lilium candidum*, but shows the three characteristic floral pieces of the iris.

The present *lys* is almost certainly a misreading by Nostradamus of the word *lige* = loyal (compare to the English: liege man). *Daussois* instead of *d'Aussois* was rather frequent. *Aussois* is the correct spelling of the word now written with an "x": *d'Auxois*, because we have forgotten that the "x" represented the group "us" or "ls". And so *Axois* pronounced [*Aussois*] became *Auxois* pronounced [*Auksois*]. In the same way *Brxel* pronounced [*Brussèl*] became Bruxelles to the French. Daussois means "from Auxois", the region around Auxonne, and sometimes "from Auxerre", which should in fact be spelled Ausserre.

Near Auxerre was situated one of the main Templar commanderies of the province (*baylie*) of Burgundy, which derived its wealth from the production and even more from the trade of Chablis wine. Dozens of Templar commanderies are enumerated in the *Centuries*. This litany is of course justified if the poem was written by Yves de Lessines in the beginning of the 14th century. But what prophecy has Nostradamus concealed in this list that in his time was already totally obsolete?

> IX 34 *Le part soluz mary sera mittre*
> *Retour conflict passera sur la thuille*
> *Par cinq cens un trahir sera tiltre*
> *Narbon et Saulce par contaux avons d'huille*

A first remark: the spelling of *Narbon* shows that the nasalizing of the "o" had not yet occurred, and hence that the text is noticeably anterior to Nostradamus. *Narbonne* has always been pronounced [*onne*] even when spelled [*on*] because in those days each [*on*] was pronounced [*onne*].

The jokers who saw Narbon in the neighbourhood of Saulce, or vice versa suspected an Inscrutable Prophetic Mystery, but Revelation maintained a stony silence. And then, finally, at long last, along came Anatole Le Pelletier, obsessed by Napoleon. Bungling on fanatically, he doused the *Centuries* in a Napoleonic sauce and came up with the surprising conclusion that Sauce was the surname of the innkeeper of Varennes-en-Argonne who betrayed the King, Louis XVI, to the revolutionary troops. In fact it was the name of the local attorney.

Anyway: astonishment, admiration and reverence: Nostradamus, The Greatest Prophet of All Times, in one flash of sight, had even revealed the name of the traitor. Anatole's argument, moreover, was irrefutable: in the same line we see the word *huile* (oil). And oil, his explanation went, is sold in a grocery store. Sauce, being a publican-grocer, was sure to have some in his establishment and this is the unquestionable proof that this particular line of the *Centuries* prophesied Louis XVI's arrest at Varennes. Narbonne, well now, that was another problem altogether. As others before and after him, Anatole identified this as a reference to the Count of Narbonne trying to save the monarchy.

Unfortunately, one word eluded all intelligence. Anatole was unable to grasp *contaux*. At his wits' end, he changed it to *cantons*. Had I had the rare joy of knowing Anatole, I would have murmured into his ear that *contaux* is the plural of *contal*, which is a barrel or a cask. Today, we are still using the related word *quintal*, the meaning of which is more restrictive but equally medieval. In short, Anatole succeeded in making a division of land from a plain, ordinary barrel.

I cannot compel you to believe me, but I can assure you that I have seen this sauci-stupidity dished up by a whole tribe of nostraddicts, up to and including the most recent.

Before giving a more sensible explanation, prefaced by the formal statement that Sauce is not the landlord of Varennes-en-Argonne in whose inn Louis XVI was arrested, I feel compelled to praise two or three brilliant nostraddicts. Although I think it might be more correct to say that one or two borrowed their idea from the genius of one of the three, who did indeed have a stroke of genius. Anyway, it so happened that all of a sudden, one nostraddict had the insight that the word "huile" might be a metaphor. He dared to suggest that it was possibly not the fat substance extracted from olives, beech-nuts, rape-seed, poppy, ricinus, whale, crude oil or cod-liver but rather the Judas reward, the thirty pieces of silver rightfully paid to Sauce for his ignominious behaviour. It is a fact that being a swine without reaping a profit is a stupidity a real swine would never perpetrate. In the exponent's mind, the idea was still hazy, the ghost of an idea, the shadow of an apparition seen through the fog. Never mind though: the proto-embryonic idea was correct.

During the Middle Ages, the *huille*, the word itself or an allusion to it, is used in a number of highly picturesque expressions the subject of which is often money, and more specifically money, riches, or valuable objects that a cunning man has managed to whisk away right from under the nose of a powerful or rich man, preferably somewhat stupid. As for *sauce*, it is not necessarily the savoury accompaniment to meat, fish, pasta and desserts that eventually makes us avoid the scales. The *sauce*, *saulce* or *saussaie* is a place where willows (*saules*) grow, formed in the same manner as *quesnoit* or *chênaie*, which refers to the habitat of the oak (*chêne*), *fresnoit* or *frênaie* referring to the habitat of the ash tree (*frêne*), *vernaie* the alder (*aulne*), *hêtraie* the beech (*hêtre*), *boulaie* the birch (*bouleau*), …

In brief, *La Saulce*, i.e. the place where willows grow, was the huge chief commanderie of the province of Burgundy. La-Saulce-sur-Yonne is now situated in the Auxerre district.

Since we also know that the chief commanderie of the Temple province (*baylie*) of Septimania was located at Narbonne, we can afford the luxury of a word by word translation: *from Narbonne and from Saulce, we received* (avons) *money* (d'huile) *in barrels* (par contaux).

Meanwhile, it is high time for us to return to the department Meurthe-et-Moselle.

> IX 18 *Le lys Daussois portera dans Nansi*
> *Jusques en Flandre Electeur de l'empire*
> *Neuve obtenue au grand Montmorency*
> *Hors lieux prouves delivre a clere peyne*

Portera dans Nansi: the verb *porter* (to carry) is nowadays always a transitive, or active verb. In this instance it is intransitive, or inactive because during the Middle Ages most of the verbs that are now transitive were also intransitive, and vice versa. This usage had disappeared by Nostradamus' time.

Here is no room for doubt: *Flandre Electeur de l'empire* – Flanders Elector of the Empire is the Imperial Flanders. This mysterious territory consisted mainly of the county of Alost and its annexes, sited between the Dendre and the Scheldt, the southern part of which comprises the seven villages of the "tenement d'Inde", the already mentioned *Terre des Débats*. The Count of Flanders paid homage to the King of France for his estates on the left bank of the Scheldt. The County of Alost and the Flemish enclaves in the County of Hainaut on the other hand belonged to the German Emperor, who was elected. Hence the poet's expression.

In Nostradamus' time all this had lost its political meaning. Emperor Charles V was also Count of Flanders, his own liege lord in a sense; he paid homage to himself. Moreover the world of the mid 16th century had nothing in common with the situation prevailing at the beginning of the 14th. Nostraddicts' eyes are fixed firmly on events that post-date their idol. If, moreover, they are French, they know that words such as Germany, England and Austria exist but, to them, they have no meaning. Outside their divine Hexagon, the world is a hazy, misty region they know little about.

They could never imagine that this quatrain describes the values of the feudal system, that was already falling into decline in Philip the Fair's time and had vanished completely a quarter of a millennium later. By the time their hero was beginning his illustrious career, the only remaining memory were the taxes to be paid. In Nostradamus' time, at the end of the reign of Charles V, nobody worried that in theory, the Emperor had to take the oath of fealty to himself as regards the villages of Wodecq and Ellezelles. What the people were interested in was whether they paid taxes to Mons or to Ghent – because the rate was different – or whether in a lawsuit, the common law of Alost would be applied or that of Valenciennes, because the choice helped to determine if you stood to win or lose your case. Whatever the eternal circumstances prevailing at the time, one always defines one's attitude according to what one perceives as the most important thing at the time of which one speaks.

Why would the author of the *Centuries* react differently? In the Old Monk's time, at the beginning of the 14th century, this Imperial Flanders had been periodically causing trouble with the Germans for about a hundred years. Moreover, the war for the possession of the *Terre des Débats* was still raging. The end of the battle between the Avesnes and the Dampierre was not yet in sight. In fact, this war really started in 1280 when the Count of Flanders, Gui de Dampierre, refused to pay homage to Rodolf de Habsbourg. The latter retaliated by investing Jean d'Avesnes, Gui's half-brother, with the County of Alost. Hence, the concept "Flanders Elector of the Empire" was an everyday reality, painfully present in Yves de Lessines' life, whereas Nostradamus certainly had not the slightest idea of what it meant.

Le lys Daussois portera dans Nansi
Jusques en Flandre Electeur de l'empire

Translates as follows: *The loyal from Auxerre will take care of the transport through Nancy as far as the Imperial Flanders.*

It should be remarked that this itinerary would be unthinkable, in normal circumstances. The most usual way would be to follow the Yonne and the Seine up to Paris, where four possible routes offered themselves:

1) one could sail down the Seine up to Rouen, which acted as terminus for the coastal trade, continue north and moor at Nieuport if the destination was Ypres;
2) if one wanted to go to St Léger, one could hug the Flemish coast up to the Hont passes, and after transhipping somewhere along the river, sail up the Scheldt to the vicinity of Pecq;
3) at Conflans-Ste-Honorine, one could also board a ferry that commuted along the Oise; at the end of the navigable channel of this river, two short day's marches would take you to the Haine that could be sailed down to Condé; from there, the Scheld would carry you to St Léger;
4) from Paris, one could move straight on to Cambrai where one could either sail up the Scheldt, or go on marching.

To us, these itineraries seem far-fetched and unnecessarily complicated and tortuous; in the old days, they were the least tiring and the least expensive way of travelling. We can hardly imagine the hustle and bustle that would have been going up and down the streams and rivers. The waterways were the highways of the Middle Ages.

A point of importance: travelling through Nancy was *the only logical road from Burgundy to Flanders if one wanted to avoid the territories of the French King at the time of Philip the Fair*, because at that time Lorraine belonged to the Empire. The detail is revealing; it is one of those small true things, too insignificant to be a result of calculation, and which definitely authenticate a story.

Chapter Eleven – A Light to show the way

Neuve obtenue du grand Montmorency

At the end of the 13th century the lord of Montmorency, in Ile-de-France, had bought a fief at Ellezelles corresponding to what is still called "le Neubourg" (the new district). In the Old Monk's time this could easily be called a new acquisition. I do not think that many places in the world are named in this way Since the Old Monk indicates the geographical environment – Imperial Flanders – it becomes rather difficult to claim that the Neubourg is not the Montmorency fief.

We have now reached the last line of this quatrain:

Hors lieux prouves delivre a clere peyne

Prouver is to endeavour, to taste, or to prove, and also to test, to try. *Delivrer* means to (set) free and to hand over goods. *Clere* is simply the 14th century spelling of *claire* (bright, clear, light); *peyne* is a form of *pene* or *pegne* of what is now called a *pignon* (a pointed façade). Therefore the first meaning of the line is: *Outside of the known places recover freedom at the light-coloured pointed façade.*

The second meaning is just as revealing if one keeps in mind the three major events that had upset and dismayed the people: the attack on the Papacy by the King of France, the battle of Groeninge, and the destruction of the Temple. With the very same words, the author also wrote: *Outside the places subjected to suffering* (the kingdom of France where the Templars were imprisoned, tortured and some killed), *the thing is handed over at* (brought to) *the light-coloured pointed façade.*

Addressing someone who knows what is meant, the light-coloured pointed façade will make him think of a white construction, and hence of the Blanc-Scourchet. In our Picard, a *scou* (secours = help) is a shelter, and a *scourchet* is a small shelter, a small protection. The word has taken on a few figurative meanings, but the *blanc scourchet* is the small white shelter, a white building. Nothing else.

And now, my friends, what about a little romantic walk along the bank of a babbling brook? In June, when the grass grows high, and the setting is right to further any matter at hand…

This preamble takes us to a line of quatrain I 13:

Whenever he speaks about a *mine* (the mine) the author uses the feminine. For example:

> I 53 *Las qu'on verra grand peuple tormente*
> *Et la loi sainte en totale ruine*
> *Par autres loix toute la Chrestiente*
> *Quand d'or d'argent trouve nouvelle mine*

In the Romance languages, French, Italian, Provençal, etc. *"la mine"* is always a feminine noun. All predecessors duly noted that in the quatrain above, it is a masculine noun; the most illustrious dismiss it peremptorily, calling the detail negligible. The more obstinate rummagers of nostradamology are not so easily satisfied: *le* mine has given rise to an immeasurable outpouring of ink. They may be forgiven though: the riddle was totally, absolutely impossible to break.

Once more the Old Monk treats us to an impressive example of his craft: to render the line incomprehensible, he does nothing, literally nothing. He is taking a chance on the fact that nobody will grasp the significance of the masculine article in *le mine*. The economy in the means of expression can be held up as an example for many a writer.

Because *le mine* is very simply the old name of a brook that even in Yves de Lessines' time was more generally referred to as the brook of the "Tordoir", the brook of the oil press, a name it still goes by today. The oil press, the *"tordoir"* is also still there. The name Mine was erased from memory about seven hundred years ago; it is impossible that Michel Nostradamus should ever have heard of it. The following photo, nonetheless, is one of the said brook and its grassy bank.

The *Viel Rentier d'Audenarde*, which is kept at the National Library in Brussels, but a copy of which I was allowed to peruse in the Archives of Oudenaarde, mentions this brook a number of times by the name *Minebèque*. *Minebèque* is not even a transposition, but simply the Picard way of pronouncing the Flemish *Minnebeek*.

L tena	Libers Tricos, 20 s., de 1 bonier de tere, à Minebèque, tenant au manage le Contesse.
G bert	Gérars li Escuiers, 12 s., de demi bonier de tere, à Ghillebertmont.
Je Poil	Jehans de Hauteville, 12 s., de demi bonier de tere, à Poillewaignon, tenant à le tere Gérart l'Escuier.
G dem	Ghéluis de Hautevile, 6 s., de demi jornel de courtil et demi jornel dehors sen courtil, à Minebèque.

That the name is Flemish is not surprising. The area is a language boundary region to the north of the *"Civitas Nerviorum"* and owes most of its place names to the Franks, more specifically all our village names. We were situated in the heart of the Salic country.

The significance of the Flemish toponym is charming: *"minne"* is the old word for *love*. But what if the long-awaited does not speak Flemish? No fear, Yves de Lessines being the man he was, had foreseen this and gives the same information in Picard: *Amour a legre non loin pose le siege* (X 38). The cherry on the cake? In Flemish, the word *"minne"* is a *masculine* substantive.

Mettront: The Old Monk uses the verb *mettre* or *mittre* more than once in its original meaning of *mittere*: to send. For instance, IX 34: *Le part soluz mary sera mittre = the part* from below will be sent by sea.

Les enmis: the words we call "false friends", that mean something quite different from what we instinctively feel they mean, are the reader's worst enemies. In this text it is our enemy that is a false friend. If, in the old language, the *enemi* (seldom spelled *enmi*) is indeed the enemy, *enmor* on the contrary means love and *enmi* is the friend! *Par* may mean along and also in the direction, in the vicinity of.

As usual, the line has at least two meanings:
1) Secretly they will send the friends along the Mine;
2) Secretly they will lodge the friends in the neighbourhood of the Mine.

Let me remind you that the future tense must automatically be converted into the past tense. When the poet says: they will send, this means that they have sent. Yves de Lessines himself suggests that we proceed in this manner to understand his message.

We continue our walk along the Mine. At a location called "Pont d'Oc" (the bridge of Oc, or Wodecq), on our right side, a light is shining:

VIII 8 *Pres de Linterne dans des ton-nes fermez*

Linterne is the old, normal Picard form of our lantern. "La Lanterne" is the name of the hamlet situated between the Mine and the Blanc-Scourchet. Could the Old Monk have lit our way more clearly then by writing *Linterne*, with a capital L. Oh yes, he has done better.

This is a magnificent example of the efficiency of an enigma in the hands of a genius. Casually said: *Pres de Linterne* is a simple, innocuous re-mark. But the hamlet bordering on Lanterne is called "Hameau Du Pré" (hamlet of the meadow). We will see that Yves de Lessines speaks emphati-cally about the little white shelter. This little white shelter is built on the meadow of the "Hameau du Pré" (still registered by that name at the land registry office), near la Lanterne. The Old Monk did not miss the superb word play. And so the light is shed on the Lanterne. The name existed a long, long time before the flashlight was even invented. Whoever doubts this will immediately be put back on the right track by the *Viel Rentier d'Audenarde*.

C'est li rente de Waudèke, ki vint de chiaus d'Oubertmeis.

Li oir Stévenon de Ribaucourt, 20 s., d'entor 7 jorneus de tere, à Ribaucourt, desseur leur manage, tenant à le tere Gérart l'Eskievin, entre Ribaucourt et Hanekincrois.

Jehans li Starkis, 10 s., de demi bonier de tere, tenant à le Haizète.

Jehans de le Lanterne, 7 s. et demi, de 1 jornel et demi de tere, tenant à le tere Jehan le Starki.

I have just named the land registry office. There is a toponymical ref-erence I am now able to add thanks to two friends working in that particular office, and doing research into the antique paperwork kept there. I had al-ready discovered dozens of place names in the *Centuries*; they added 23 more, all located on Ellezelles and Wodecq. Speaking of an abundance would be no exaggeration. They found this:

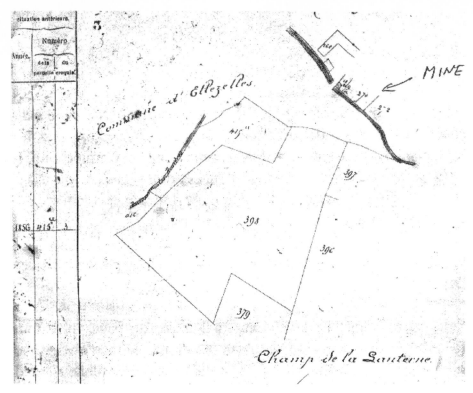

Fiat lux et lux fuit! In the beginning there was:

> IX 25 *Passant les Ponts venir pres des rosiers*
> *Tart arrive plustost qu'il cuydera*

Up to then, I had been stumbling around lamentably because when I read the line, I had thought of a barn called "Les Rosiers", a property of the Abbey of Cambron in Ormeignies, to the south of Ath. There was no logic in the matter at all, but I just could not see why not. I had fallen into a trap and would still be stuck in it, had it not been for my friends. Like a fool, I had fixated on the *rosier* (the rose bush), the daddy of the roses, and I had not thought one second of the word *ros* (roseau = reed), the synonym of *cistiel*.

As soon as they showed me the document, I remembered the line and realised my mistake. The thorny rose and the reed were spelled identically in 14th century Picard and both were pronounced [rosîr]. The *rosiers* is simply a marshy area where reeds grow, the *roselières*.

A number of years ago, before chemical progress won total victory, the marsh I refer to was indeed full of reeds.

Later on, we will see that by means of the same line Yves de Lessines alludes to the fact that the final destination of the journey is close to a

Cistercian establishment. With the right information all the pieces of the puzzle fall into place of their own accord and the itinerary is again precise and coherent.

Passing the Pont d'Oc, you walk up a gently sloping road for about 300 metres to La Lanterne. From there the road slopes down over 200 metres to the Rosières; along the old road that is no longer used, you walk up again to the Trieu, at a distance of 300 metres. But why do we have to cross the bridges? Because at the Pont d'Oc, there are two bridges, less than 20 metres from each other.

The road from Lanterne to Trieu is really very short:

> IX 71 *Aux lieux sacres animaux veu a trixe*
> *Avec celui qui n'osera le jour*
> *A Carcassonne pour disgrace propice*
> *Sera pose pour plus ample sejour*

And here it comes, the famous *"trixe"*! All those people who mustered up the courage to "explain" the "prophecy" of this quatrain were of one mind: trixe was an adaptation by Nostradamus of the Greek θριξ, θρικοσ or τριχοσ, they are not quite sure, but it means fleece, they say. So doing, they gently copy what the greatest nostraddict celebrity of the 19th century, Anatole Le Pelletier, came up with.

Anatole's philological method is utterly original, thoroughly innovating, and of an astonishing simplicity. Whenever Anatole fails to understand a word, he decrees it to be Greek. The method lights up the hypocritical skies like a brilliant sun and has proved to be exceptionally efficient in making people believe the most comical notions. The lecturers and authors who owe it their moment of success and their few savings are legion.

In fact, Anatole had stumbled across a trick and exploited it thoroughly. Waking up one morning with the conviction that Nostradamus had a knowledge of Greek, he set himself to searching for a Greek word that more or less looked like one of the words he did not understand. If it sounds the same, it surely means the same. Q.E.D. There was but a small, almost negligible problem. Our new-born expert's knowledge of Greek was limited to leafing through the dictionary. And so it happened that lots of Flemish or Picard words all of a sudden found themselves to be… ancient Greek.

As an example among dozens, the poor man saw the word *selin*, hellenised it to σελενη (selene), the moon, whereas the word *selin* exists and means… *salted* or *parsley*. As previously explained, by playing on *zele*, *cele* and *sel*, Yves de Lessines always relates *selin* to the Emperor of Constantinople, Henri d'Ancre or de Hainaut. Anatole, and all anatolians, seldom confessed followers but nonetheless industrious and furtive copiers, extracted sheaves of prophecies from this moon-selin.

On the other hand, with a rare consistency Anatole overlooks all the word plays the Old Monk really does make on basis of the Greek, because he did not realise that the Greek used by the Old Monk was primarily the language spoken in the 13th century in Byzantium, interspersed with an occasional word of Attic Ionic of the 4th century AD, the language we now call classical Greek.

The aforementioned *trixe* offers us a perfect opportunity to show their intellectual wickedness. Firstly, Anatole, who said so himself, based his demonstration on the word *trixe* without an "h" that Nostradamus would have derived from the Greek word θριξ,,: *thrix*, with an "h". You should be aware of the fact that all of Anatole's statements are derived solely from the brain of Le Pelletier. There is not and never has been the slightest indication that Nostradamus ever mangled Greek words, the meanings of which surpass the nostraddicts' intellect. If we assume for one second that Anatole's manipulating tricks were more than just that and had indeed some foundation, out of reason as well as honesty, should the helleno-maniac exponent not have referred to the word trix (trix, without h) that actually exists? If he has not done so, it is most certainly not for lack of consulting his dictionary under the letter tau, but rather because the meaning of *trix* – triple or three times – leaves no room for a prophetic vision: *on the sacred places, animals seen thrice, in triple*. What is an illustrious prophet supposed to do with that?

The mistake – the confusion between tau and theta – is typically French. Let me explain. In the Greek alphabet there are two characters that the francophones class under the "t" family, to the surprise of the Greek themselves. The first, the character τ called tau, is a true "t", whereas the second, the character θ called theta, is a false "t" that corresponds more or less to the English "th". To clarify the sense of my words, I will refer to the English language that offers a perfect similarity with the words *three* and *tree*. Le Pelletier is like someone who builds up a whole demonstration, which he considers to be indisputable and conclusive; and then, on purpose or out of sheer ignorance, begins it with a confusion between the figure three and a tree.

One last word… In his innocence, Anatole made a rather surprising statement that the nostraddicts, to Anatole's luck but their discomfiture, never noticed. The first meaning of the Greek θριξ,(thrix) is "hair", "horsemane" and "pubic hair". Which means that, if we are to believe Anatole, and admit that *trixe* is Greek, Nostradamus literally wrote: *In the sacred places* (a church, for instance) *hairy beasts will be seen*. No comment!

The line becomes clear as soon as one knows that the "x" is the spelling previously used in Picard and in Walloon among others, to first stress the pronunciation of the "h", which was somewhat like the German ichlaut; then later to write the letter groups "ls" and "us". In the Walloon of the Liège region, this spelling still exists, though with a slight variant. In the list of communes you will see Xhoris or Xhoffrais, pronounced *Horis* and *Hofrais*. The Templars for their part wrote Xrist for Christ, which was then pronounced in the Flemish way, exactly like the "schild" of the "schild en vriend" atrocity.

Let us also consult the *Viel Rentier*:

> Thiérions, li fix Franchois le Conte, 4 s. et 2 capons, d'une masure là ù il maint, encosté le tere Baudet de Téraisse, et joint là ù Williaumes de Hubermont meist.

Words written with an "x" in the spelling of that period correspond to, for example, our modern *"fils"* (son), which is pronounced *fiss* in French ("feess" in Anglophone). The local Picard evolved to *fi* (fee) by way of the intermediate stage *fiH*, that is to say that the sound of the syllable "ils" changed into a long i-sound, while at the same time the final consonants group "ls" disappeared without a trace. This evolution constitutes a minority exception in the Picard language. The normal practice consists of reducing the vowel "i" to a "y", as in "you", and adding an "e" instead of an "l". In other words, what one village pronounces *fi*, is said *fie*, pronounced *fieu* (fyer), by the next village.

When talking about her son, Dame Oedain never referred to her *"fix"* (feex) and neither did François Lecomte. Similarly, Anatole's Greek fleece was pronounced [*triH*], [*trîls*] or [*trius*] that evolved from *trîls* to *triH*, and then *trî*, still used in Wodecq and surroundings. The word means a fallow stretch of land: *∂n tér a trî*. There is just one shadow hanging over this: we thought to get closer to the sun by copying Louis XIV and started writing the word *trieu*, while still pronouncing it [*trî*]. The proof will be found in one of the numerous works by Julien Loix, part of his monumental history of Wodecq and Flobecq. *Trîls* evolved to *trî* via *triH* in the villages of the *Terre des Débats*, whereas the adjoining regions call it *trieu*.

> Gillos dou Buis, li fix Dame Oedain, demi bonier verghes, vers les Sars.
>
> Gossuins de Avesnes, 1 jornel, es Sars.
>
> Thiérions, li fix Franchois le Conte, 4 s. et 2 capons, d'une masure là ù il maint, encosté le tere Baudet de Téraisse, et joint là ù Williaumes de Hubermont meist.

" Louis LOIX, au lieu de Joseph FOURDIN, ci devant Pierre le LEUX
du dit Wocq, sur sa maison, grange, étable, jardin applanté
d'arbres contenant un bonnier gisant au hameau de la Pierre, tenant
au camp du parcque par derrière à la ruelle allant au dit camp et
à Quentin WINDALLE et au chemin menant au <u>triel</u> a l'estaque. Item
de même un journel et demi au camp devant la dite Pierre, tenant
au chemin allant au hameau d'Aillemont, à Philippe LISSON, à Sacre
FONTAINE et à la chapelle du Très Saint Nom de Jésus en l'église
Saint Martin à Ath.

Templars are quite a different species, as the sceptics will say. Let us once again consult the *Viel Rentier*:

C'est dessous le pire dou Lonc Triés.

Gilles li Boutilliers, 3 jorneus et 44 verghes de tere, tenant à le tere ki fu le maieur, d'autre part le pire, dessous le voie, ki est del més dou Lonc Triés, 5 d. et obole, et 2 sestier d'avaine, le quarte part d'un sestier mains.

C'est encosté le Lonc Triesch.

Li oir Galiot, une obole et 1 capon, de 1 cortil, à Lombard[1] Ponchel, entre le Lonc Triés et le tere Monsigneur d'Audenarde, ki fu Monsigneur Phellipon de Rodes.

Exactly the same piece of land is referred to.

When you are in the sacred places, you will see animals on the fallow land. That is the meaning of the line and it makes sense. In those days the herds were put out to graze on fallow lands. Besides providing fodder, the procedure also offered two other vital advantages. The first that comes to the mind is that the animals provided natural manure for the soil. The second is less obvious but more important still. In those pre-herbicide days weeds were a real plague. The land yielded poor crops anyhow and if weeds were not kept in check, as likely as not, the farmer reaped less grain than he had sown. Sheep and cattle were put to graze on the land with their preferred weeds, before they ran to seed, and helped clean the soil.

The line, such as it has been written by Yves de Lessines, has two meanings, but the *double entendre* only made sense during the Middle Ages. Around the middle of the 14th century, crop rotation was introduced in this region. This is an agricultural practice that replaced the one that consisted of letting land lie fallow, and had been invented in Flanders in the course of the 13th century. As of that moment, the *tri* became exceptional; their memory only survives in the toponymy. This line is constructed on a pattern similar to the one referring to Moustier. In both cases, Yves de Lessines uses an everyday word (monastery, fallow land) that is also a toponym. In his days, the banal sense prevailed and the Old Monk uses it cleverly as a lure.

Having seen the cows on the *trieu*, we may now admire the moon on the Blanc-Scourchet:

> IV 31 *La lune au plein de nuit sur le haut mont*
> *Le nouveau sophe d'un seul cerveau l'a veu*
> *Par ses disciples estre immortel semond*
> *Yeux au midi les siens mains corps au feu*

Except when it is new and cannot be seen, solely because at that moment it moves between the sun and the earth, the moon sails continuously above almost all the mountains of the world, and has been doing so since the dawn of Time. The truism is such that I can hardly imagine the Old Monk taking the trouble to write it down. If I had not been vaguely studying astronomy and astrophysics for twenty years, I would never have understood a single word of his astronomical notations shaped as riddles. I have mentioned previously that Yves de Lessines was capable of calculating the day and the ground line of a solar eclipse 670 years before the event actually happened – the famed "prophecy" for 1999. Without a computer, without a calculator, without even the help of a good old slide rule, the performance is not likely to be equalled easily. At the end of the second volume, in the chapter dedicated to Yves de Lessines, we will pay a well-deserved and substantiated tribute to his astronomical talents.

Taking into account that the moon moves a little more than a half degree per hour on its orbit around the Earth, he knew perfectly well that on the day of the full moon, if the moment it becomes full is close to midnight, at midnight true time, the moon is due south. Now, in these particular circumstances, seen from the Blanc-Scourchet, at midnight true time of Wodecq, the full moon lies exactly over the high mountain of Mainvault. I was able to verify the fact carefully during Christmas Night 1996. On that date, the moon was full a few minutes before the local true midnight, and at midnight true local time, I was granted the opportunity to verify Yves de Lessines' notations in ideal conditions: the silvery light of the moon was strewn freely over the snowy fields. Since the Old Monk certainly did not have a watch that could have been of some help, he must have based his calculations on angle measurements; another achievement that deserves our due admiration.

If a pair of eyes suffices to determine the day of the full moon, to define its precise point in time is quite another problem. At the beginning of the 14th century, to determine a hour during the night when the sky was clear was not an easy task. If the weather was overcast, you did not stand a chance. Who can say for certain on a dark or misty November day whether it is eleven, twelve or one o'clock if you have no expedient such as a watch, the radio, the passing of a train? And on a dark night?

A long time ago I wrote a few articles on the history of time measurements and the various ways to tell the time. In the monasteries, for instance, in order to know how long one had to wait before waking the brethren up to send them out into the cold night to chant matins, a few monks were drilled to sing psalms in a constant rhythm. The results of the drone were then compared with the data of an hourglass and a so-called calibrated candle. Does this whole procedure surprise you? As a means of precise time measurement the hourglass was not much more trustworthy than the singers. And if the monk in charge of turning the hourglass around happened to fall asleep on the job, you had a problem. As for the candle, I am sure you all know that there is no rule regulating the speed of its burning down.

The fact that no means existed to keep a correct track of the passing of time has seriously impeded the emergence of science based on precise measures. How can a candle, a water clock or an hourglass be calibrated accurately if the best tool for measuring time that you have at your disposal is a sundial? How a minute or a second can be measured by means of a sundial? A correctly calibrated obelisk is necessary to make a more or less correct measurement. Then how can time be read when it drizzles or the rain pours down? To determine the exact point of midnight is equally uncertain.

That is why we must understand that Yves de Lessines has made this detour to situate the Blanc-Scourchet. He mentions a remarkable feature on the horizon and indicates its position by alluding to a compass-point.

In this instance the manner he uses to make an enigma departs however somewhat from the normal one. The meaning of this so banal line is as follows:

1)   *La lune au plein*:   the full moon
2)   *au plein de nuit*:   at midnight
3)   *sur le haut mont*:   on the high mountain,

hence, the mountain lies due south.

Le nouveau sophe d'un seul cerveau l'a veu

The *sophe* of course is the Greek sofos (sophos): the sage, the scholar, the initiate. It is also fos (phos): the light. *L'a veu*: as usual, the tense of the verb must be reversed: *the new initiate will understand in one thought.*

Par ses disciples estre immortel semond

Par: Nostradamus certainly has read *par* instead of *por*. I will not be the one to blame him. I know from experience how difficult it can be to distinguish between the two prepositions in old manuscripts. Most of the time, if not always, the answer is provided by the context and not by the spelling of the word itself. "*Por*", the old spelling of "pour", seems more appropriate. The verb "*semondre*" means to warn, to invite, to convoke and to order. We keep these four meanings simultaneously in mind. The line means: *For his disciples he is an immortal warning, invitation, summons and command.*

Yeux au midi les siens mains corps au feu

Yeux au midi: looking in the southerly direction, what else will the *new sophe* think of other than France, that in those days could be reached in less than two days marching, or a few hours' horse ride? In the region, something from the south means "from France". Our elders almost always talked about "the wind from France" when they meant a wind blowing from the south. "Vent du sud" was considered to be pretentious, belonging to the vocabulary of doctors, notaries and other "men wearing hats"!

Les siens mains: Some have sadly translated these three words as "*ses mains*" (his hands), thereby inadvertently accusing their Idol of writing gibberish. Their translation is indeed of an eyebrow-raising intelligence: *his hands and his body in the fire!* It is common knowledge that the Middle Ages were not averse to atrocities of all kind. But as far as I know, each time they burned someone's body, they also burned his hands. We cannot charge his exponents with this stupidity since Nostradamus was the first to think that "*mains*" referred to the part of the body usually asked for in marriage.

Our *mains* is an interesting clue. It is the past participle masculine plural of the verb *maindre*, a form of the verb *manoir* that means to stay, to remain. *Mains* means simply *remained*. But Nostradamus could never have used it himself because the word had long since disappeared and there were no dictionaries that could have taught it to him or helped him understand the meaning. Even in the beginning of the 14th century it was already archaic and survived only in a few dialects. The mage from Salon-de-Provence was the first one to be led up the garden path by the similarity in spelling. Let us therefore learn a lesson from the Nostradamian misunderstanding and make our point clearer with an example. Originally, the verb *partir* meant to share. There is a French popular poem called: "*La Housse Partie*", The Shared Quilt. Now imagine that a would-be Nostradamus presents this fable to you as his own brainchild and that in the course of your conversation you suddenly realise that the "author" believes the poem is called "The runaway quilt". Would you still trust him?

Les siens mains corps au feu: "his own (people, friends) whose body remained in the fire." Who does not perceive the allusion to the Templars burned at the stake by Nogaret and his gang?

Yves de Lessines' idiomatic word plays cannot be grasped by anyone who does not speak Picard. We will take this opportunity to stress once more the immense richness of information that can be hidden in a medieval text. Yves de Lessines also wrote some work on theology. Hence, he is familiar with exegesis, i.e. he knew all about the mental gymnastics required to write a whole book to explain three words of the Gospel. That he is also capable of doing exactly the opposite is only normal. In the *Centuries* he gives in to this reverse tendency, condensing his text to the point of saying six different things in three words.

The word group *yeux... les siens* was pronounced [ieuss les sîn (yerss lay san – Anglophone)] and corresponds to the old Picard *euss... lê sin* (they who belong to him), which in some cases equals "les miens" (mine). The logical consequence of this is that the line: *Yeux au midi les siens mains corps au feu* means quite literally: "Mine who were in the south, remained with their body in the fire"; and "Mine remaining in the south, their body in the fire." But not their souls: they were martyrs who ascended to heaven and not heretics doomed to eternal hellfire.

Chapter Twelve –
Vestal Virgins not far from Athens and the Pyrenees

There is a lot of talk about the Templars in the *Centuries*. I have been the first one to be surprised. I had always ironically discarded the incoherent tales about the Templars that regularly pop up. That is why it took more than two years for me to admit the reality of what my eyes were seeing. I had determined when the *Centuries* had been written; even a hidden allusion to the Order of the Temple did not fit in. As a matter of fact, the King of France was not the sole beneficiary of the abolition of the Order.

His people… mine… Yves de Lessines considers himself a brother of the Templars. When he talks about their fate, his grief meets the sorrow of the *new sophe*, the *long-awaited* who arrives from there, who has escaped the horror: the warrior-monks arrested, imprisoned, tortured, burned at the stake; the Order destroyed. He knows that the King of France and the French aristocracy, closely followed by the Pope's favourites and the assorted rulers of all countries, had moved in for the kill and not left a single piece of the prey.

Nothing has changed: in the 14th century as well as in the 21st, the true scoundrels of both sexes enjoy their malice, allowing nobody to uncover what they are or what they do. They will use all means, sugary if possible, brutal if need be, to silence each and everyone who ventures to remark upon the pretty picture they paint of themselves. Only in darkness do they thrive; naming their evil is a formidable weapon. The powerful of the year 1307 proceeded exactly along these same lines. Until the middle of the 14th century these human vultures maintained a true anti-Temple terror, so that even alluding to the Templars became life-threatening. This is why, during the period 1309-1350, when a bold author alluded to the White Cloaks once in a while, this was always done with the necessary precautionary detours.

If I had come across an allusion to the Order of the Temple from time to time, I would not have been particularly surprised, so long as that these allusions were brief and scarce. Their abundance and their precision, together with what they seemed to disclose, made them improbable and, without beating about the bush, absolutely impossible to believe. So, for more than two years, I obstinately refused to admit that the so-called prophecies of Nostradamus might be a poem about the Templars. In fact, that expression is too weak. I absolutely refused to imagine that some day, maybe, I might come to believe it. Writing a Templar poem of 4000 lines in the period 1323-1328 would have been not only a bold act of foolhardiness but a recklessness bordering on suicide on the part of the author.

It is true that I had read a few Templar related matters in manuscripts from the 12th and the 13th centuries, but I had given it little attention. I had an idea about the affair but my knowledge in this respect was no broader than that of the rest of the history of the 11th-14th centuries. I knew decidedly less about the Knights Templar than I did about other domains of literature and history of that period. And finally, I must be honest and admit that I do not fall for fancy tales; any story too pointedly Templar orientated only roused my distrust. In short, I am not inclined to esoteric obsessions. On the other hand, failing to admit the evidence, the text remained incomprehensible to everybody, especially to me.

I knew the smallest details of the circumstances in which the opus was created, I knew the name and function of its author, since he himself discloses them. And yet, all this certainty could not keep me from straying into reverie. The main problem of this text, that I could understand almost effortlessly, was that it told an unbelievable story: the story of the end of the Templars. And that story, I just did not believe. I accused myself of becoming derailed, of rowing without oars on a sea of delusions for which I could find no good reason. Had I knocked my head rather badly? Had that caused my brain to enjoy dwelling in an esoteric Templar fantasy? But the truth was not to be silenced: in almost every quatrain, I came across an indication, an anecdote, an allusion, all pointing in the same direction: Christ's Army, *Sacer Exercitum Templi.*

I confess I felt uncomfortable and did not want to look ridiculous. The whole story was so absurd. In the end, I solved the dilemma my way. Since I restrict myself to explaining and translating a text, the only sensible attitude to take is to say: this is the translation of the *Centuries* based on historical and philological explanations. This is a difficult text to understand and all attempts to explain it have resulted in incoherent, mendacious or plain stupid verbiage; if one accepts it as a Templar-related text, the oeuvre has sense and meaning, and is coherent from the very first to the very last word. I will leave it up to you to conclude.

Let us get back to the quatrain. The new initiate was standing at the Blanc-Scourchet gazing up at the full moon. The Old Monk refers to the new initiate: *le nouveau sophe.* Let us pay a little visit to the Croix Philosophe.

Who could tell us why this place was given such a bizarre name? What eccentric from days long past planted there, in the middle of the fields, on the highest spot of the old Cambron estate, visible from far and near, that extravagant and now centuries old weeping willow, broken by storm and tempest, but still heroically standing upright?

Because it was said to bring misfortune, the weeping willow was a rare species until deep into the 19th century. Whoever had it planted on his grounds, displayed his progressive mind and his disdain for what the 18th century called "superstition".

The modern scientific name of this species is *salix alba tristis*, the sad white willow, but not that long ago it was still called *salix Babylonica*, the willow from Cairo (if in a medieval text you read the "Soudan de Babylone" this means the "Sultan of Cairo"). At the time of the Crusades the saying went that the Templars imported the species from that part of the world. Whether this is a historical fact or not, has no bearing on our story. The only important fact is that then the people did not doubt the reality of their belief.

This willow is a symbol, a sign. The name is not given innocently. In the 13th century, geography was not a science but a phantasmagoria. Babylon lay somewhere over there, far away, near to Paradise; and the willow of Babylon is the tree that weeps on the sin of Adam at the gate to Paradise.

The shape of the tree is explained in the Sacred History. Today we reject this reasoning as stupid and infer that the people who believed in it were naive and idiotic, which is totally wrong. It reflects their conception of the world, which, for the rest is perfectly coherent, but fundamentally different from ours. What seems naive and unrealistic to us is simply the way our medieval ancestors gave expression to the idea they had of Causes and Causality, from which we are completely estranged. The upheaval of the foundations of this thought pattern caused a revolution in the world view and the metamorphosis of outlook. To a medieval mind everything is a symbol, everything is interrelated, the whole of Nature is a homage to God, each object conceals a religious meaning, each event is a message, each thought comes from the hereafter or tends towards it. The sublunary or terrestrial world, the heavenly spheres and God's kingdom are the three stages of Creation, in perfect and total harmony. This macrocosm is reflected point per point in the human microcosm: the body, the spirit and the soul.

To the Templars, the weeping willow was their symbolic tree, more so than the omnipresent thorn trees. Adam, fallen through eating the apple, had been chased from Paradise and as a result, found himself with no fixed abode. An angel armed with a flaming sword was appointed by God as guardian of the entry. A somewhat superfluous precaution taken by a divine but wasteful show-off: considering the strong personality of the first human male, a catapult would have done the trick. Anyway, the angel was standing underneath the willow.

The Order of the Temple identified with the figure and the role of this guardian angel. The White Cloaks, *privee mesnie de Deus*, (God's private army), were God's earthly army, the exact replica of the celestial army. The Order even had its fallen angels: the Templars who had "lost the House". This is the true symbolism of the Temple.

Let us take this opportunity to stress a fundamental truth: the Temple symbolism is *always* religious and *never* esoteric, alchemical, astrological or magical. Imagining that they might in any way be involved in practices clearly forbidden by the Church, is a gross insult. Assuming they would have had knowledge of it, any religiously licentious interpretation would be rejected in horror. The Templars were monks who offered their lives in the service of Christ. Each man dying under their robe in the battle against the infidels was a martyr, ascending immediately to Paradise.

Hence the subterfuge of many a lord, determined to lead a life of total debauchery up to the very end, and pulling a last trick on the threshold of eternity. Feeling death approaching, they asked to be laid upon a Templar's robe. Never doubting God's stupidity, they were of the opinion that expiring in the white robe obliged the Almighty to open the gates of heaven wide to welcome their dark souls. Even this pitiful comedy is pure symbolism. The sign (the martyr's robe) erases the reality (the sins). The biggest fault of our times is to consistently label all symbols as esoterism. We do not realise that by laying our modern conceptions over past times, we fall into a particularly defective anachronism. The pseudo-scientific esoterism, such as it is presented to us now, made a very timid start in the course of the 15th century and did not really started developing until the 16th century, i.e. after the

Middle Ages had ended. Hence in the medieval system no room for these notions existed. Symbols, on the other hand, occupied all room available. They abounded and overabounded. Literally everything was symbol.

Primarily, symbols of religion. Religion was at the heart of everything, each individual was drenched in it, at every moment of his life. The Christian act of worship itself is centred upon a powerful and mighty symbolic deed: partaking of God's Body. Everything was explained by the acts of God, the angels and the devils; everything has been said in God's Word, in the Scriptures of the Fathers of the Church and in the Tradition. Each object, each event paid homage to God, and the religious symbolism explained this reverence while at the same time being part of it.

The Middle Ages also knew a civil symbolism, or more specifically a lords and guilds symbolism: that of the family arms and the seals and the distinguishing marks of the craftsmen. Its only purpose was identification. There is not the smallest trace of intellectual refinement in this imagery; the only thing that it cultivated zealously was the coarsest and most trivial evidence of clanship or craft.

Related to religious symbolism, and present everywhere, literary symbolism covers a much wider range, from the most subtle to the most ordinary, if not vulgar. It was brought to an extraordinary level of delicate expression, of imaginative potency and richness of meaning by the Irish filid such as Dallan Forgaill or Fland Mainistrech and, as far as Scandinavian literature is concerned, by the skalds like Bragi Boddason, Egill Skallagrimsson and Snorri Sturluson.

It is common knowledge that the medieval paintings, sculptures and architecture were loaded with symbolism that was moralising as well as religious. Even the scatological sculptures decorating the capitals of many a Romanesque cloister or church taught a moral lesson, if the clerks of the time can be believed.

To complete the picture, there was also a scientific symbolism, more developed that one might think, but one that rather quickly became sterile by melting in the religious symbolism; the latter really did not take kindly to science. Worse, it smothered every intent to understand in an incoherent babbling that pretended to have all the answers. Theology wanted to be sole queen by divine right and rule over all the domains of knowledge.

Eventually freedom was born from mathematics. The progressive increase of mathematical symbolism, with its laconic way of expression, devoid of all emotions, prudently drove a mental wedge between the stated law and the real fact. Thereby it gradually separated the Creator from the creation, then denied God his role as immediate cause of all events, and finally imposed the idea of a natural world governed by miracle-proof laws. This nature was open to analysis, with itself as the only point of reference because it concealed in itself all causes of objects and events.

One must also be aware of another purpose of medieval symbolism: it was an *aide-memoire*. Indeed, reciting a poem or singing a song is the most efficient way of memorising a craft's techniques, whether it be the carving of stones, the brickwork of a cathedral, the assembly of its frame or the art of painting. Mastering a craft was equal to a life insurance, if not the certitude of a certain wealth. It was a jealously coveted treasure, protected against undue curiosity and kept hidden by the craftsman, even from his own helpers. Theoretical instruction consisted of teaching the accepted apprentices little stories and songs, without revealing the deeper sense of the anodyne-looking texts. Then, if the apprentice proved to be worthy, when the time came, little by little the keys of the interpretation were handed over. In this way the craft of the builders was transmitted so that men who could scarcely read and write, if at all, were able to acquire the skills of a trade and erect the masterpieces of pure art and intelligence that are the Gothic cathedrals. A stranger to the guild never got to learn any of its secrets.

The initiation of the mate (the word being used in the sense of learning a trade) was done on the basis of songs and stories. Although not involved in their creation, the Templars protected and developed the *crafts* and the *guilds* through their system of *confratres*, or affiliates. This had far reaching consequences. A papal privilege had been issued whereby it was forbidden to any non-Templar jurisdiction, whether civilian or religious, to judge, or even to call upon as a witness, a confrater of the Temple without the formal authorisation of the Order.

The transmission of "secrets" through tale-telling or song-singing was therefore very well known within the Order of the Temple, and we must admit that the method used by the Old Monk is strangely similar to the one used in those days by the *confratres* of the Temple.

In this system, the function of the symbol was triple:

1)   to memorise important things;
2)   to draw the attention of the long-awaited;
3)   to serve as a secret gathering sign.

A Templar knew, of course, that his Order was designated amongst other things by LIX (Legio Iesu Xristi). When he sets eyes on the SALIX, the Temple tree – as he has been told time and again – he will understand automatically *Signum Agri Legionis Iesu Xristi*: the sign of the spot (the area or the field) of the Legion of Jesus Christ. That is all there is to the secret of the Temple willow.

The Temple tree at Wodecq is visible from afar. And what if this tree, so unusual and unexpected, had been planted there on purpose, to beckon the long-awaited? Is this a coincidence? Or does the poem provide indications corresponding to the local landscape and the toponymy? If we found in the *Centuries* a reference to the location where our willow grows, we would of course have the most conclusive proof. What has the Old Monk got to say in this instance?

> II 17 *Le camp du temple de la vierge vestale*
> *Non eslongne d'Ethene monts pirrennees*
> *Le grand conduit est cache dans la malle*
> *North getez fleuve et vignes matinees*

Not far from Athens and the Pyrenees? Now this is absurd! How could one simultaneously be in the vicinity of Athens and the Pyrenean mountains, when it takes weeks of sailing to go from one place to the other?

Under its anodyne, innocuous and humorous aspect this quatrain conceals one of the best constructed and most subtle enigmas of the *Centuries*. Thanks to a long dispute with one of my Latin teachers, nicknamed "Le Pélo" whose grumbling deafness we had to survive for a whole long year, I will never forget the Latin name of Ath: Athensis. Confused by my mocking smile and infuriated by my remarks, one day when I had been particularly active, he lost his temper. The punishment that issued spontaneously from his over-boiling rage consisted of a Latin translation exercise of one sentence, outrageously stupid: "when it rains in Ath, the sun shines in Mainvault" (the latter is a village adjacent to Ath). Believe me, since that day, I have known Athensis.

But there is more serious evidence to corroborate our knowledge than the exercises ordered by an old man whose only goal it was to force me to think along his own lines. All medieval men of letters used to play the *Etymology* game à la Isidore de Séville. This is not the time or the place to detail the astounding influence of etymology on all domains of medieval thoughts. Paradoxically, the errors made by the etymologists generated the greatest effects. Their fundamental mistake lay in the fact that they interrelated words on the basis of their resemblance instead of proven affiliation. That was just a small start of their wanderings that led to the most surprising results. Do you know for example why Adam and Eve bit into an apple? Chapters 2 and 3 of the book of Genesis make a reference to the *fruit* of the tree of the knowledge of good and evil. The etymologists have determined that the species was an apple tree: the Latin word for both evil and apple is *malum*.

In fact, this is a delusion. *Malum* = evil is pronounced with a short "a", while *malum* = apple has a long "a". That they are apparently the same word is purely coincidental; it results from the converging evolution of two Indo-European words that have no connection. Their identical spelling is due to the fact that Latin had no specific sign to indicate the difference in the length of sounds. In French, the cases of converging evolution are numerous; apart from the four "sô" (*saut, sot, seau* and *sceau*), *croire* et *croître* for instance are identical in the third person singular indicative present, though we make a difference by placing a antiquated circumflex on one of them, (*croit* and *croît*). "Je peux peu" is a simple spelling trick.

And so it happened that the lettered men of the Middle Ages were all convinced that the small town of Ath owed its name to the illustrious city of Athens. Why would they have been in doubt? The Counts of Hainaut, and those of Flanders as well, proudly presented a family tree firmly rooted in the Trojan war. Of course, they were all the direct descendants of the heroes of the said war. In the registers of St Peter of Rome or Santiago de Compostella, pilgrims from Ath were noted as coming from Athensis, Athenis, Athenes and sometimes even Ethene or Ethen, an obvious spelling mistake by the clerk in charge of delivering the pilgrimage certificates. Maybe the man misunderstood the names because of the rush of people filing past his desk, or he was slightly deaf, or absent-minded, or a little bit drunk, who is to say?

But of course, Yves de Lessines, a long-time neighbour of the Chatellenie of Ath and having an almost daily contact with the county administration, knew the correct name of the town on the three Dendres. We must never forget that a medieval artist seldom commits an obvious, glaring mistake because he is stupid or negligent. On the contrary, the error or the clumsiness is almost always a means to tell the attentive reader or spectator: "Look out! Here comes a hidden message." This is true in each artistic domain, without exception. The Old Monk wrote Ethene as a means to tell us: "Of course you will think of Athens, but be careful, this Athens is not the Athens everyone will think of." To discover the Old Monk's Athens, one needs to know the Latin name of Ath, as you already know.

On the other hand, one needs to know Picard instead of Latin to see the Pyrenees lying in front of us. The first thing that catches the eye when reading the line is that "pirrennees" is spelled with two "r", immediately followed by the fact that the word has three sets of double letters: three sets of twins, exactly as in Moustier. Is Moustier close to the Pyrenees?

Philippe Demets was born in the Pyrenees… not the Ariège ones, but those of Renaix, Belgium. These Pyrenees are situated on the south-east flank of the range of hills enclosing the town of Renaix. Today, the toponym refers exclusively to the well-known Catalan-Andorran-Navarran-Basque mountain range, but originally there was no relation whatsoever between the Renaix place name and the Cirque de Gavarnie. The old-Picard *pire* (pîr) is a paved road; the *pîr rennees* means quite literally: the road to Renaix; and the so-called mountains are simply the chain of hills where the road to Renaix passes through. A two-minute stop at the specific place plus a three-minute explanation, and you will never question the logic of the name again.

We must also emphasise the oral word plays based on resemblance. Whoever knows Picard will easily understand what I mean: *pirrennees* is the anagram of *pri renee* meaning "près de Renaix" (close to Renaix) and the homophone of *pî* (de) *renee* meaning "pied de Renaix" (foot of Renaix). Another meaning, another sign: in the old language the *pîr rené* is also the foot of the Kingdom or the road to the Kingdom. More than once Yves de Lessines calls the Order of the Temple *le règne*, a word that, in his days, also meant the Kingdom.

When the Old Monk was alive, these two place names did not refer at all to two small, remote, provincial towns: Ath was one of the most powerful strongholds of Hainaut, and Renaix was the fourth largest town of Flanders, judging by the amount of taxes it paid, Flanders itself being the wealthiest region of Europe. It is also noteworthy that Yves de Lessines, in one and the same line, refers to a landmark in Hainaut (Ath) and a landmark in Flanders (Renaix). You will remember that we are in the *Terre des Débats*, object of a violent dispute between the Counts of Hainaut and Flanders. Coincidence?

If you ever go and meditate at the Croix Philosophe, you should be well aware that *ATHens* lies hidden less than ten kilometres from the place where you are, behind the ridge to the south, and also that to the west, at a distance of about four or five kilometres, lie the *monts pirrennees*. Also note that the Old Monk spells *Ethene* with a capital letter and *pirrennees* with a lower case: his coherence never fails.

Except for one instance, each time the Pyrenees are mentioned in the *Centuries*, this always refers to the Renaix range. There is an even more surprising element in the identification of our Pyrenees, an element that by giving a key to the hidden game, also demonstrates that Yves de Lessines clearly intended to exploit the same sound of the two places.

As is still the case today, during the Middle Ages the name of the hill range differs depending on whether you look at them from Ellezelles or from Renaix. Leaving nothing to chance, the Old Monk also gives the Flemish name of the ridge of the Pyrenees: the Bronneberg, the mountain of the spring. At the end of the 13th century, and the *Viel Rentier d'Audenarde* as a whole bears witness thereof, the written language of this region was infected with a violent urge to frenchify all place names, and this toponym became: *le mont Lebron*. Take a look at the *Centuries*:

> *Du mont Lebron proche de la Durance (Duranne)*

Maybe the word play existed originally, but it would not surprise me too much if Nostradamus himself changed Duranne into Durance for profit. The Durenne, Durine or Duranne is a vast rural area situated on the outskirts of Renaix and Saint-Sauveur, at the foot of the "mont Lebron", in other words at the foot of the Pyrenees.

Nostradamus' followers owe it to themselves to take things a few steps further than their master. Hidden zealots of Anatole Le Pelletier, they fervently apply the anatolian method: everything that looks more or less alike is the same, and everything that is not too far off, is at the same place. There is no mountain bearing the name Lebron close to the Durance? No problem. Lebron is effortlessly changed to Leburon. And during the Third World War, the one that was predicted for the years 1980 – after the assassination of John Paul II at Lyons on a 13th December, and the famed passage through the Swiss tunnels – the Iraqi have attacked and conquered the Albion plateau sited, or so it would appear, in the mountains of the Lubéron, where the French keep their nuclear missiles. Excuse me, what did you say? Have you already forgotten that terrible war? And the noise of the atomic explosions? I dare say you must suffer from amnesia…

And are not Lebron, Leburon, and Lubéron the same? Will you please stop nit-picking? And hair splitting? Can't you just for once try and convince yourself you are wrong, and trust Mr. AA? Blindly.

> III 99 *Aux champs herbeux d'Alein et du Varneigre*
> *Du mont Lebron proche de la Durance (Duranne)*
> *Camp de deux parts conflit sera si aigre*
> *Mesopotamie defaillira en la France*

The six place names mentioned in this quatrain refer to Flemish places, more specifically to places located in Renaix. What a pity that the nostraddicts, who are decidedly convinced they know it all, had no knowledge of the Flemish language!

But we are not yet finished with our Athens-Pyrenees quatrain:

> II 17 *Le camp du temple de la vierge vestale*

Non eslongne d'Ethene monts pirrennees
Le grand conduit est cache dans la malle
North getez fleuve et vignes matinees

What, for goodness' sake, is a vestal virgin doing at the Croix Philosophe? Vestals ceased to exist a long time ago. In ancient Rome, the Vestales were virginal young girls who guarded and maintained the sacred fire. During the whole of the Middle Ages, St Bernard was depicted with a flaming red mane. According to his flatterers this represented the flames of the Holy Spirit, the pre-eminent Holy Fire, and the saint whose first name means 'Bear's heart" was symbolised by a flame. The *vestal virgin* guards this flame, hence protects St Bernard and, by extension, the monastic order of which he was the magnificent figurehead: the Cistercians. The *vestal virgin* is Our Lady of the Cistercians. The *temple of the vestal virgin* is a Cistercian church or abbey.

And *le camp*? In Wodecq vernacular, a *camp* is simultaneously a camp and a field (champ). *Le camp du temple de la vierge vestale* refers in the necessary roundabout way, to the field of the Cistercian Abbey.

Cambron is a Cistercian Abbey. At the Croix Philosophe we are not only in the heart of the estate of Cambron, but the field on which the old weeping willow grows is called *Champ de la Mère Dieu*: the field of the Mother of God. The environs of the field of the temple of the vestal virgin is the only place on earth where one can be close to Athens *and* the Pyrenees. The Old Monk could not have worded it more beautifully. At the expense of literary acrobatics, why would he use the word *temple* here, if it were not to make something clear to us?

Le grand conduit est cache dans la malle

The *conduit* means the provisions for a journey, but also the safeguard; *malle* has a double meaning: the marl (the soil, the earth) and the crop of a bird; *the great provisions, the great safeguard is hidden in the ground*. On the other hand, the crop of a chicken is the organ where the food that is gathered hurriedly is stored. The second meaning of *malle* suggests that the collecting had been done in great haste.

North getez fleuve et vignes matinees

North is not English! *Getez*: We misread what Nostradamus has not understood when he modernised and frenchified the text. The word is *wété* or *wéti* and means to look. When a Flemish or Picard text was frenchified, the "w" was generally changed in "g" or "gu"; for instance, *warte* becomes *garde*. The same was true for Italian; in Dante's *Hell*, an allusion is made to the great dyke of Flanders:

> *Quale i Fiamminghi tra Guizzante e Bruggia,*
> *Temendo il fiotto che in ver lor s'avventa,*
> *Fanno lo schermo, perchè il mar si fuggia*

> ... *tra Guizzante e Bruggia: between Wissant and Bruges.*

As in Latin, a *fleuve* is a watercourse, without an underlying restriction as to the width or capacity. It is flowing water. The word is derived from the Latin verb *fluere*, to flow. We must be well aware that the Old Monk had a daily practice of spoken and written Latin; he is used to thinking of words in this way. Moreover, the use of the word *fleuve* is not without reason. It is an introduction to the Rosne that we will come upon later.

Matinees: *vignes matinees*: Mixed vines, meaning a vineyard enclosed in other cultivated areas. With the usual subtlety in the choice of the words; *matiner* is to ill-treat, literally to treat like a dog (a *mâtin* is a fierce watchdog). The *matinees* are also the matins, i.e. the first prayers of the day chanted by the monks in the deep of the night, in the hope and the certitude that a new morning will soon break. Hence we must also understand that the hope lies on the location that Yves de Lessines is telling us to look at; and the indications he gives are the simplest of all: *look to the north, past the watercourse and the mingled vines.*

If we look to the north, standing at the Croix Philosophe, we will see beyond the brook, on the southern slope of La Pierre, left of the old Roman road, the field that in the Middle Ages was called the "Champ de la Vigne" (field of the vine); and beyond the "Champ de la Vigne", right in the middle

of the countryside, lies what is called in Picard the "blanc scourchet", the small white shelter.

Let us lean against the tree for a while and look at the landscape:

> V 85 *Par les sueves et lieux circonvoisins*
> *Seront en guerre pour cause de nuees*
> *Camps marins locustes et cousins*

The Sueves were not just the ancient barbaric tribe from Arioviste, celebrated since their skirmish with Caesar, the one and only, famous Julius of the Gallic wars. It was also the name given to the inhabitants of the southern part of a territory. The *Terre des Débats* is sited in the south of the County of Alost, hence its inhabitants are *suèves* without a capital letter. The *Champ des Nuages* itself lies in the south of the *Terre des Débats*, exactly on the border of Flanders and Hainaut.

Par les sueves et lieux circonvoisins Seront en guerre pour cause de nuees: *in the south and environs they will fight a war over the Field of the Clouds.* To be at war because of a field: is this not a splendid hint at the petty aspect of this war?

Camps marins locustes et cousins

Camps marins is a mistake attributable to Nostradamus. However, let us be fair. In the original handwriting it is extremely difficult, even for the best-informed professionals, to distinguish between *camps marINs* and *camps marNIs*. In most cases the sense is given by the context. The Old Monk has certainly written *marnis* but this is a word Nostradamus could not know. So he came up with his startling oceanic fields.

The *camps marnis* ou *marlis* – both words are used at random – are fields where *marne* or *marle* (marl, a type of clay soil) is found. The proof that they were thus called and that they were situated near the *field of the Clouds* comes, once again, from the *Viel Rentier*: as *Mallières au Noage.* Note that, just like Yves de Lessines, the scribe of the *Viel Rentier* also uses a plural.

The *locuste* or *laouste* is the grasshopper, the locust. From the Croix Philosophe, we can see the *camp du Crikyon* (the field of the cricket) and the *marlire Criquette* (the marl pit of the grasshopper). The Old Monk writes *locustes*, the plural form. Is more explanation needed?

> Thiris li Roche, 10 s., seur 1 jornel de tere et demi jornel de pret, à Minebèque.
>
> Adans li Fèvres, demi bonier et demi jornel, as Mallières au Noage, et à Bracle en est li jorneus.
>
> Jehans Hurdut, 5 s., seur 1 jornel de tere, au Buis.
>
> Watiers Mossons, 5 s., seur 1 jornel de masure, au Buis.
>
> Ernous de le Bare, de Evrart Caisnoit, 9 s., seur 1 et demi jornel, à Brouc Espine.

The *cousins* might designate members of the family. They are also gnats and mosquitoes. Moreover, a *cousen* or *cousin* was also a fief held in common. This was the status, in the beginning of the 14th century, of a stretch of land rather close by, and that is still called *Commont* today.

And so, assembled on a minuscule patch of the *Terre des Débats*, and visible from the same spot, we find all the places corresponding to these toponyms that are rarely found, to say the least.

Why so many indications? As well you know, the words Templars, pirates, Pharaohs, Martians and Atlantis serve as starting blocks to treasure hunters of all sorts and conditions, chasing after the umpteenth chart – and this time it is really the one (!) – that gives them the exact place where the treasure is hidden. The author of the *Centuries*, however, knows better: drawing a map to show the location of a storage is putting the stored objects at the disposal of the first lucky prospector to come along. Since he is intelligent and free of generally accepted ideas, he prefers to indicate a place without naming it or mapping it out, simply enumerating a number of hamlets. The whole range leads to identification. If he wanted to refer to London, or San Francisco in the same manner, he would not name the town but list a number of streets.

Yves de Lessines' method is a result of his religious convictions, which gave it its reason and its meaning. From the eagle to the worm, from the oak to the nettle, from the stars to putrefaction, the whole Creation, down to its smallest details, lies in God's hand. Divine will or Divine permission is the direct cause of everything that happens in the universe. The devil, for his part, is crafty and cunning but lacks intelligence. Discovery is beyond his reach. By expressing his message in a way so subtle that it surpasses the intelligence of the malicious, Yves de Lessines protects it against the evil one and his servants, because only God's envoy will be given the light. This whole philosophy is eminently medieval.

Which train of thought did the Old Monk follow when elaborating his stratagem? First of all, the same place name, whether old or not, can be found in various different places. Almost every town or city has its own Liberation Square, Revolution Plaza, Victory Avenue, Main Street or Lovers Lane. On the other hand, the rarer and more characteristic a toponym is, the better it defines a precise location. One isolated place name, however, will not lead to absolute certainty. One must indeed account for coincidences and the risks related to the passing of time. It is never prudent to erect a building on only one point of support. Only a whole set of toponyms, logically and strongly interrelated, will give a trustworthy and meaningful result. Using place names in any other way is raising a stroke of luck to the level of science.

The *Centuries* contain a profusion of old and rare toponyms, bedded in less exceptional but profuse place names. Yves de Lessines enumerates dozens and dozens of them. Is it really a coincidence to find them all together on the territory of Wodecq and its close environs, while there is no chance of finding four similar ones for miles around?

We can end the topographical explanation of this quatrain. In a distance of not more than six or seven kilometres, restricted to only one access road, we have encountered twenty-one place names, all quite unequivocal and backed up by pertinent physical evidence, the reality of which cannot be denied, except by ignoring the existence of what all eyes can see. An average of three names per kilometre is ample to satisfy the most demanding questions. Statistically speaking, there is not one chance in a thousand billion that the same ensemble of toponyms should reproduce itself at another place on the planet. And we must limit our search to its French speaking part because there is no suggestion anywhere in the *Centuries* that the numerous enumerated hamlets might refer to places in Germany, Poland, the Oman sultanate or the island of Java.

Chapter Thirteen – The Locked Room

Now, with infinite patience, the Old Monk is trying to tell the long-awaited that he has reached his goal.

> IX 40 *Pres de Quintin dans la forest bourlis*
> *Dans l'Abbaye seront Flamens ranches*

Quintin: the name of the church of Wodecq was, and still is, Notre-Dame de Wodecq or… Saint Quentin. *Bourlis*: Burned or burned to the ground, but also flattened (as with a roadroller) when speaking of the ground. Modern Picard calls it *bourlé*. In the years when the Old Monk was writing, the large wood that stretched from the village square of Wodecq to Cambron-chaux was cleared. Seeing burning scrub and kindling at such a place is quite normal. With the other sense of the word in mind, it suggests an image of a torn-down forest that has been crushed by a steamroller.

That particular part of the village is still called *∂l Bouy* (pronounced booy), which was frenchified to *Buis* (boxwood). Although it was spelled *Buys* or *Buis*, pronounced *boojs* or *boolls* in the subject-case, which disappeared, it meant in fact "*wood*". In the object-case (which was maintained), the word was spelled *Buy* and pronounced *booy*. The peasants, mostly illiterate, could not care less about the written form and they kept pronouncing *booy* since only the object-case survived. When the end-declension began to disappear, the foreigners and the lettered men did not understand that the word spelled "*Buis*" was in fact the subject-case of *Buy*. They read the word *à la français* and simply believed it referred to the shrub, the twigs of which are consecrated on Palm Sunday. We may blame the medieval French-adoring clerks directly for having turned the great Wodecq forest into a small shrub.

The expression *forest bourlis* is historically correct as far as the village is concerned, on the condition that it is placed in the right context, i.e. Yves de Lessines' period. All that remains of this once mighty forest are a few meagre rows of poplars, with a pollard-willow here and there.

Dans l'Abbaye seront Flamens ranches

At the ancient forest's edge stood the Abbey (*Cambronchaux*), which we are certain was used to lodge (*rancher*) Flemings, either freely as occupants or as prisoners during the famed war *because of the clouds*. There is no doubt about this: the facts are mentioned in Flemish documents – archives, chronicles and even accounts – dating from the beginning of the 14th century. The verb *ranchîr* (corresponding to the old-French *rancher*) means, in Picard, to pile up in a small, cramped room. The word is related to *"ran" de pourchô*, the pig sty. Not so very long ago, this used to be the smallest, darkest place on any farm. "*Ranchîr*" means massed like pigs. *Near Saint Quentin in the felled forest, in the Abbey where Flemings were crammed together.*

The capital letter of *Abbaye* shows that the author was certainly not speaking of just any abbey; as to the forms *Quintin* and *Flamens*, they derive from the Picard as well as the Flemish.

Let us stay in our woods one moment longer:

> IX 87 *Par la forest du Touphon essartee*
> *Par hermitage sera pose le temple*

And here we come across once more one of those so-called mysteries, renowned in the circles of nostraddicts, who have been looking everywhere for an untraceable forest, especially in Brittany, and to the farthest corners of King Arthur's mystical wood. Thus the Touphon remained hidden behind the foliage of Broceliande. In Picard, *bouchon* is still used, meaning a shrub or a tiny wood, a little Bouy. A *touphon* was a *touffe*, i.e. a small wood that today we usually call "*∂n stokéé*", a word directly adapted from the Flemish.

We are therefore faced here with a twofold word play. "*La forest du Touphon* (with a capital letter) *essartee*": the forest of the Shrub or the Buis. This finesse, however, can only be understood if one transports oneself mentally to the end of the 13th and the beginning of the 14th century. To a Nostradamus, living 220 years later, this line makes no sense. It was no longer possible at that time to grasp the toponymical significance: the history of the deforestation that took place near this village was only re-discovered by modern historians. Moreover, the great European deforestation was done during the 11th, 12th and 13th centuries. The clearings at a later date were but trifles when compared to the medieval enterprise. This notation in the *Centuries* is once more proof of the fact that the text was written at the beginning of the 14th century and not after 1550, when the clearing of a whole forest was no longer the order of the day. Clearings were undertaken again at the end of the 18th and the beginning of the 19th centuries, but on a much smaller scale. Only an eyewitness or someone living in the years following the deforestation, when its memory was still vivid, would write this line and actually believe it would be understood.

Let us end our explanation of the Touphon forest with the usual details: *∂l forest toufon*, pronounced in Picard, has two other meanings:
1) "the wood lies at the bottom (of the valley)", which is the exact location as far as the Wodecq Buis is concerned;
2) "the strong (the strength, force in old Picard) lies at the bottom (of something)".

From the wood we walk over to the hermitage:

> *Par hermitage sera pose le temple*

Hermitage may be considered to be the Abbey, or more exactly the barn of Cambronchaux. Taken in its literal meaning, it is an isolated, remote, secluded, hidden spot. It may also refer to what was then called an *"écart"* or a *"retrait"*, a retreat.

> "At the remote spot... or else
> In the neighbourhood of the Abbey
> the Temple will be put"

The compilation of both senses heightens the efficiency of the location.

Furthermore, it should be noted that during the Middle Ages the verb *poser* and all the verbs that derived from it had a subtle underlying sense of a *limited period of time. The Temple will be installed for a while*, is what the line conveys; in the author's mind the situation is a temporary one, pending the return of happier days. The accumulation of numerous language subtleties such as this one, used unwittingly, confirms on the level of more or less deliberate allusions, what the Old Monk expressed clearly in several other parts of the text: he hopes for and awaits a glorious revival of the Order of the Temple.

Another location? Standing at the Croix Philosophe and looking more or less in the direction of the church of Wodecq, you will see the Grand Champ, that the Old Monk calls, in the singular, *l'arpen long labourable*. It is this singular form that creates the finesse. The "arpent" is an old unit for measuring an area, equivalent to about a quarter of an hectare. Unless the "arpent" has the width of a footpath, it is impossible to plough it in long stretches. A farmer will see this logic immediately. In the Wodecq dialect, the word became synonymous with a very small field. Sometimes it is even used instead of courtyard.

The enumeration of topographical indications could go on almost indefinitely, and yet we must put an end to it sometime. Let us add just one more, to duly honour its profusion. Yves de Lessines obviously enjoyed setting his traps so much that we really owe it to him to smile knowingly just once more.

We are still at the Croix Philosophe. I must admit that my joy in describing this to you is exceptionally great. The line filled many a nostraddict with dismay, and caused them to come up with one absurd prophecy after the other.

Near the end and the beginning of the Rosne

The game the Old Monk plays is identical to the Athens-Pyrenees one and, as we will see, from exactly the same location. Let us not forget that the art of the enigma is based on revealing hidden things by means of, amongst other things, strange enunciations and impossible associations.

Indeed, how could we be at the source and the delta of the Rhône simultaneously? The Old Monk is talking nonsense. If my memory serves me right, the total length of that stream is somewhere in the neighbourhood of 800 kilometres, but I do not seem to recall that its valley forms a large circle allowing the Rhône to flow out into the sea… in Switzerland. Until further notice, the Swiss-French river still wells up out of its glacier near the Furka-pass, deep in the Swiss Valais, and streams out over the Camargue beach, drowning all the nostraddicts in their Rhône as a result.

Yet the solution is almost unbelievably simple: the Rosne is not the Rhosne. We have "Rône" galore and one flows slowly past our eyes: about 500 metres further on the Ronsart traverses the whole countryside.

The watercourse the Old Monk told us to look at a few pages ago has been called the *Ronsart* for a couple of centuries. A "sart" is a cleared place and later on the brook was named after a particular spot of its valley. This way of naming features is very common. So is the reverse order: Sterrebeek, for instance, a village on the bank of the Sterre. Another outcome of this same custom caused the Minne to be called the Tordoir, because of the oil press, the "tordoir", that had been erected on its bank, and that still exists.

Hence, to understand the name of the Ronsart, the idea of a circular field should be banished at once from one's mind. By the way, did you ever stop to wonder how it would be ploughed? I challenge anyone to try it with a team of oxen or horses. Whoever has driven one will know what I mean; they will also know that the plough will *never* stay in the furrow. To understand the name, one should pronounce it as it was done in the Middle Ages: ∂*l rône sarte*, i.e. literally the cleared spot near the Rône. Standing at the Croix Philosophe, you will discover the whole course of the Rône, from its source to its confluence with the Minne, from which point the two together form the Ancre. The Blanc-Scourchet is sited exactly midway between both brooks.

The Old Monk was right once again. It is not difficult to get *pres de la fin et principe du Rosne* (near the end and the beginning of the Rosne) if the Rosne in question is only about three kilometres long! Let us admire the superb turn of phrase to avoid the word "bouche" (mouth) and, in doing so, the confusion with the great river that he uses to trap the undesirable: *Pres de la fin et principe…*

The Croix Philosophe and the Blanc-Scourchet are the only places in the world where one can be not too far from Athens and the Pyrenees, and near the end and the beginning of the Rône. Ath lies ten kilometres away, the Pyrenees between five and six, and the Rône flows at about 500 metres. As far as I know, Yves de Lessines must be the only man ever to have noticed this topographical curiosity.

Let us resume the stroll the Old Monk invited us to take. He requested us to look north, where the watercourse flows and the vines grow. He now spurs us on to do a little climbing.

V 75 *Montera haut sur le lieu plus a droite*

Is there any way he could have told us more clearly to go to the Roman road that slopes up towards La Pierre, situated at 200 to 300 metres further up, to the right of the Champ de la Vigne, at 300 metres to the right of the little white shelter?

In those days we could not have failed to notice the dolmen erected there, nor the gigantic oak in the shadow of which it stood, and after which the village was named. The Old Monk would have used them automatically as landmarks. However this time he did not and he must have had a good reason for not doing so. So at this point, we shall simply note that he located the feature most visible at that time, i.e. the enormous oak and the dolmen that were the real eye-catchers, by referring to what was much less visible, the little white shelter, and not the reverse. Is this a subtle hint to make us see that what is the most important here is not the most visible?

This hamlet, "La Pierre", is a crossroads. Which direction should we follow?

A l'aise n'ira le Buy ne retournera

In old Picard a *aise* is a plank. At the crossroads of La Pierre, when coming from the Croix Philosophe and walking straight ahead, we will arrive first of all at a spot called *Anaise* and the next hamlet of some importance is *La Planche*, which also means "The Plank" or *l'Aise*. Turning right at La Pierre will bring us back to the *Buis*. In the *Centuries* the word is written with the correct old spelling of the object-case, with its Picard pronunciation: *Buy*, pronounced [booy].

If we may not go on to La Planche, nor return to the Buis, we can only do one thing: turn to the left, towards the Blanc-Scourchet. But before doing so, we must comply with another instruction: have a rest, which we will gladly do:

V 75 *Demoure assis sur la pierre quarree*
Vers le midi pose a sa senestre
Baston tortu en main bouche serree

Remain seated on the hewn stone. Because the Picard word *pîre* sometimes meant a paved road, a few particularly obstinate people persisted in claiming that there never was a dolmen. According to them, the spot owed its name to the Roman road. This is wrong.

In the first place, grammar tells them so: *∂n pîre* = une pierre (a stone) is a feminine word, while: *é pîre* = un chemin (a path) is masculine. When we refer to the hamlet, we all say *al pîre* (feminine) and never *au pîre* (masculine). Moreover, the whole local toponymy is based on a stone and is incompatible with the sense of a road. The old maps are revealing: next to the crossroads of La Pierre, we find the sign that, traditionally, represents upright stones of any kind.

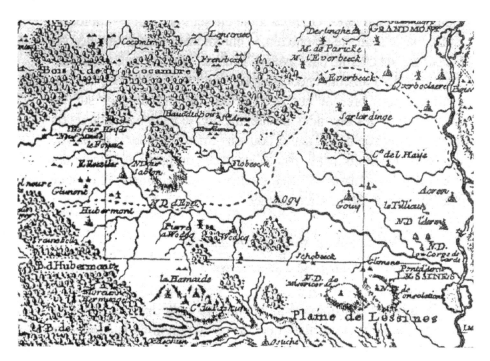

And of course, the *Viel Rentier* is always there to confirm the indications of the old map:

> Thiris Godefrois, de tere ki siet au Caisne à le Pierre, seur le cauchie, encosté le maison Adan le Fèvre, 5 s.
>
> Liebers Tricos, 9 s., de demi bonier de tere, ki gist à le Haisète, ki fu Watier le Baubot.
>
> Thiris li Fèvres de le Pierre, 1 capon, de une maison là ù il mainnent ens, à le Pierre, devant le Caisne.
>
> Gilles Bue(s)sès, 1 capon, de le masure là ù il maint, à le Pierre.

Since one more piece of evidence will not harm the demonstration in the least, let us add a very ancient chronicle that refers to this hamlet. In the year 885, the Norsemen on their tour through the region, had put up camp at this exact spot that their chronicler mentions in Latin: *lapis*; and *lapis* means a stone. If La Pierre had been a road, he would have used the words *via calcaria*: the road paved with limestone. The road itself still goes by the name: the *Cauchie*. During the 18th century the dolmen in question was still standing at La Pierre. On basis of the research and the books written by Julien Loix, I have no doubt that it should not be too difficult to excavate most of its elements. The traces from the past and the text of the *Centuries* confirm each other in an obvious way, and that really is our first concern.

> *Demoure assis sur la pierre quarree*
> *Vers le midi pose a sa senestre*

There is no lexical difficulty in these two lines. *Quarree* means "hewn" and "square" simultaneously. *Senestre* is the old word for "left"; in the form *sinister* and with a drastically reduced meaning the word still exists. We should not overlook the sober expression *hewn stone* to describe the flat table of a dolmen.

If the long-awaited sits down on the stone, with the south on his left side, he cannot but face the west. What lies there for him to see? The small white shelter, the *"blanc scourchet"*, hardly a stone's throw away.

Now, be careful not to be deceived by the naive look and the soft wording of the following line:

> *Baston tortu en main bouche serree*

If you have kept in mind the Old Monk's habits, you know this line must have at least two meanings. In stark opposition to its appearance, this line is not easy at all, and you must not expect to grasp its full richness without an effort. To explain the unusual lack of mystery of the fourth line, the first thing to be noticed is the strange construction of the third line: "Vers le midi pose a sa senestre." When imagining the long-awaited sitting on the stone, the south to his left, we have not taken the word "vers" (towards) into account, and we did well. He would have been ordered to remain seated *vers le midi*, i.e. facing the south, but the south would be *on his left side*. Try to be facing fully southwards while keeping the south on your left side! The Old Monk once again states an obvious impossibility.

This might be the right moment to stress that the enigma is, by its very nature, the most carefully constructed literary genre ever. One neglected detail will make it absolutely incomprehensible and the whole thing falls apart. The intended result will not be achieved, and the author will inevitably go through the rest of his life feeling pitifully foolish. The genre brooks no weaknesses. Hence we must not consider the suggested contortion to be a sign of indolence or an unfounded artifice: the author started the third line with a word that makes logical sense in the fourth.

The medieval literati immediately seized on the reason for this strangely placed preposition *vers*; in Picard or in French this construction is faulty, or rather intolerable; on the other hand, in Latin poetry it is quite normal. What is Yves de Lessines' message? Using a Latin versification pattern, he wants his reader to understand the French *and* the Latin meaning of the word.

Versus derives from the Latin *vertere*, meaning to turn. It is the Old Monk's own beautiful way of suggesting that we should turn the quatrain to discover the hidden path, in the same manner one turns over the stones in a brook to discover the life underneath. The more so that, if the word *vers* has the same meaning in the old language as today, i.e. the basic unit of versification, it more often designates the stanza as a whole, whatever its name or length: laisse (i.e. the stanza of a chanson de geste), quatrain, sixain and so on. In another meaning, *versus* is the furrow the plough traces in the soil. Once again we are to think of turning over the soil and of tracing a path.

"The road I mark out is long and difficult," the poet chants to the long-awaited, whom he has accompanied the whole way and now sees resting on the *pierre quarree*.

If we add to the Latin meaning of *versus* the sense of the French preposition *vers*, the trap contained in the words is revealed instantly: *Vers le midi pose a sa senestre*, does not imply that one must be facing the south, but that one must be turned in such a way that the south lies to his left. The long-awaited, having the south to his left, is turned towards... what? Towards the white shelter, as we have said previously. Yves de Lessines, however, proposes another complement to the preposition heading the line: *baston tortu*.

What can be more trivial, less interesting and less inspiring than a stick, that is not even straight? Wait just a little and you will see. The stick is one of the richest of medieval symbols. We will not draw up a complete catalogue of all the uses of a stick in the Middle Ages, but a few are necessary. First of all, the stick could be the symbol of weakness: the white stick was carried by the blind, the disabled, the beggars and the pilgrims. In direct contradiction, the stick was also a symbol of authority: from the lowest city guard or police officer to the marshal and the king, everyone in a position of surveillance or command carried a stick, the splendour and cost of which served to proclaim the social status of the happy owner. Which category does the crozier belong to, the so-called pastoral staff which, I am glad to say, appears more and more often between the sticks of the poor?

There are three staves in which we are particularly interested: the Abbot's staff, the staff of the Prior of the monastery, and the command staff. At the time of writing this quatrain, Yves de Lessines carried the Prior's staff. Little did he realise that very soon he would be given the Abbot's staff. These staffs are both crooked. And so was the command staff of the *centurio* (we are reading the *Centuries*, remember), in principle a vine. There is one more left, not the least, which is also crooked: the "abacus", the staff of the Master of the Temple.

Who should we infer from this crooked stick? Yves de Lessines describing himself, carrying his Prior's staff? This is more than just an image: it is perfectly consistent with feudal customs. The investiture *par rain et par baston* solemnised a mission: one was invested by *the branch and the stick*. Yves de Lessines watched his own father being invested thus with the castle of Lessines. Here let us remember that, in the second quatrain of his oeuvre, Yves de Lessines has compared branches to a reed, and that reed is called *cistels* or *cistiels*, and later on *cistiaus*. Yes, indeed, the "Ordre des Cisterciens", more commonly called the "Ordre de(s) Cistiaus" means literally "Ordre des Roseaux" (the Order of the Reed)! I think now is the right time to recall the line: *Passant les Ponts venir pres des rosiers...*

Of course, Prior Yves sees himself in the symbolism of his time: he is *rain* (cistel) and *baston* (prior) at the same time. And, what is more, how could we misunderstand what he conveys to us by alluding to the customs of that time, when the remittance of a stick was the solemn sign by which someone was entrusted with an important mission. How could we misunderstand that he, Prior of a Cistercian Abbey, considers himself to be *invested* "*par rain et par baston*" in this adventure.

But perhaps we are thinking of the wrong person. Maybe the one implied is the Master of the Temple and his *abacus*. Jacques de Molay, last Master of the Temple, imprisoned by Philip the Fair, no longer has the said *abacus*, the sign of his authority, in his hand. Should *main* be given another meaning than the strictly anatomical one? In the Middle Ages as often as not the word meant a house, a dwelling (derived from the verb *manoir*, to remain, to live at). The line can therefore be translated: *the crooked stick is in the house*. Is this house the little white shelter that the long-awaited can see from his *pierre quarree*?

The two last words of the quatrain reveal capital information.

Let us first of all take the word *bouche* (mouth) in its purely anatomical sense. The apparent meaning of this word group *bouche serree*, "closed mouth", is easy to understand; evoking his title and his mission, Yves de Lessines confirms that he has remained silent, that he kept the secret. But we must also take into account the other meanings of *bouche* and *serrer* that are correct here and the means by which we must never forget – because that is the way in which sentences were understood – the purpose of literature was to suggest an idea, or an indication by giving a number of elements that will stimulate the reader's reflection. It is never a discourse constructed on our way of thinking, academic and demonstrative.

The *bouche* is an opening in the most general sense, whether for aeration or of an oven, a sewer, a stream… but always with the secondary underlying idea of matter in motion. Forced to it by the etymological mania of the period, we must add the meanings of the word *bouge*, almost always spelled *bouche* elsewhere and *boche* in the region. *Boche* means:

- the convex or the concave part of an object (to be compared to the Flemish "*boge*": vault arch);
- a room for dumping waste;
- a sort of small side room, usually without a window, next to a larger room;
- a muddy spot;
- a hump;
- a leather pouch;
- a trunk, a purse;
- To which we must add *bouchel*, a barrel, a cask.

The verb *serrer* means to close with a rod or a lock, to keep closed, to keep locked in.

This exploitation of the lexicon leads to different translations of the line, with the *abacus*, the staff of the Master of the Temple, as point of departure:

1) the crooked staff is in the house and the opening is firmly closed;
2) the crooked staff is in the house where a small room next to a larger one is kept closed;
3) simultaneously, we must think of locked-in barrels and a closed dumping room.

Blinding whoever is not supposed to see nor to know, enlightening the envoy from heaven, Yves de Lessines has led the long-awaited to the end of his voyage. Sitting on the hewn stone, the stranger beholds the white façade of the shelter, a tiny Temple enclave saved by a brilliant ruse from the greed of Philip the Fair's prowlers. Having hidden their essential belongings before the final disaster, the Templars immediately sold the property to a brewer by a clever financial technique. This ancestor of the mortgage loan allowed the seller to recover the sold goods within a predetermined period of time (usually thirty years), simply by reimbursing the sales price to the buyer.

It would have sufficed for an envoy to present himself with the agreed amount and the second copy of the sales deed to return the property to the Templars, without any further justification. But, in the meantime, neither the shelter nor the surrounding field belonged to the Order of the Temple, hence they could no longer be seized. No prowler could prey and the new owner was not entitled to sell before the end of the agreed term.

Did the long-awaited actually sit on the square stone? Did he enter the old house? Has he been watching, as I do, at sunset *"Mont Aventine brusler nuict sera veu, Le ciel obscur tout a un coup en Flandres"*? Or did he walk past the white shelter without understanding? Our century will know the answer when the *"bouche serree"* is discovered and opened, revealing the presence, or the trace thereof, of the *"grand conduit"*.

The road of the old monk

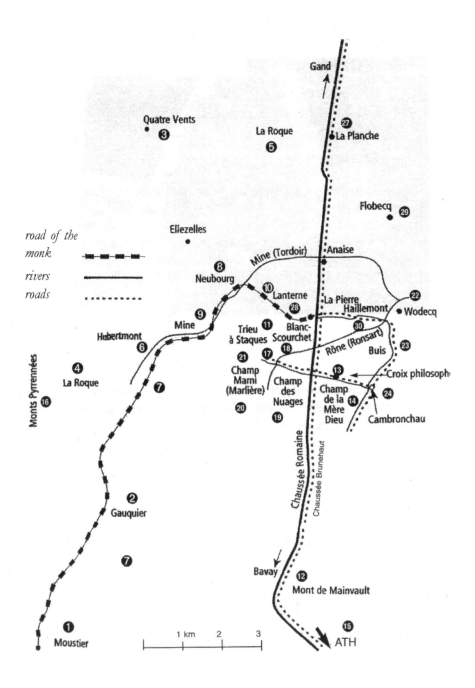

Nexus Magazine
Steamshovel Press
World Explorers' Club
RIAP Bulletin

**Nexus Magazine Europe/
Steamshovel Press Europe/
RIAP Bulletin World Headquarters:**
Frontier Sciences Foundation
P.O. Box 372
8250 AJ Dronten
the Netherlands
tel: +31-(0)321-380558
fax: +31-(0)228-312081
    email: info@fsf.nl
    www.fsf.nl

World Explorers Club Europe
Pannewal 22
1602 KS Enkhuizen
the Netherlands
tel: +31-(0)228-324076
fax: +31-(0)228-312081
email: info@fsf.nl
www.fsf.nl

Steamshovel Press UK:
Frontier Sciences Foundation
P.O. Box 13722
North Berwick, EH39 4WB
Great Britain
email: info@fsf.nl
www.fsf.nl

World Explorers Club
World Headquarters
403 Kemp Street
Kempton, Illinois
60946, USA
tel: 815-253-9000
fax: 815-253-6300
email: info@wexclub.com
www.wexclub.com

Nexus Magazine USA:
NEXUS Magazine
2940 E. Colfax #131
Denver, CO 80206
USA
tel: 303 321 5006
fax: 603 754 4744
email: nexususa@earthlink.net
www.nexusmagazine.com

Steamshovel Press USA:
P.O. Box 23715
St. Louis, MO 63121
USA
email: editor@steamshovelpress.com
http://www.steamshovelpress.com

THE STONE PUZZLE OF ROSSLYN CHAPEL
Philip Coppens

Rosslyn Chapel has fueled controversy and debate, both recently in several worldbestselling books as well as in past centuries. Revered by Freemasons as a vital part of their history, believed by some to hold evidence of pre-Columbian voyages to America, assumed by others to hold important relics, from the Holy Grail to the Head of Christ, the Scottish chapel is a place full of mystery.

This book will guide you through the theories, showing and describing where and what is being discussed; what is impossible, what is likely... and what is fact.
At the same time, the book will virtually guide you around all enigmatic and important aspects of the

chapel. The history of the chapel, its relationship to freemasonry and the family behind the scenes, the Sinclairs, is brought to life, incorporating new, forgotten and often unknown evidence.

Finally, the story is placed in the equally enigmatic landscape surrounding the chapel, from Templar commanderies to prehistoric markings, from an ancient kingly site to the South, to Arthur's Seat directly north from the Chapel – before its true significance and meaning is finally unveiled: that the Chapel was a medieval stone book of esoteric knowledge.

*120 Pages. Paperback. Euro 14,90 * GBP 7.99 * USD $ 12.00. Code: ROSC*

SAUNIERE'S MODEL
André Douzet

After years of research, André Douzet discovered a model from Sauniere.

Douzet reveals that Saunière spent large amounts of time and money in the city of Lyons... trips he performed in the utmost secrecy. Douzet finally unveils the location indicated on the model, the location of Sauniere's secret. Almost a century after Sauniere's death, the mystery of Rennes-le-Chateau is beginning to reveal itself.

*116 Pages. Paperback. Euro 14,90 * GBP 7.99 * USD $ 12.00. Code: SMOD*

CROP CIRCLES, GODS AND THEIR SECRETS
Robert J. Boerman

In the more than 20 years that mankind all over the world has been treated with thousands of crop circle formations, nobody was able to explain this phenomenon. You can read how beside a scientific and historical section the author links two separate crop circles. They contain an old Hebrew inscription and the so called Double Helix, yielding the name of the 'maker', his message, important facts and the summary of human history. This resulted in the commencement of cracking the crop circle code.

*159 Pages. Paperback. Euro 15,90 * GBP 9.99 * USD $ 14.00. Code: CCGS*

From the same publisher

DARWIN'S MISTAKE
Antediluvian discoveries prove: dinosaurs and humans co-existed
Dr. Hans J. Zillmer

Yes, there were cataclysms (among them The Flood) in
the course of history, but no, there was no evolution.
The Earth's crust is relatively young and no more than
a few thousand years ago; its poles were free of ice.
Published in nine languages, this international bestseller
puts the latest discoveries and new evidence against
Darwin's Theory of Evolution. The author, who owes
his insights and expertise to numerous excavations he participated in, describes recent findings that - in line with suppressed results of scientific research
- prove what seems unthinkable to us today: *Darwin is wrong.*
"Impact is what Earth scientists call the incident when a large cosmic stone
mass penetrates the Earth's atmosphere and hits the Earth's surface. And this is
just about what happens to those who read Darwin's Mistake - like a massive
meteor, Hans J. Zillmer's view of the world probes into the convolutions of
his reader's brain, effectively and thoroughly shaking the logically explained
and established world image of Darwin and Lyell, leaving his readers in utter
amazement why for so many years we have taken these scientific explanations
as gospel."
*292 pages. Heavily illustrated. 36 Picture Pages. GBP 14,99 * USD $ 19,95*

THE TEMPLARS' LEGACY IN MONTREAL, THE NEW JERUSALEM
Francine Bernier

Montréal, Canada. Designed in the 17th Century as the
New Jerusalem of the Christian world, the island of
Montreal became the new headquarters of a group of
mystics that wanted to live as the flawless Primitive
Church of Jesus. But why could they not do that in
the Old World?
After several journeys in Europe and in Africa,
Francine Bernier realised the history of her hometown
contained a hidden dimension so far gone unnoticed and unrecorded. Her
unique, detailed, three-year long and on-site analysis uncovers the secret
history behind the foundation of a city in the French New World. Its destiny
was to become the refuge of the most virtuous men and women who expected the return of a divine king-priest; a story connected with the mystery
of Rennes-le-Château, and the revival of a heterodox group whose marks,
and those of the French masonic Compagnons, are still visible today, both in
the old Montréal city... and underneath.
*360 pages. Heavily illustrated. GBP 14,99 * USD $ 21,95*

Available from the publishers

Write for our free catalog of other fascinating books, videos & magazines.

Frontier Sciences Foundation
P.O. Box 372
8250 AJ Dronten
the Netherlands
Tel : +31-(0)228-324076 / +31-(0)321-380558
Fax : +31-(0)228-312081
email : info@fsf.nl

website : www.fsf.nl

Adventures Unlimited
P.O. Box 74
Kempton, Illinois 60946
USA
Tel : 815-253-6390
Fax : 815-253-6300
email : auphq@frontiernet.net

website :
www.adventuresunlimitedpress.com